IMAGES
of America

MANCHESTER STREETCARS

IMAGES
of America

MANCHESTER STREETCARS

O.R. Cummings
and the Manchester Historic Association

ARCADIA
PUBLISHING

ISBN 978-0-7385-0412-4

Published by Arcadia Publishing
Charleston, South Carolina

Printed in the United States of America

Library of Congress Catalog Card Number: 00-100094

For all general information contact Arcadia Publishing at:
Telephone 843-853-2070
Fax 843-853-0044
E-mail sales@arcadiapublishing.com
For customer service and orders:
Toll-Free 1-888-313-2665

Visit us on the Internet at www.arcadiapublishing.com

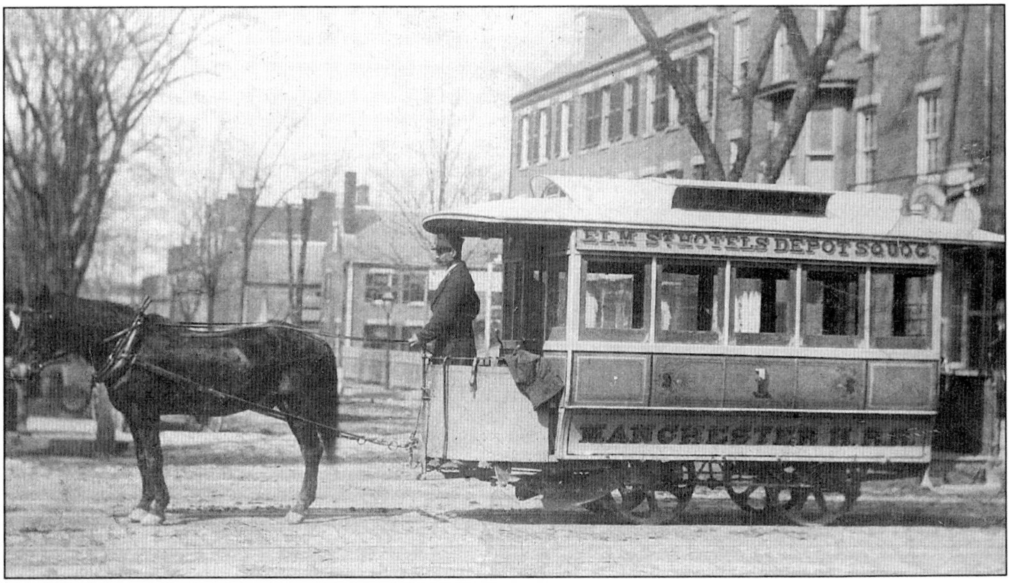

Six four-wheel, closed horsecars were placed in service when the Manchester Horse Railroad commenced operation on September 15, 1877. Three of the cars, Nos. 1, 3, and 5, had 10-foot bodies; three others, the Nos. 2, 4, and 6, had 12-foot bodies. They had respective seating capacities of 14 and 18 passengers. Number 1, drawn by a single horse, is southbound on Elm Street at Stark Street. Each car carried a one-man crew, the driver, and was equipped with a fare box into which passengers deposited coins or tickets. Because the cars initially could be drawn from one end only, turntables were provided at each end of the line and at the carbarn at Traction and Franklin Streets. However, these turntables were removed after modifications to the cars were completed. All six cars still were on hand at the time of electrification in 1895 but were discarded shortly thereafter.

Contents

Acknowledgments

The preparation of *Manchester Streetcars* would have been impossible without the enthusiastic cooperation of the Manchester Historic Association. Founded in 1896, the association made available a number of excellent views of horsecars and trolleys from its extensive collection of Queen City photographs, ancient and modern. These are individually credited by the initials MHA.

Most of the illustrations come from the author's own extensive collection of Queen City horsecar and trolley pictures. The majority of these were provided over a more-than-40-year period by a large number of fellow street railway hobbyists, including Clayton D. Sargent of Goffstown; the late Gerald F. Cunningham of Silver Spring, Maryland; the late Charles A. Brown of Sutton, Massachusetts; the late Charles A. Duncan of Danvers, Massachusetts; the late Earle W. "Bill" Maier of Mount Dora, Florida, originally of Manchester; the late Donald E. Shaw of Springfield, Massachusetts; the late Stephen D. Maguire of Belmar, New Jersey; the late Roger Borrup of Warehouse Point, Connecticut; the late Larry Scannell of Manchester; and others. Additional photographs were copied from views in the files of the Public Service Company of New Hampshire and the Union Leader Corporation.

Manchester Streetcars is respectfully dedicated to the memory of Betty Lessard, librarian of the Manchester Historic Association from 1969 to 1997 and an expert on Queen City history. Her assistance to the author over a long period is gratefully acknowledged, as is the help cheerfully given by Eileen J. O'Brien, the association's present curator of library collections, in this current project.

—O.R. Cummings

INTRODUCTION

The streetcar era in New Hampshire's largest city began on September 15, 1877. On this day, the Manchester Horse Railroad Company commenced operation over its initial 2.5-mile route from Elm and Webster Streets in the North End to South Main and Varney Streets on the West Side. It ended nearly 63 years later, on May 25, 1940, when the last trolleys were run over the remaining seven lines of the Manchester Street Railway. Just three years earlier, on December 31, 1937, the Manchester Street Railway had been absorbed by the Public Service Company of New Hampshire. Motor bus operation was inaugurated on May 26, 1940, by the Public Service Company and continues to be maintained today by the Manchester Transit Authority, which began operation in 1973.

Expansion of the horsecar system began as early as 1878. By mid-1893, the Manchester Street Railway, which had succeeded the Manchester Horse Railroad Company in 1889, owned nearly 10 miles of 3-foot gauge track. All existing lines were electrified in 1895, when the track was changed to the standard 4-foot-8.5-inch gauge. During the next 12 years, the trolley network grew steadily: new lines were being built within the Queen City itself, from Manchester to Goffstown, from Manchester to Nashua, and from Manchester to Derry. The very last extension was opened in November 1912. As of June 30, 1913, the Manchester Street Railway and its affiliates (the Manchester & Nashua and the Manchester & Derry Street Railways, all subsidiaries of the Manchester Traction, Light, & Power Company) provided electric car service over 49,223 miles of first main track, 10,079 miles of second main track, and 5,280 miles of sidings and turnouts, totaling 65.252 miles of track. Collectively, the three companies owned 51 closed cars and 54 open cars. The open cars were used during the summer months, when there was heavy riding to and from a pavilion and theater at Massabesic Lake and the very popular pleasure resort Pine Island Park, which opened in 1902 at Goffe's Falls.

Connections were made at the Manchester-Hooksett boundary with the Concord & Manchester Electric Branch of the Boston & Maine Railroad; at Shirley Junction on South Mast Street, Goffstown, with the Uncanoonuc Incline Railway and Development Company; at Derry with the Chester & Derry Railroad; and at Hudson with the Nashua Division of the Bay State Street Railway and the Massachusetts Northeastern Street Railway. Indeed, it was possible at this time to continue by trolley from Hudson to Boston via Lowell, and from Hudson to Salisbury, Seabrook, and Hampton Beaches on to Portsmouth.

Both the horsecar and trolley lines provided year-round vital and reliable local transportation within the Queen City for a long time. Passenger traffic on the Manchester Street Railway increased almost annually from 1890 to 1917, when 12,658,888 riders were carried—an all-time high. After fluctuating for six years, patronage declined steadily after 1923 as a result of growing competition from private automobiles, which rolled off assembly lines in ever-increasing numbers and at progressively more attractive prices during the Roaring Twenties.

The never-profitable Manchester & Derry Street Railway was abandoned in August 1926; the Manchester & Nashua discontinued service in September 1931; and the Concord Electric Railways, formerly the Concord & Manchester Electric Branch, called it quits in April 1933–– bus service being substituted on all three routes. Because of deteriorating track conditions, trolleys on part of the Manchester–Goffstown line were replaced by motor coaches on January 8, 1938. On April 1, 1939, the Public Service Company of New Hampshire, which had absorbed the Manchester Traction, Light, & Power Company in 1926, petitioned the state Public Service Commission for authority to motorize the remaining streetcar routes. The commission flashed the green light on January 31, 1940, and the last trolleys pulled into the carbarns before midnight on Saturday, May 25, 1940.

Today, six decades later, only Manchester's senior citizens remember the streetcar era in the Queen City, and few traces of the former trolley lines remain. Fortunately, three Manchester streetcars have been preserved at the Seashore Trolley Museum in Kennebunkport, Maine, and two of them have been restored to as near their original condition as possible.

One

The Horsecar Era 1877–1894

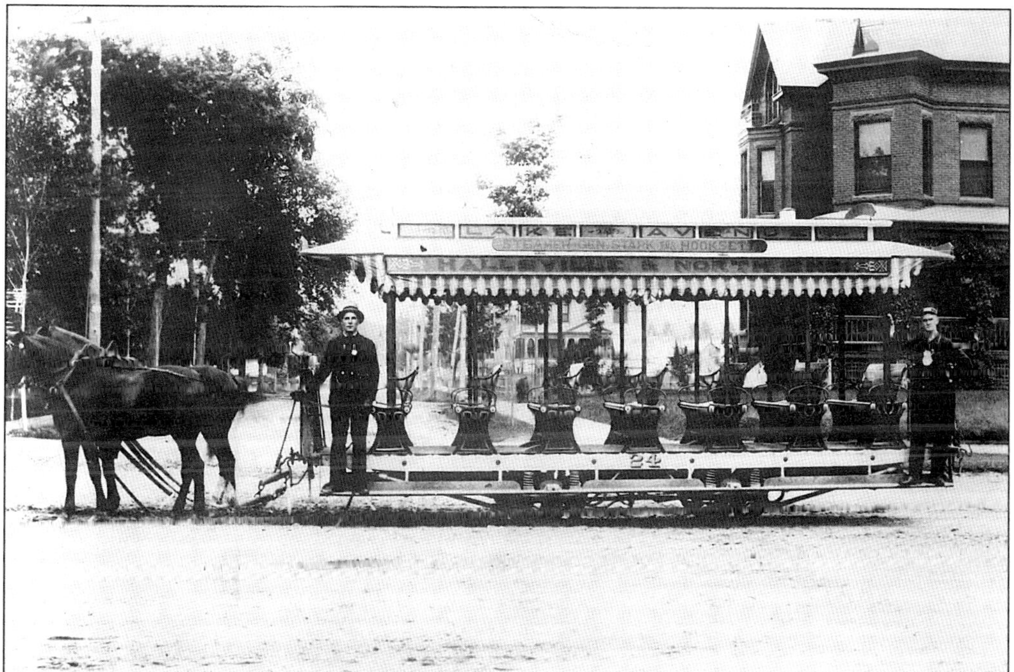

Manchester's noted photographer, the late Ulric Bourgeois, took this view of Manchester Street Railway's seven-bench open No. 24 at Elm and Webster Streets, *c.* 1890. The car, with a seating capacity of 35, is on the route between the North End and the East Manchester depot via Elm Street, Lake Avenue, and Massabesic Street.

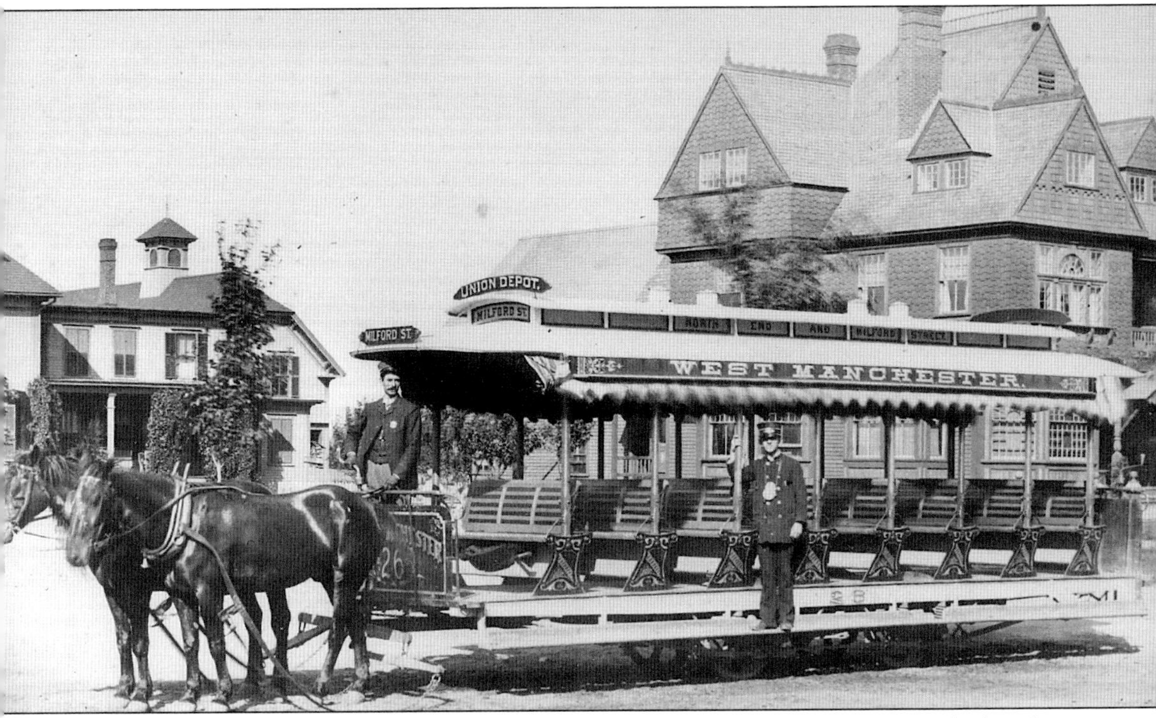

Wearing a bell punch, used to cancel tickets, the conductor of No. 26, an eight-bench open seating 40, prepares to leave Elm and Webster Streets for West Manchester, c. 1891. The building near the rear of the car is currently occupied by Allstate Insurance, at 1892 Elm Street.

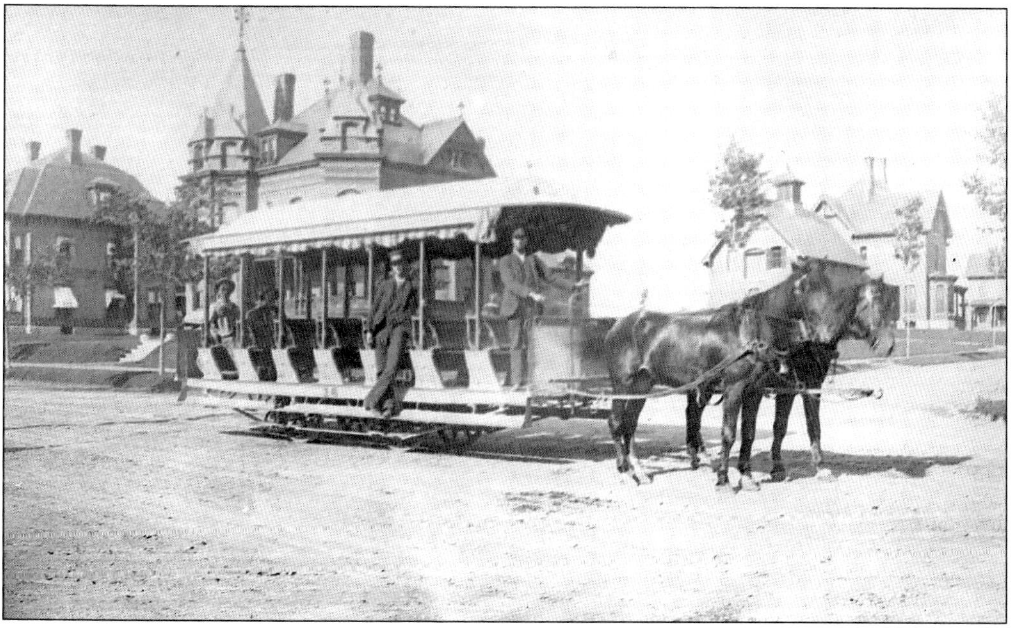

The seven-bench open No. 16 of the Manchester Horse Railroad is on Elm Street near Salmon Street, *c.* 1888. The opens were run only in summer; closed cars were operated in other seasons.

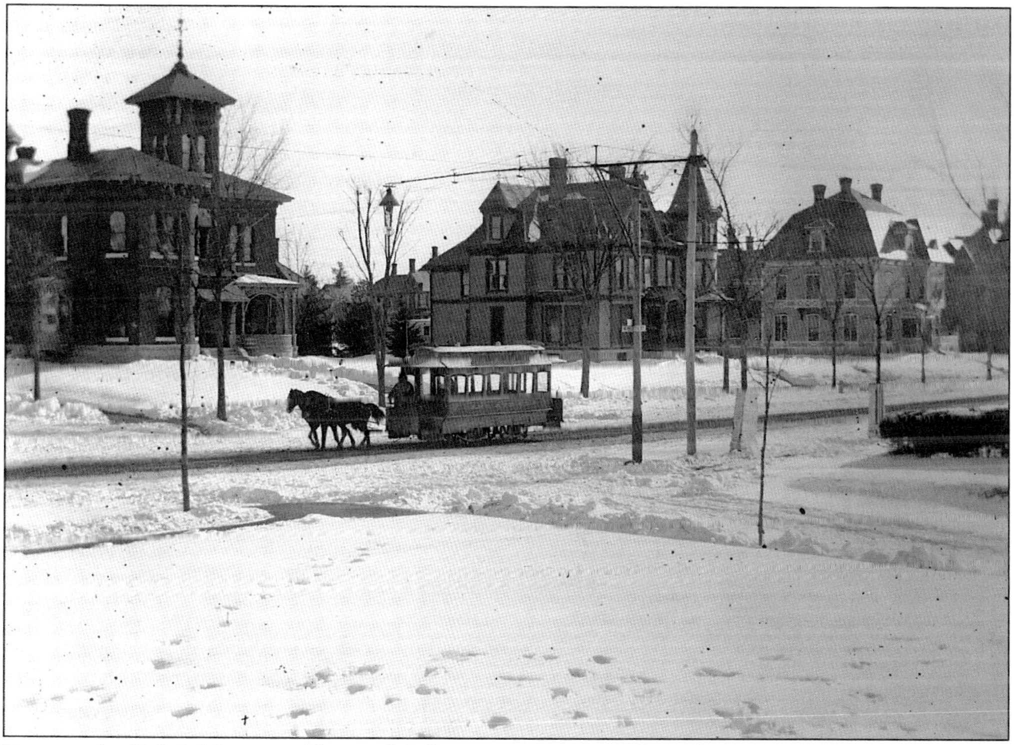

Passing the Balch House at Elm and Salmon Streets, a 16-foot closed car heads for the North End. None of the closed horsecars in Manchester were heated. Straw was spread about the floors in winter to help keep the passengers' feet warm. (MHA.)

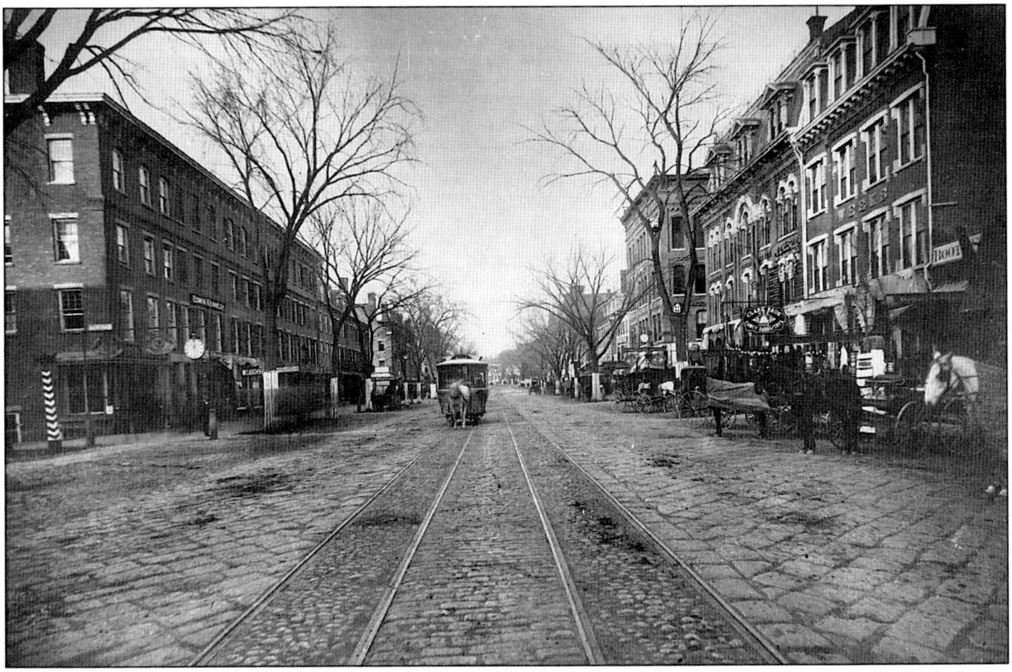

One of the original closed cars of the Manchester Horse Railroad encounters little vehicular traffic as it heads south on Elm Street near the foot of Amherst Street during the 1880s.

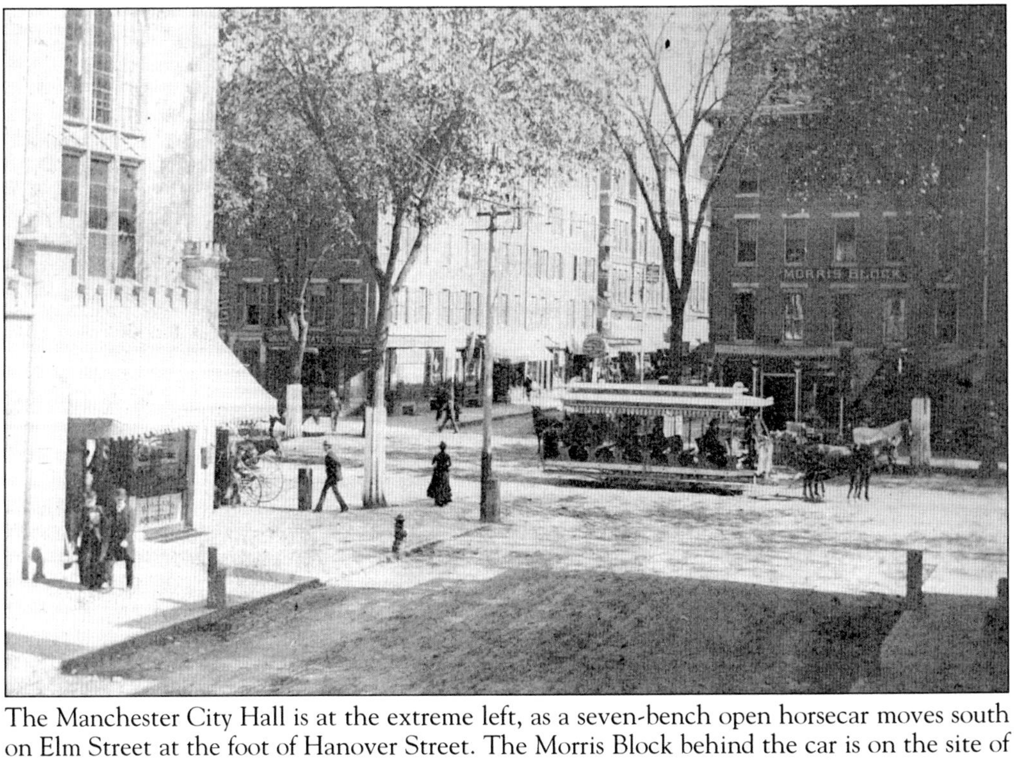

The Manchester City Hall is at the extreme left, as a seven-bench open horsecar moves south on Elm Street at the foot of Hanover Street. The Morris Block behind the car is on the site of the Amoskeag Bank, Manchester's first "skyscraper," erected in 1914. (MHA.)

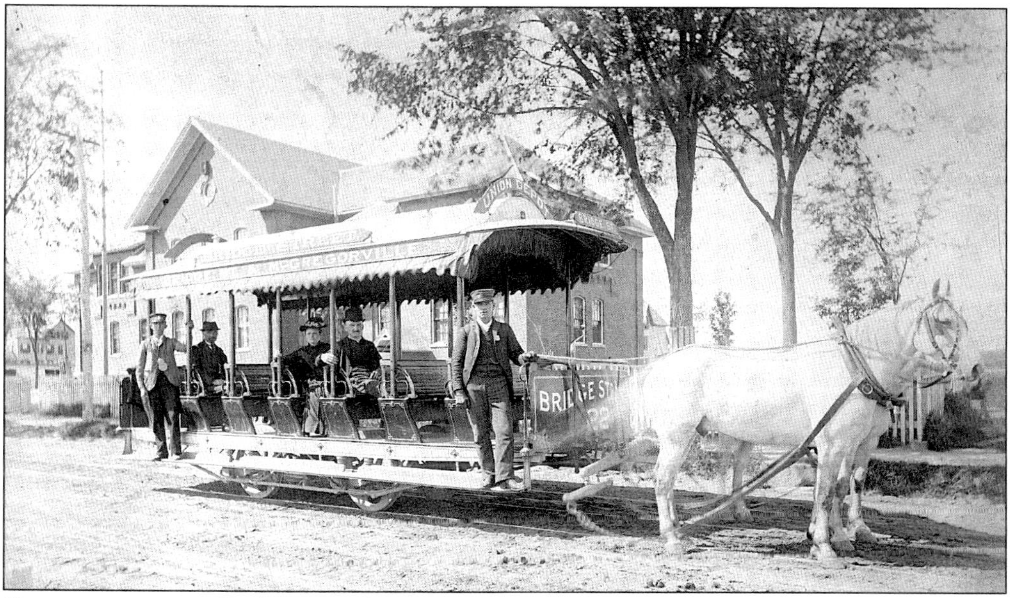

Horsecar service on Bridge Street between Elm and Maple Streets commenced June 28, 1882. By the end of 1890, Bridge Street cars were running to North Main and Amory Streets in West Manchester. This seven-bench open was photographed in front of the North Main Street School. (MHA.)

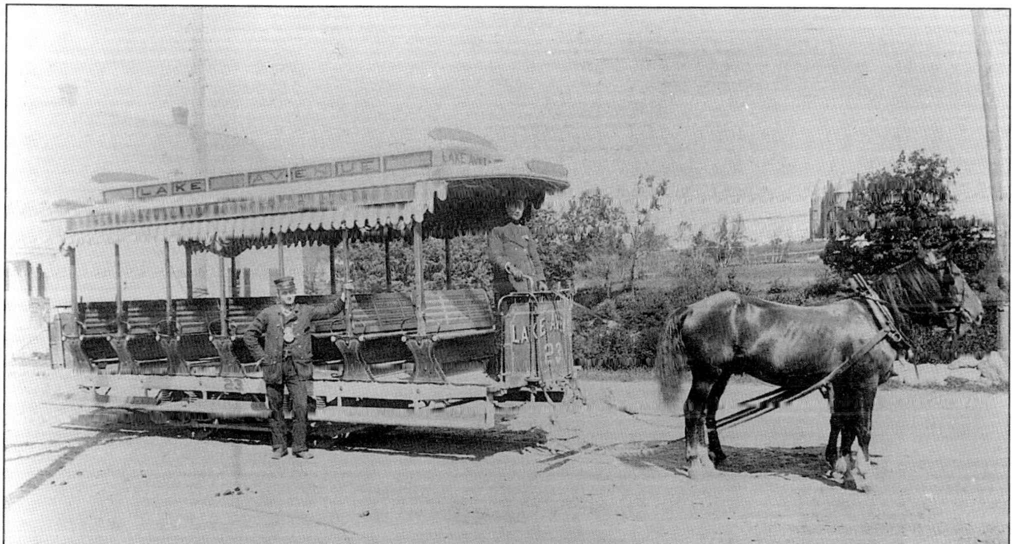

This is a c. 1890 view of seven-bench horsecar No. 23, on Massabesic Street near Cypress Street, and the East Manchester depot of the Concord & Portsmouth Railroad. Barely visible in the background is the original building of the Elliot Hospital. (MHA.)

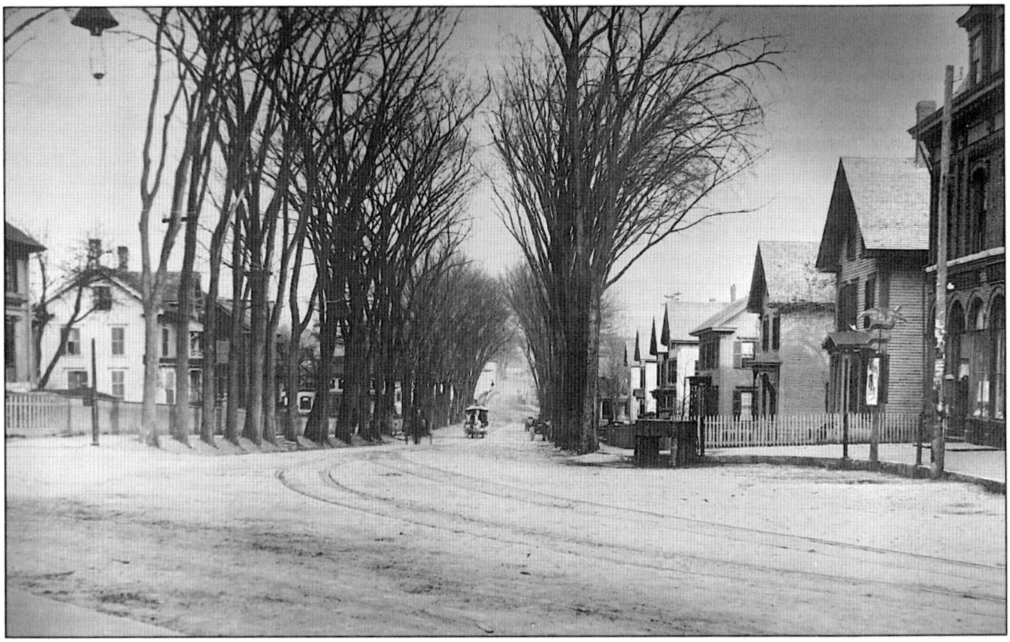

Approaching Granite Square in West Manchester is one of the Manchester Horse Railroad's original closed cars of 1877. In those years, both sides of Granite Street between the Merrimack River bridge and the square were lined with dwellings.

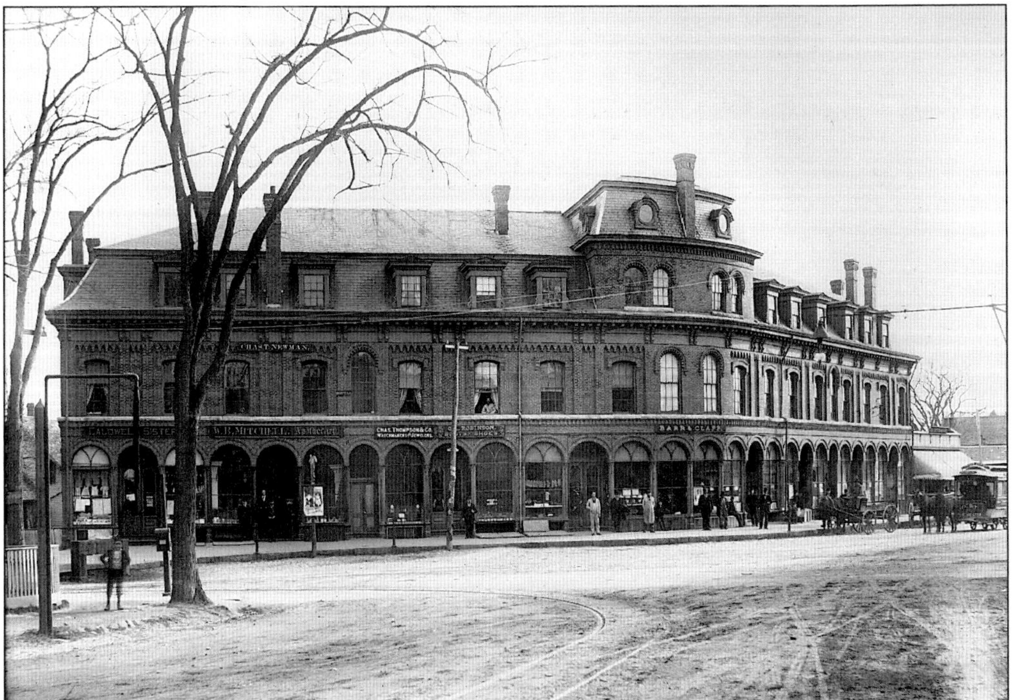

The Barr & Clapp Block was a landmark in Granite Square for many years. In this *c.* 1890 view, the closed horsecar at the extreme right is headed for the Elm Street business district and the North End. (MHA.)

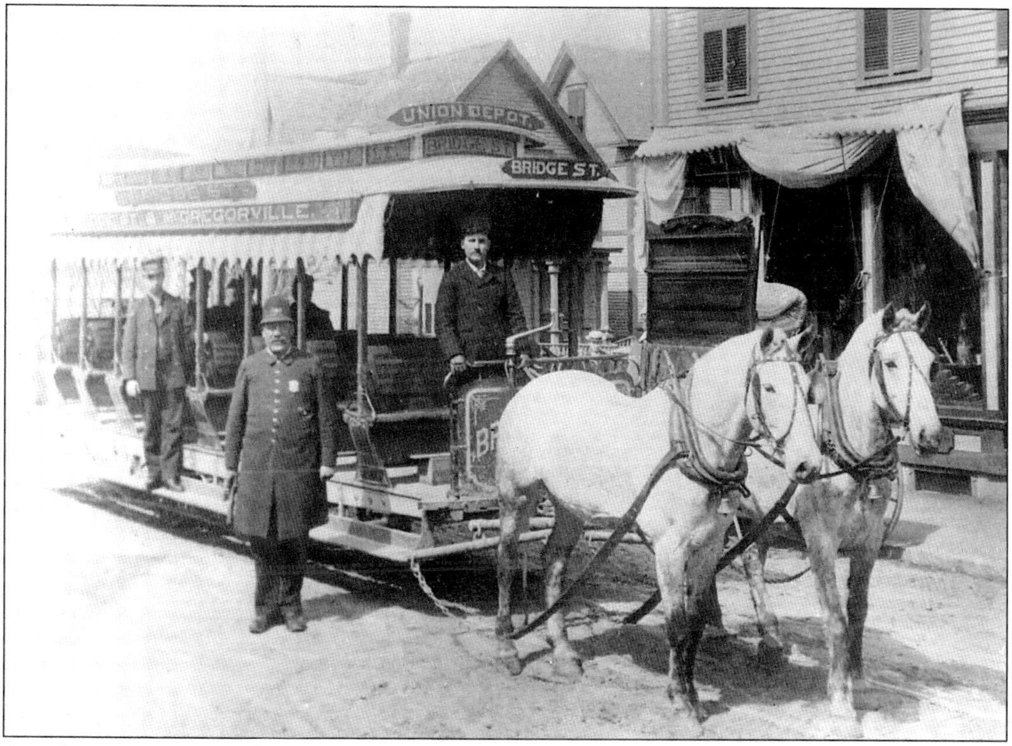

A policeman poses with the crew, as an eight-bench open horsecar on the Bridge Street–McGregorville line is photographed near North Main and Amory Streets. The brass gooseneck handle in front of the driver was turned to apply and release the brakes.

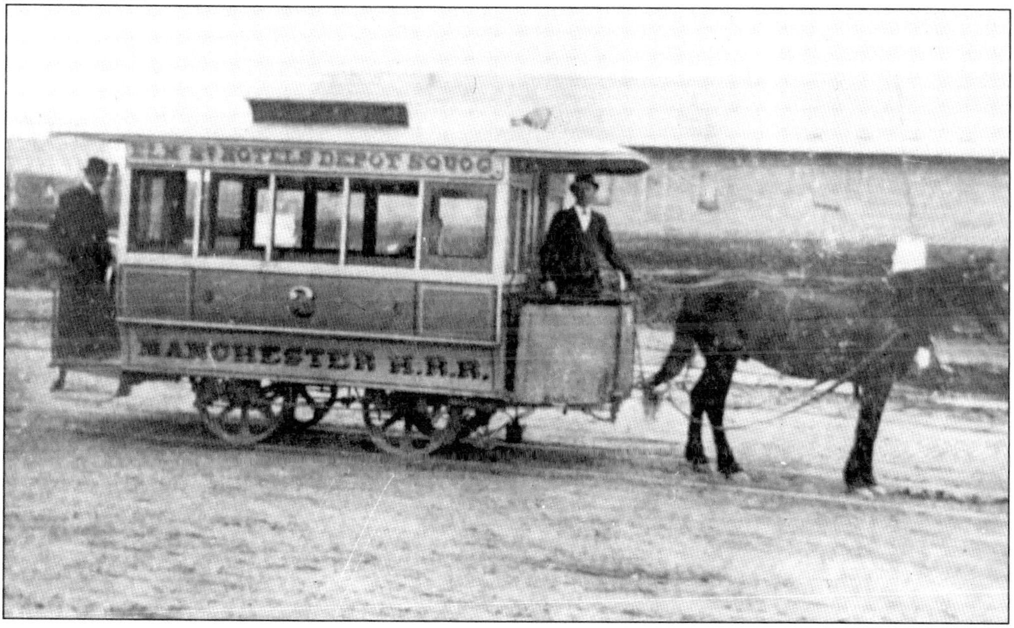

Somewhere in West Manchester is the 12-foot horsecar No. 2, *c.* 1880. The word "Squog" on the letter board above the windows was a popular nickname for Piscataquog Village in the area where South Main Street crossed the Piscataquog River.

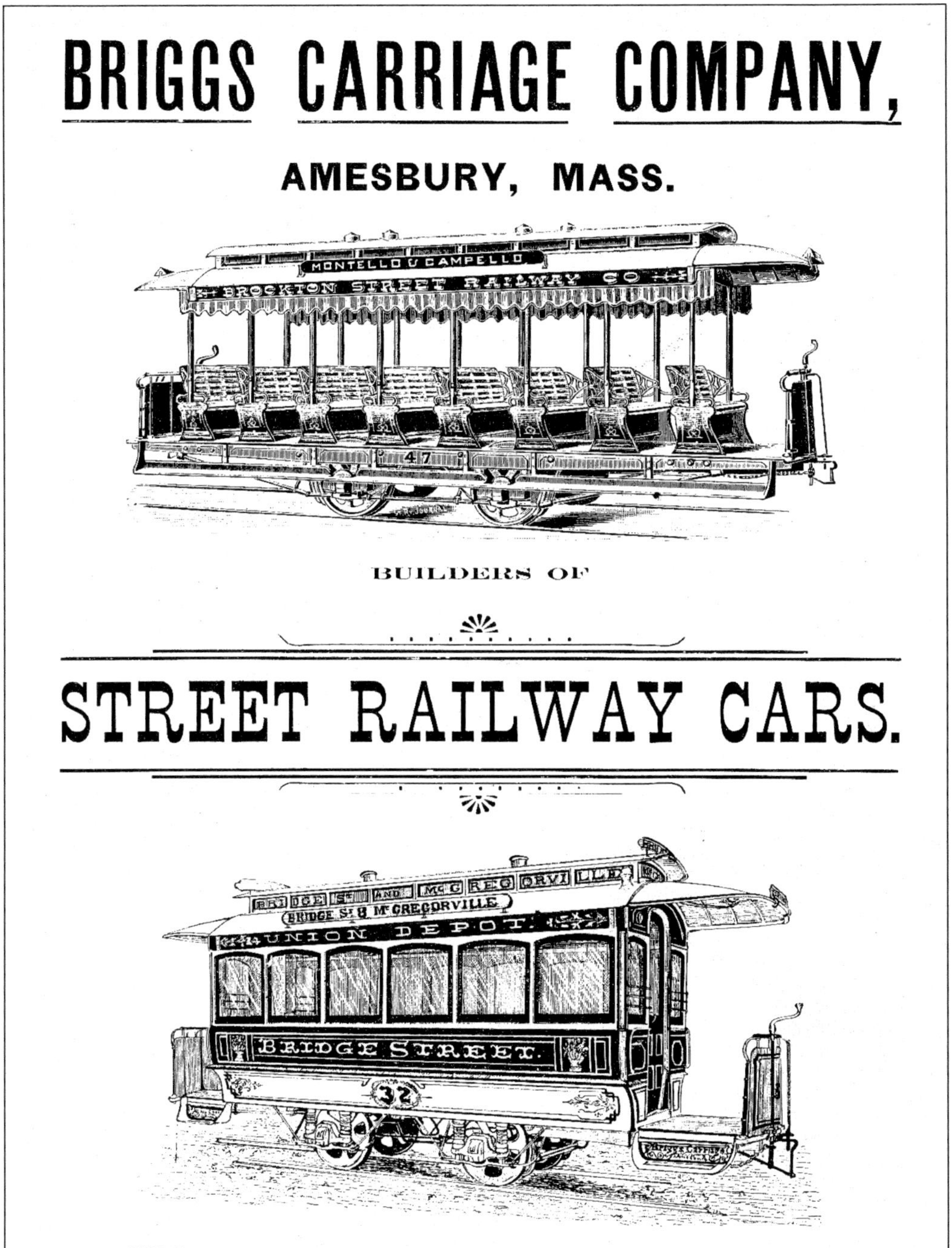

A 16-foot closed car of the Manchester Street Railway is illustrated at the bottom of an 1891 advertisement of the Briggs Carriage Company in the *Street Railway Journal*. Eight of these cars, Nos. 30–37, were built by Briggs for the Queen City in 1891–1892.

Two

Queen City Trolleys

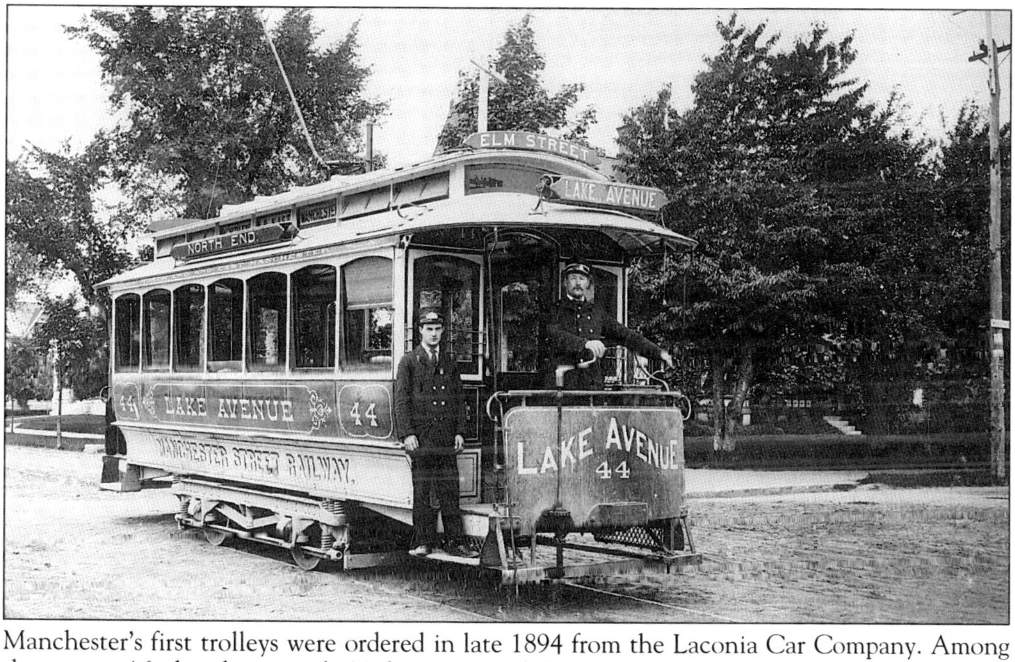

Manchester's first trolleys were ordered in late 1894 from the Laconia Car Company. Among them were 16 closed cars with 20-foot, one-inch bodies, Nos. 40–45, and Nos. 66–77. Each had two longitudinal seats accommodating 28 passengers. Number 44 is at Elm and Webster Streets shortly after being placed in service in June 1895. Four of those 16 cars were destroyed in a carbarn fire on March 4, 1905, and the remaining 12 were renumbered (even) Nos. 46–68 before the end of that year. The body of No. 60, originally No. 70, is now at the Seashore Trolley Museum awaiting restoration.

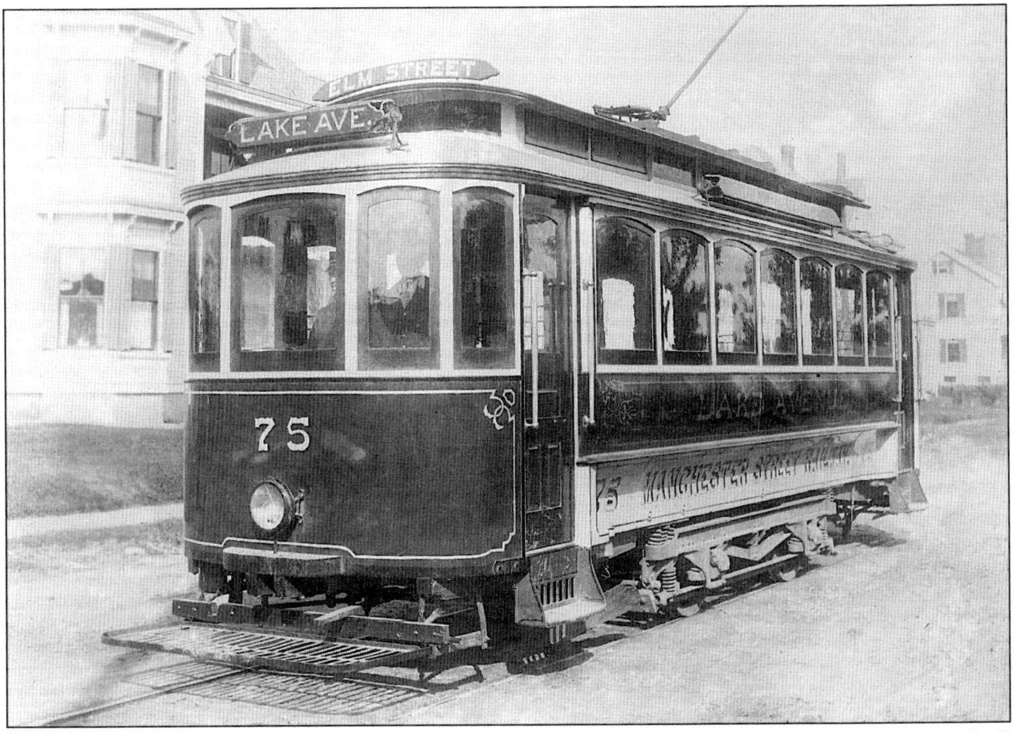

In March 1899, the N.H. Legislature mandated the enclosure of the end platforms of all streetcars regularly operated in the Granite State betwen December and March. Manchester Street Railway No. 75 is shown with its new vestibules.

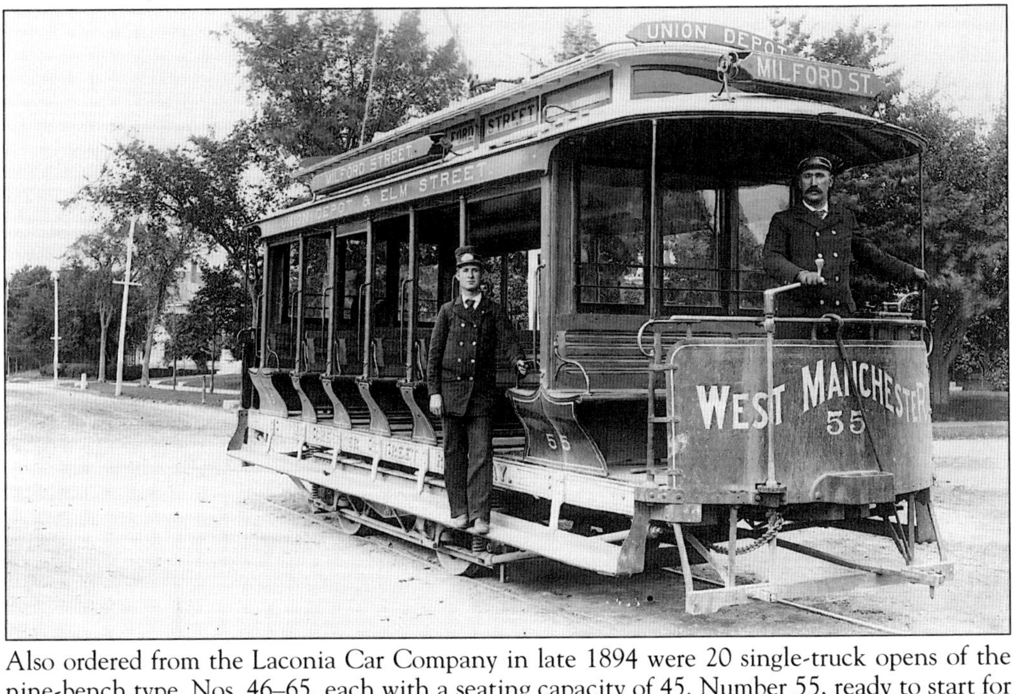

Also ordered from the Laconia Car Company in late 1894 were 20 single-truck opens of the nine-bench type, Nos. 46–65, each with a seating capacity of 45. Number 55, ready to start for West Manchester, is at Elm and Webster Streets during the summer of 1897. (MHA.)

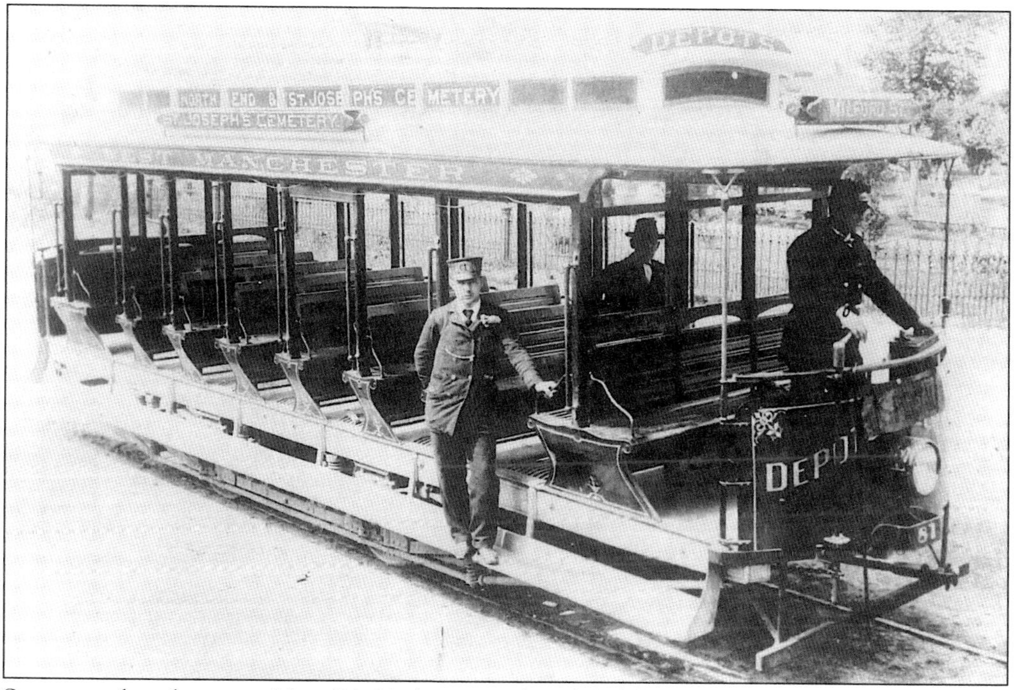

Seven ten-bench opens, Nos. 76–82, later numbered (odd) 83–95, were purchased from the Briggs Carriage Company in 1897. Each had a seating capacity of 50. Here is No. 81 at St. Joseph Cemetery on Donald Street, West Manchester, in the summer of 1898.

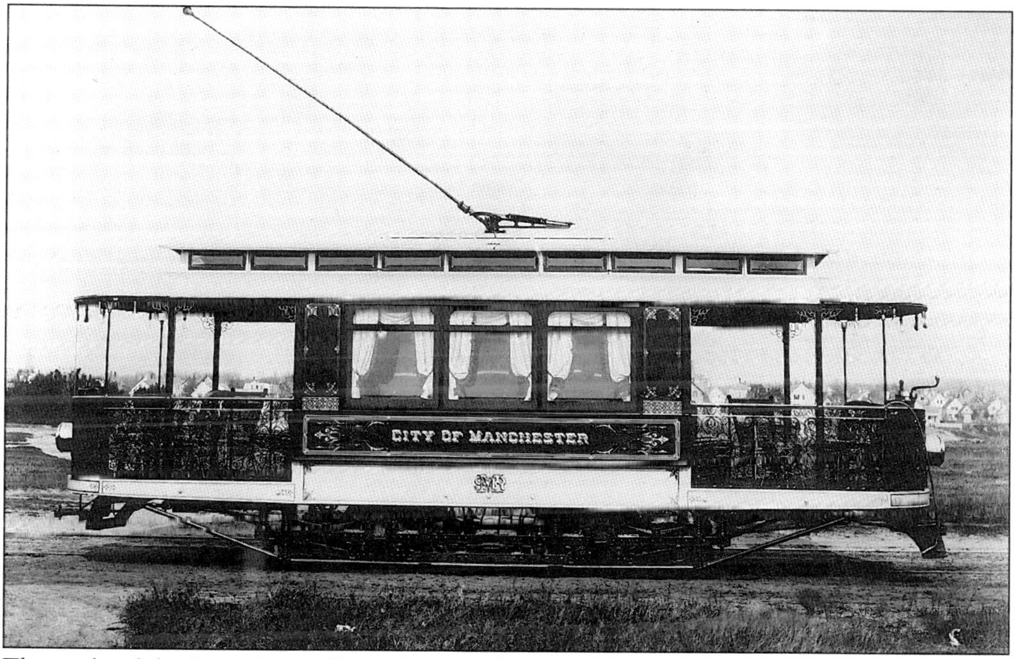

The pride of the Manchester Street Railway for many years was the luxurious parlor car *City of Manchester*, produced by the Briggs Carriage Company and delivered in August 1897. It was intended primarily for the use of the company but could be chartered by private parties at reasonable rates.

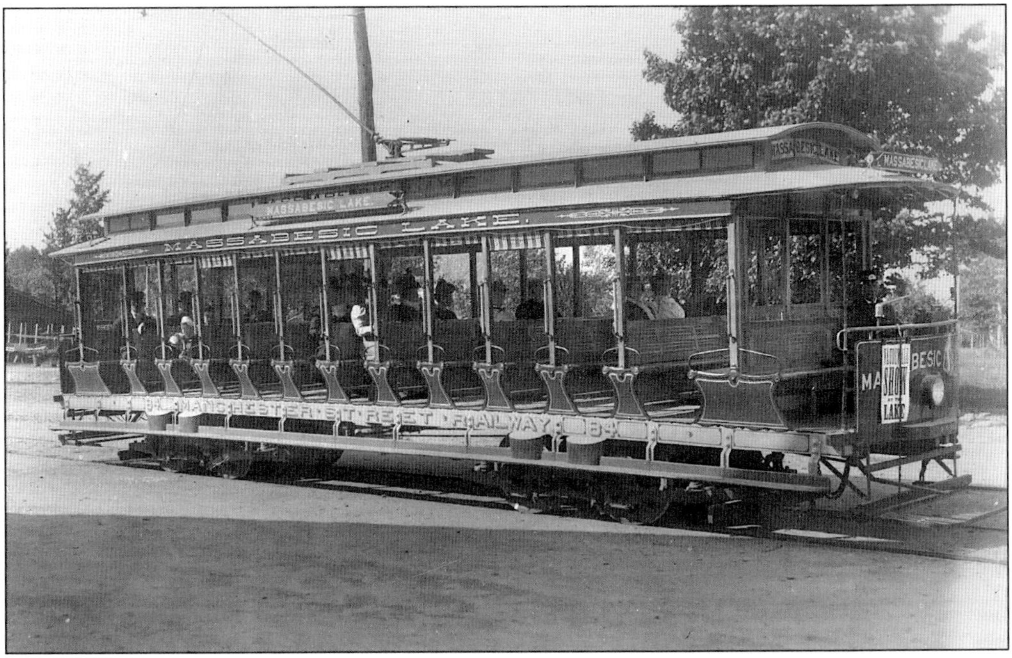

The very first double-truck (eight-wheeled) cars on the Manchester Street Railway were two of the 15-bench open type, Nos. 83 and 84. They were built by the Newburyport Car Manufacturing Company in 1899 and assigned to the Massabesic Lake line.

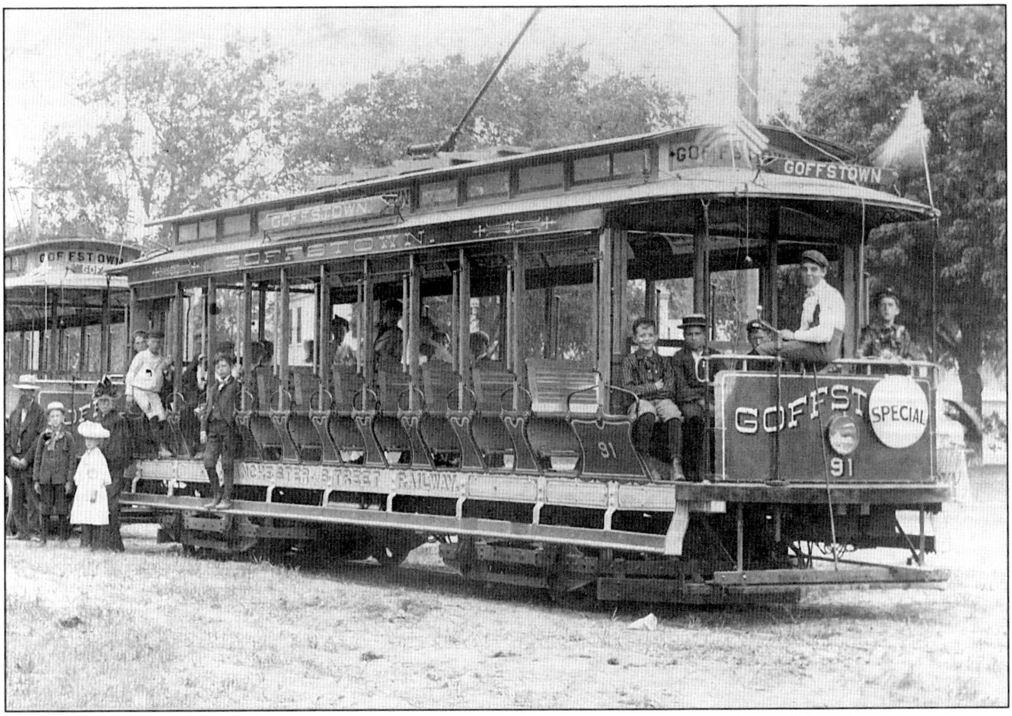

The first 9 of 33 double-truck open cars of the 13-bench type purchased by the Manchester Street Railway were Nos. 83–91, built in 1900. Each had a seating capacity of 60. Twenty-four additional cars of the same general type were added between 1901 and 1905.

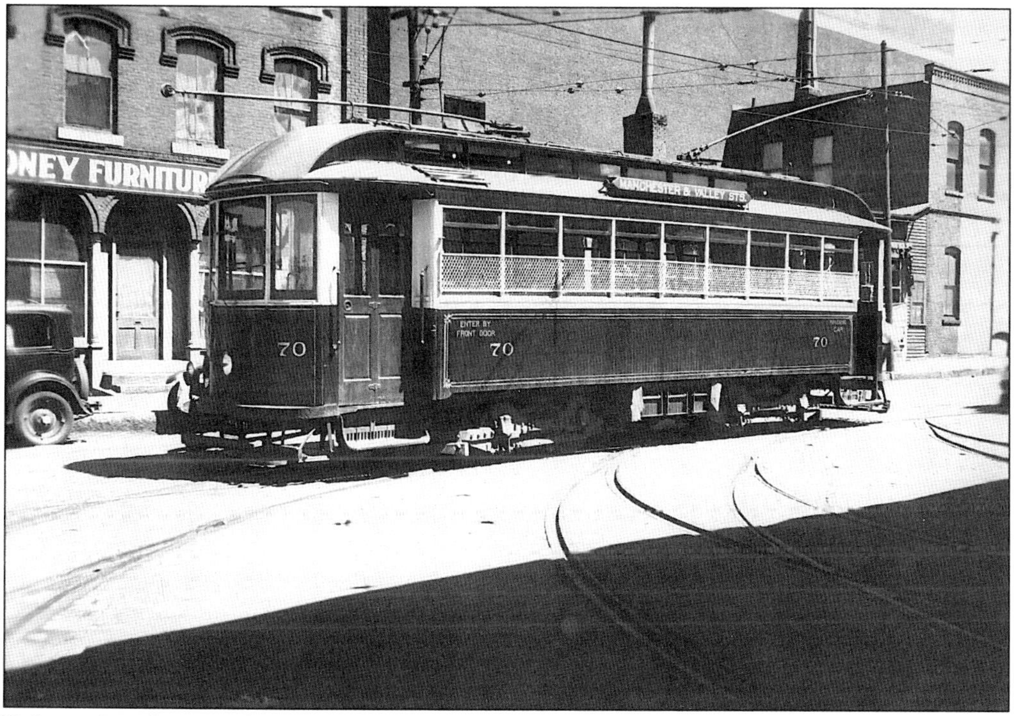

Delivered to the Manchester Street Railway in August 1900 were four double-truck closed cars with 25-foot bodies, Nos. 92–95, built by the Laconia Car Company. Two were destroyed in a carbarn fire in March 1905, and the remaining two became Nos. 70 and 72.

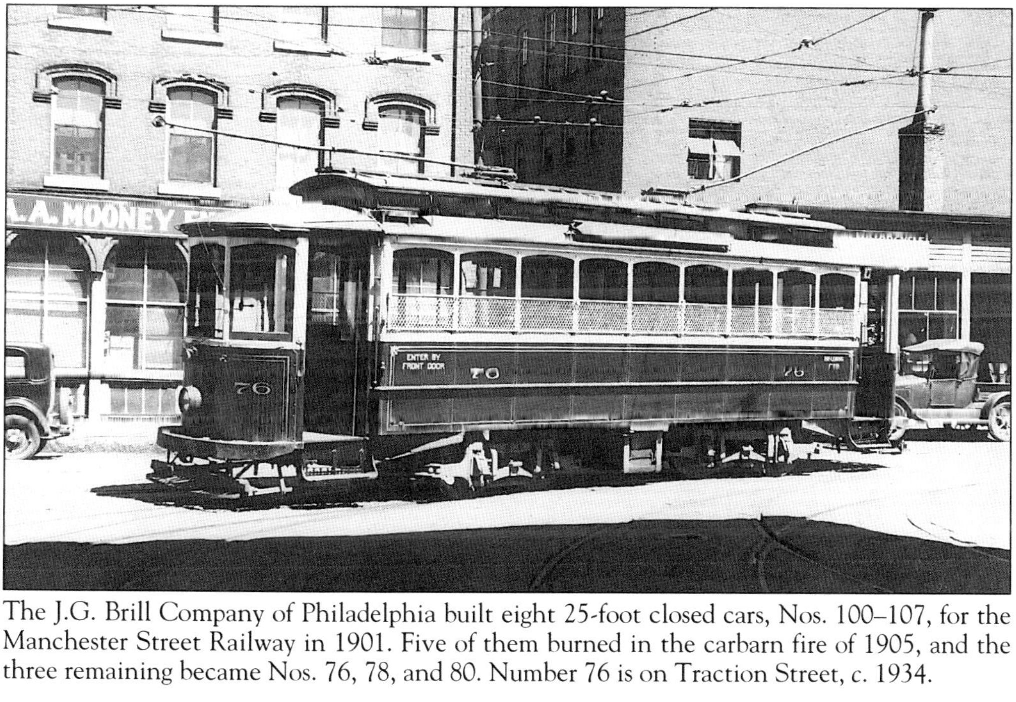

The J.G. Brill Company of Philadelphia built eight 25-foot closed cars, Nos. 100–107, for the Manchester Street Railway in 1901. Five of them burned in the carbarn fire of 1905, and the three remaining became Nos. 76, 78, and 80. Number 76 is on Traction Street, c. 1934.

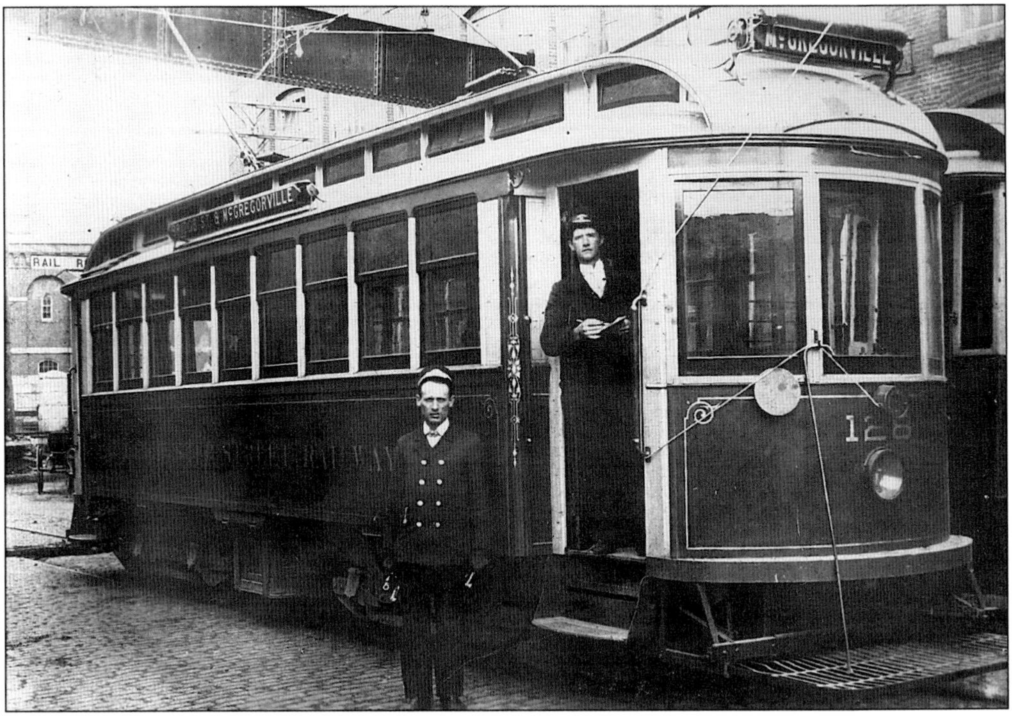

Fourteen more double-truck closed cars with 25-foot bodies, Nos. 123–136, were ordered from the Laconia Car Company in June 1903; deliveries began in early September. The six remaining after the 1905 carbarn fire were renumbered (even) Nos. 82–92.

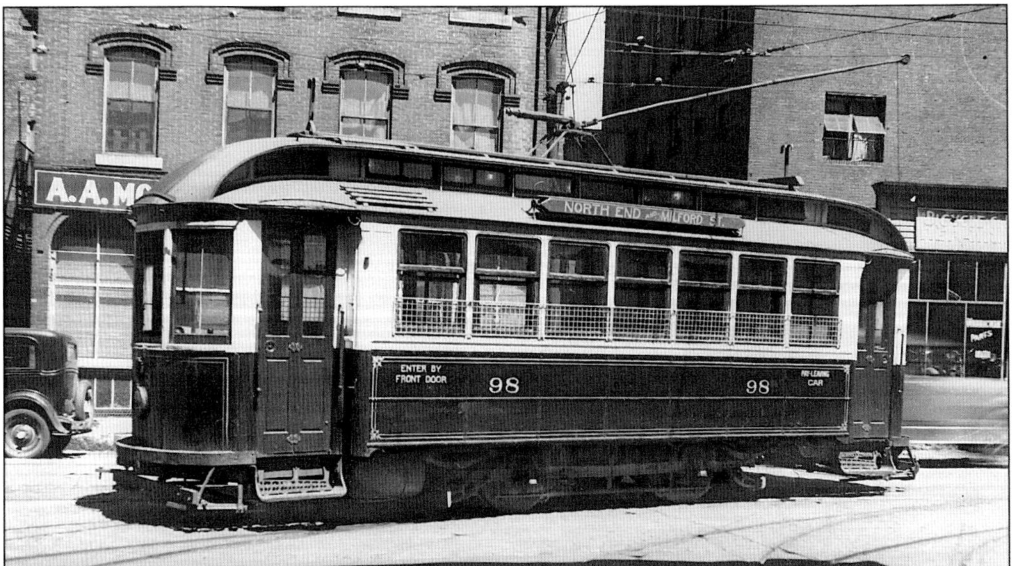

Twelve closed cars with 20-foot, 2-inch bodies, (even) Nos. 94–116, were ordered by the Manchester Street Railway from the Laconia Car Company in early 1906. All were revamped for one-man operation in 1924, and all had been retired by the end of 1938.

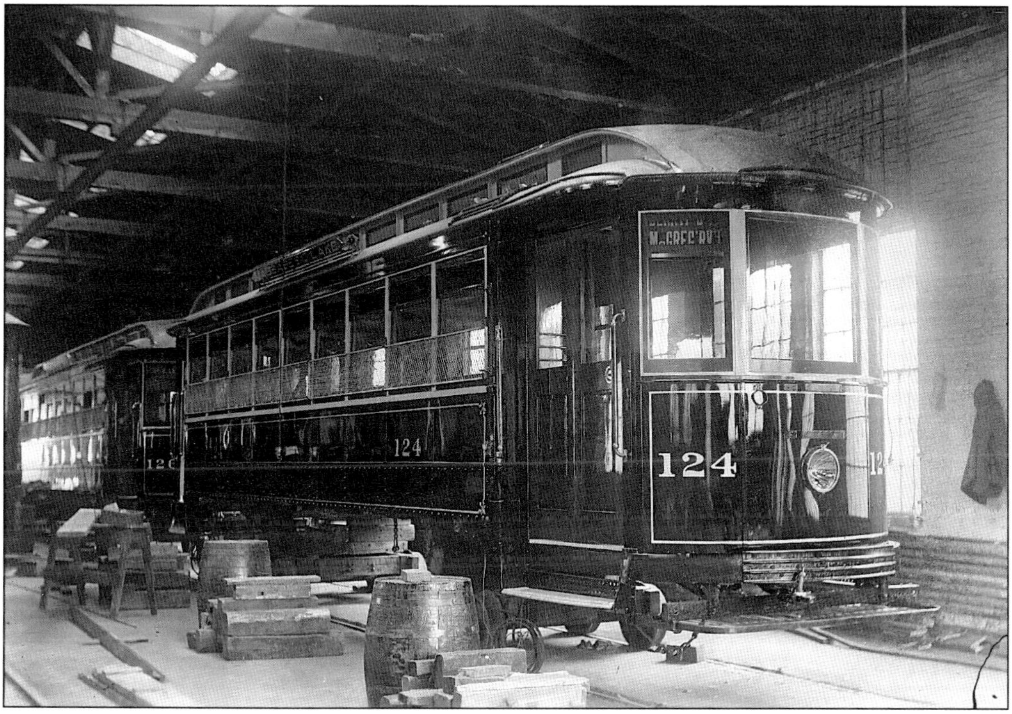

Shown in a Laconia Car Company shop are two of the six 26.5-foot double-truck closed cars, (even) Nos. 118–128, ordered from that builder in 1912. All six were still active when trolley service in the Queen City ended in 1940.

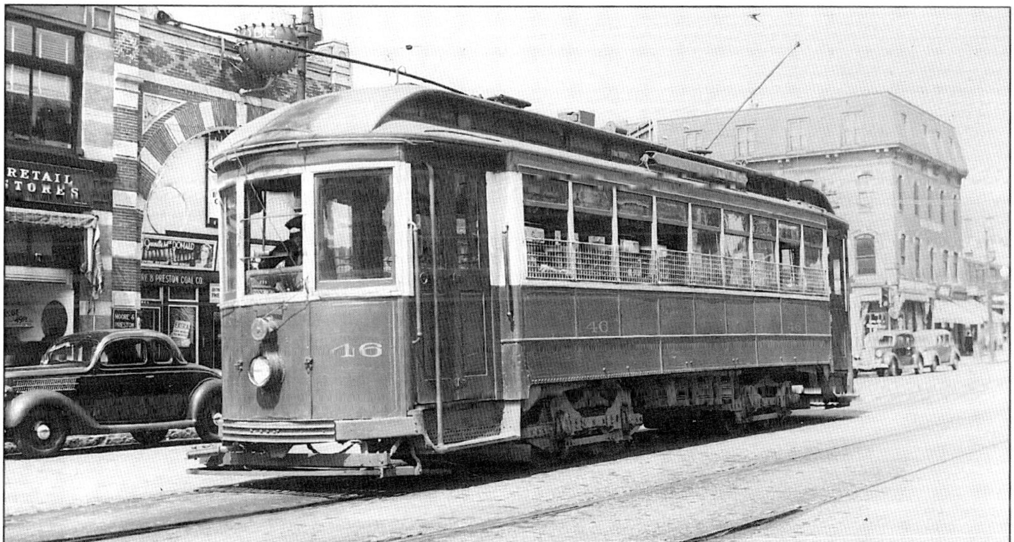

Substantially identical to Nos. 118–128 were four cars, Nos. 46, 48, 52, and 56, produced in the Manchester Street Railway shops in 1915–1916. Equipped for one-man operation in 1924, they remained in regular service until 1940. Number 46 is on Elm Street in 1938.

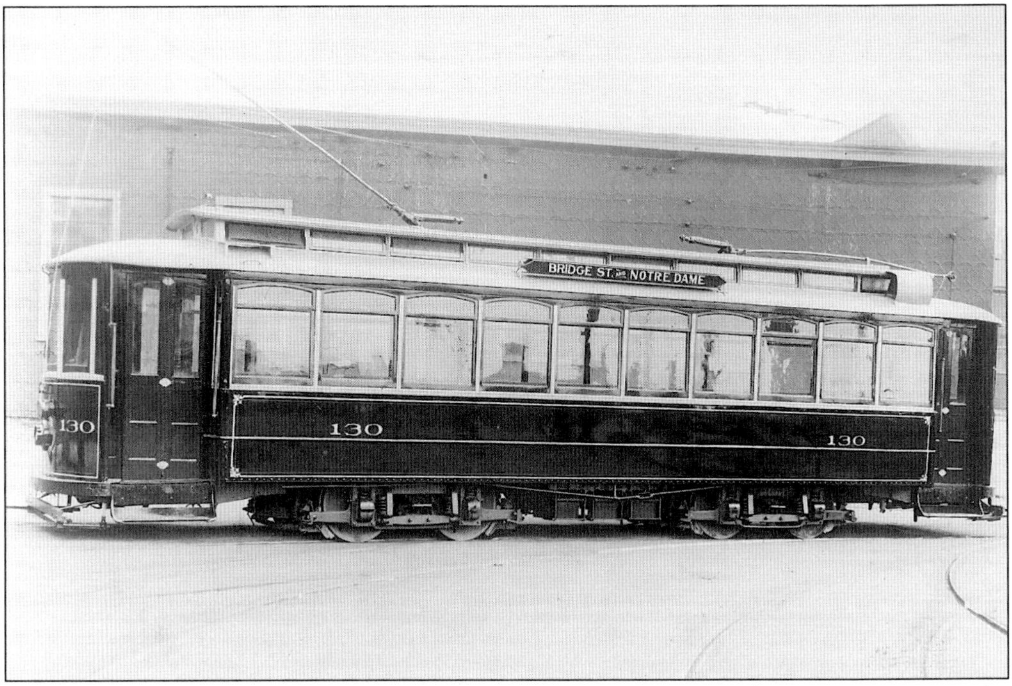

Nine ancient double-truck closed cars were acquired secondhand in Bridgeport, Connecticut, by the Manchester Street Railway in 1919. Four of them, built by Jackson & Sharp of Wilmington, Delaware, in 1897, became (even) Nos. 130–136 in the Queen City.

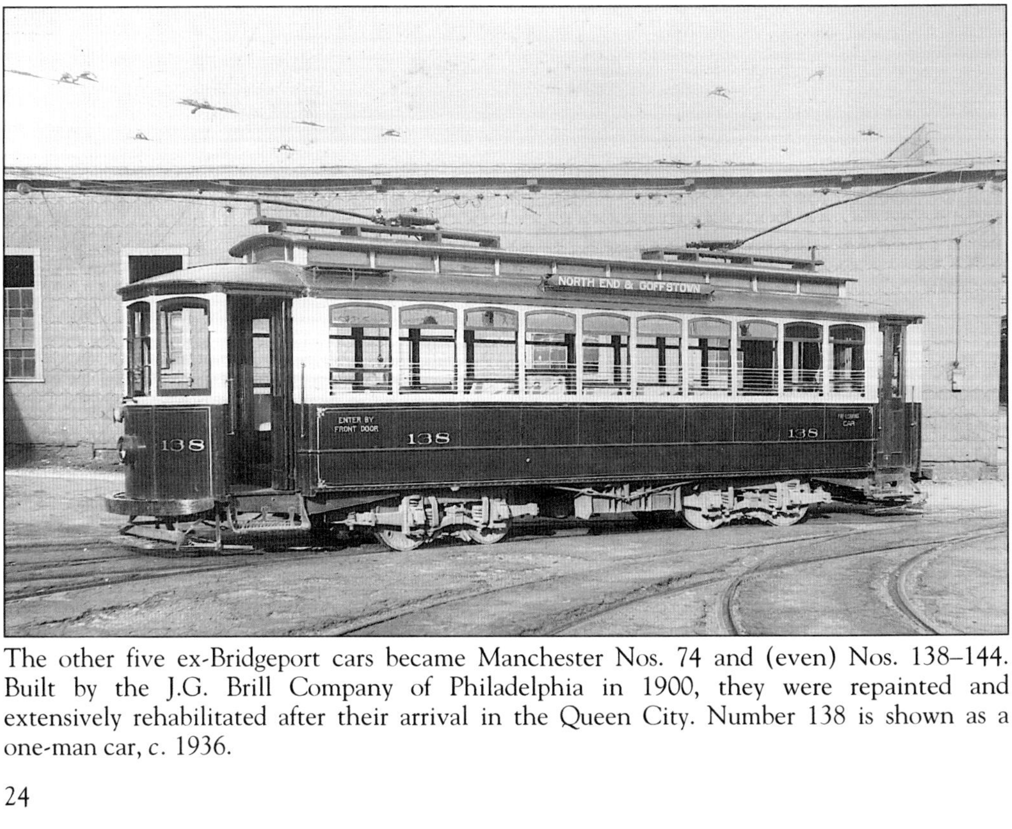

The other five ex-Bridgeport cars became Manchester Nos. 74 and (even) Nos. 138–144. Built by the J.G. Brill Company of Philadelphia in 1900, they were repainted and extensively rehabilitated after their arrival in the Queen City. Number 138 is shown as a one-man car, *c.* 1936.

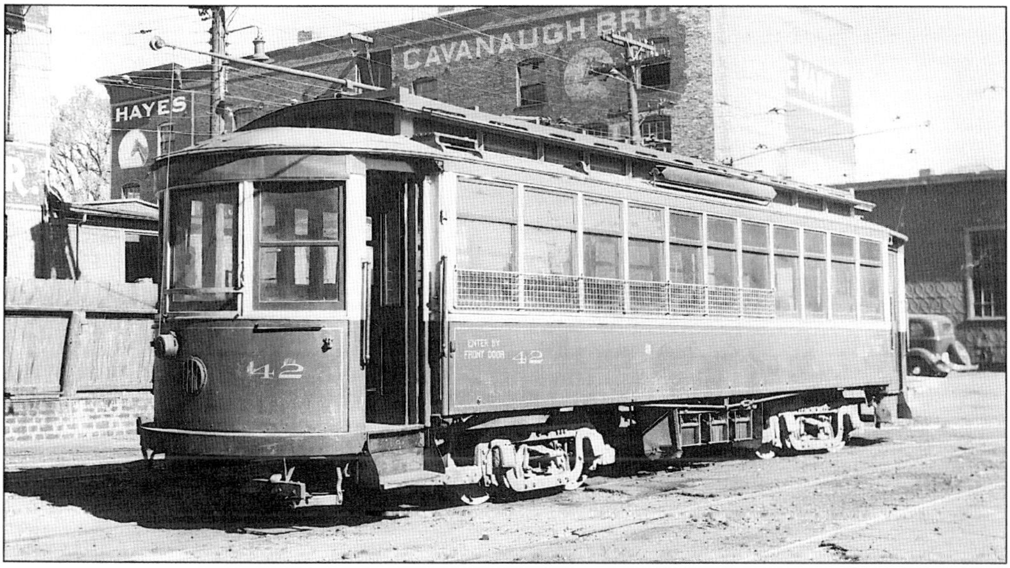

Two obsolete 30-foot closed cars, built in 1902, were purchased secondhand from the Eastern Massachusetts Street Railway in 1921. They became Nos. 42 and 44 of the Manchester Street Railway. Both cars were in service until the end, in 1940.

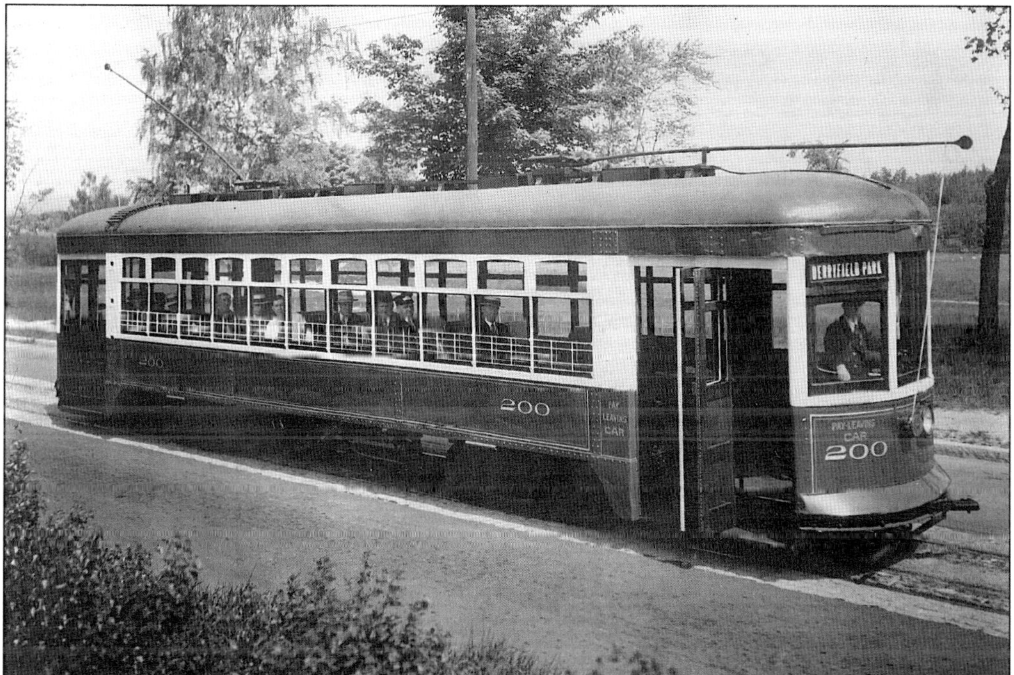

The most modern closed trolleys ever operated in the Queen City were four with 31-foot bodies. These were purchased second-hand in Muskegon, Michigan, in 1930 by the Manchester Street Railway, which renumbered them (even) 200–206.

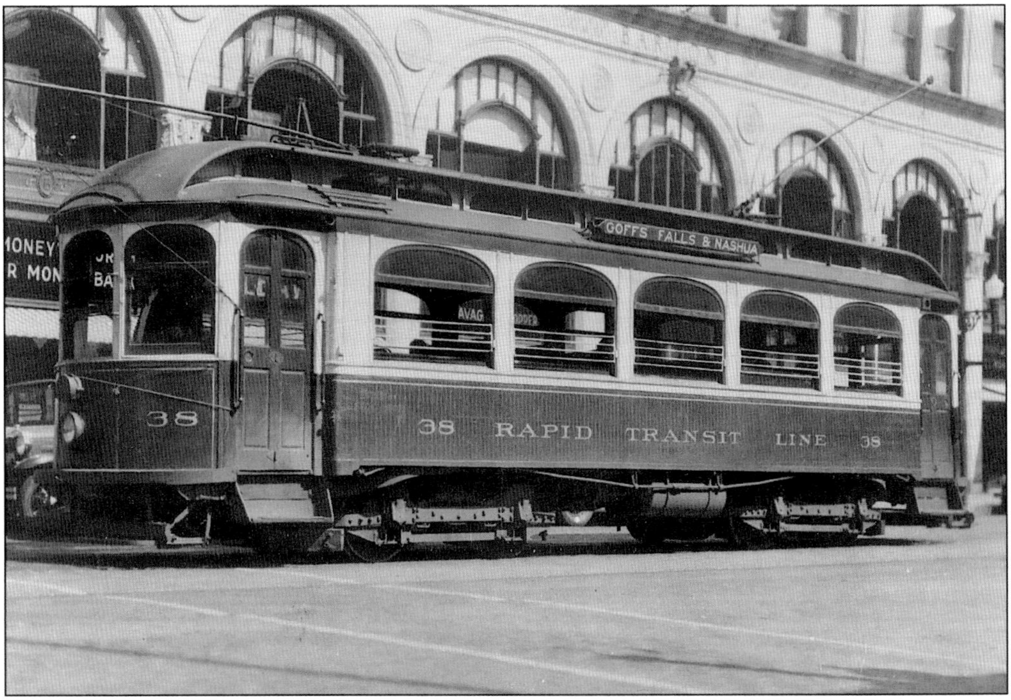

Six double-truck cars with 29-foot, 6-inch bodies, Nos. 1–6, were ordered from the Laconia Car Company in 1906 for operation over the Manchester & Nashua Street Railway. They subsequently became (even) Nos. 30–40.

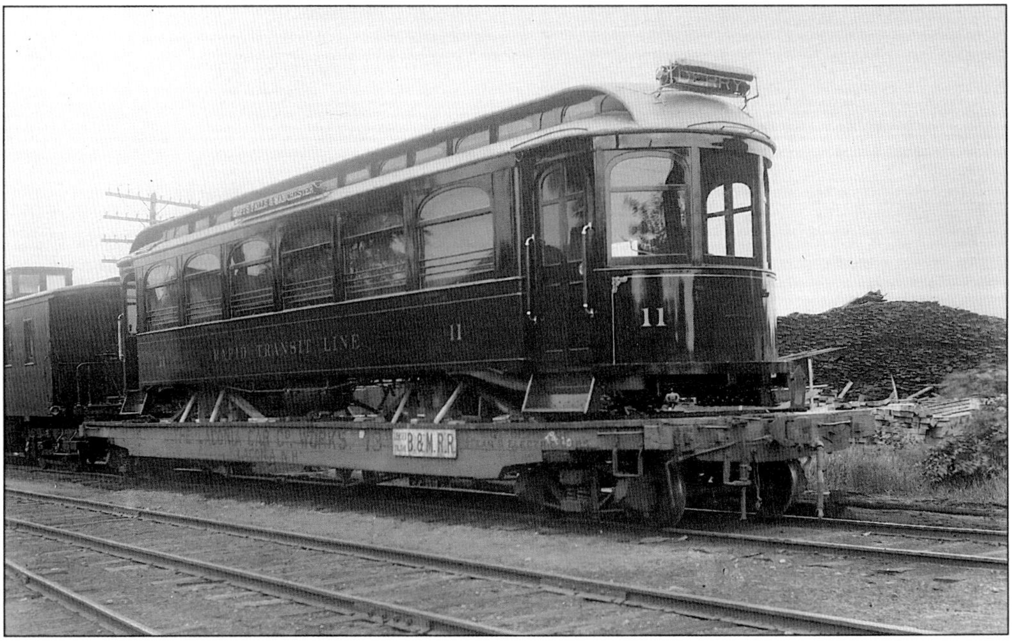

Loaded on a flatcar for shipment is one of the six 33-foot, 10-inch double-truck closed cars, Nos. 7–12, later (even) Nos. 2–12, built by the Laconia Car Company for the Manchester & Derry Street Railway in 1907. Both these and Nos. 1–6 of the Manchester & Nashua were popularly known as "Rapids."

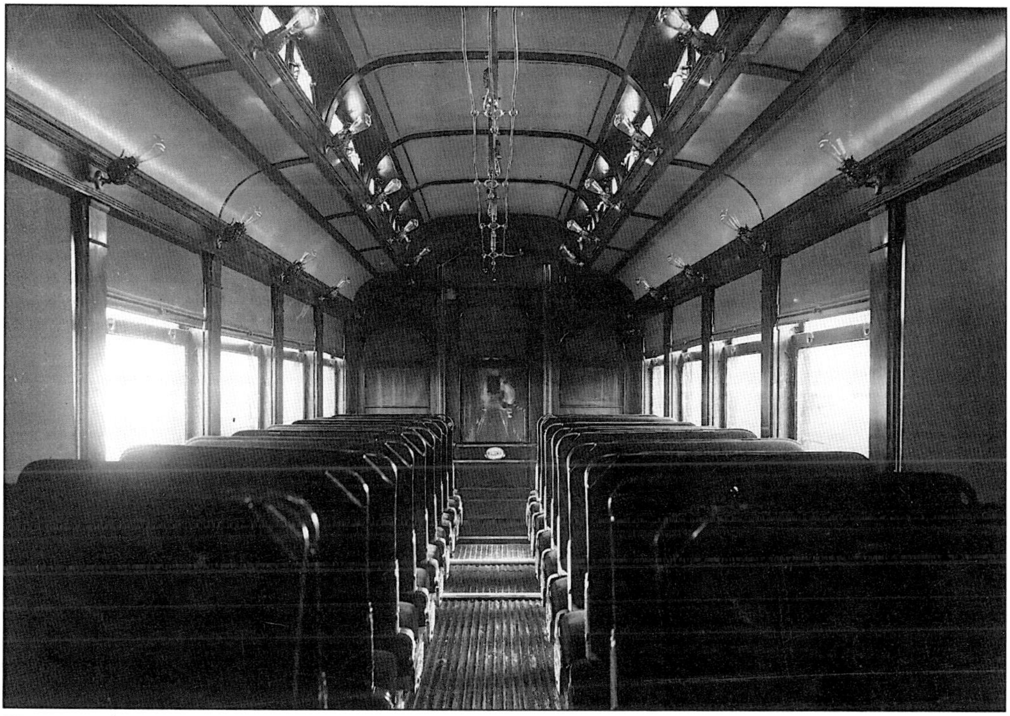

Shown is the interior of No. 11 of the Manchester & Derry in 1907. The seat cushions and backs were upholstered in green plush, and there was a single sliding door in each bulkhead. Electric heaters were provided under the seats.

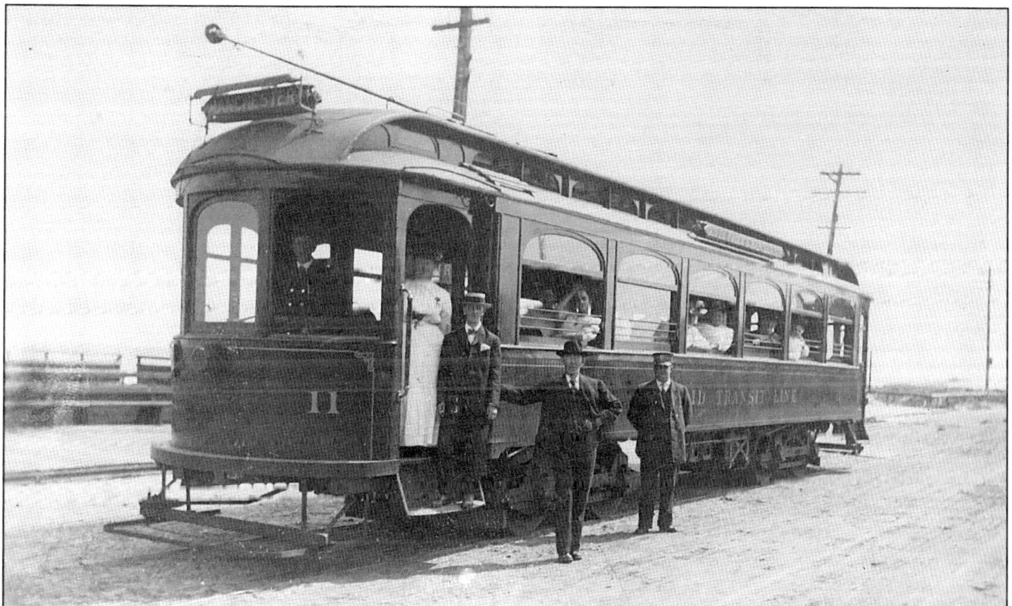

Shown at Hampton Beach *c.* 1910 is Rapid No. 11, which had just conveyed a special party from Manchester to the resort, where a casino, theater, and ballroom were among the major attractions.

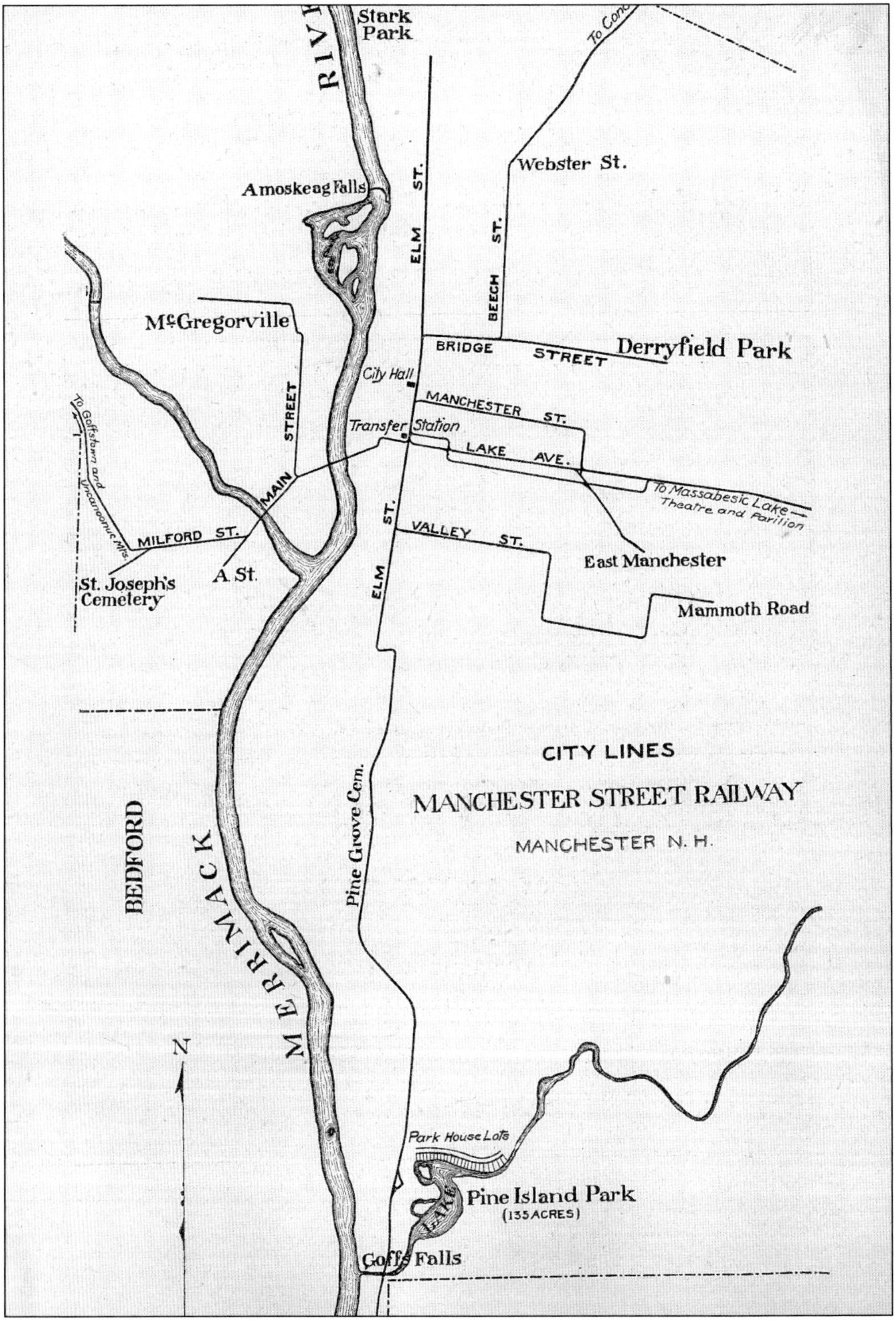

This map from a 1908 Queen City trolley guide shows the city lines of the Manchester Street Railway. There were no important changes until the advent of motor coach operation in 1940.

Three

The North End to Goffe's Falls

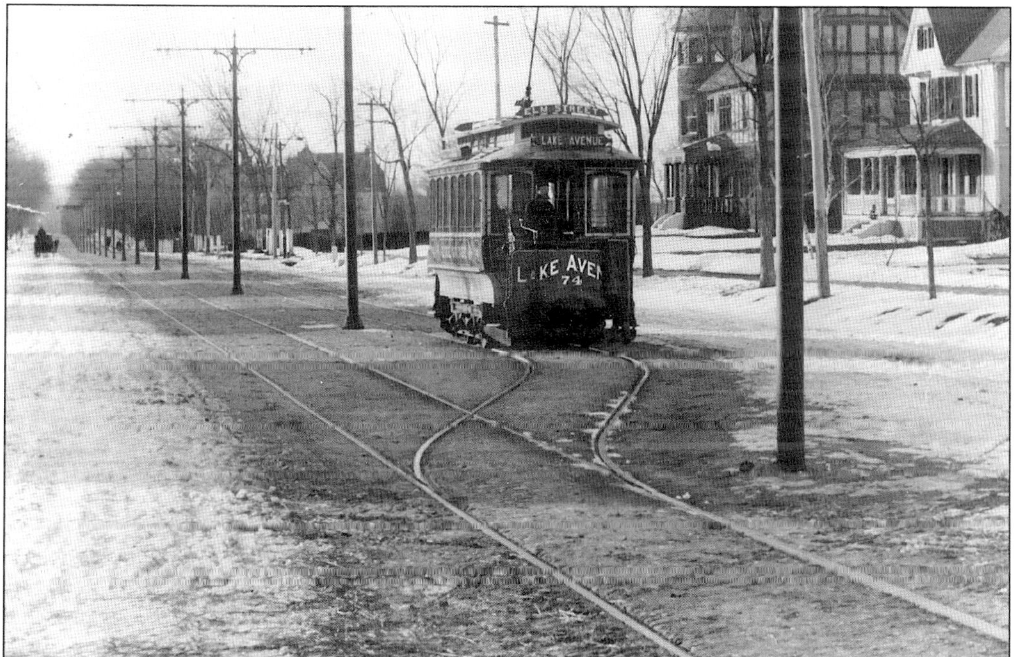

When the Manchester Street Railway was electrified in 1895, the trolley wires on Elm Street between Webster and Prospect Streets were suspended from brackets attached to center poles. These are evident in this view of No. 74 near the present Red Cross headquarters at 1800 Elm Street. Many years later, having become a traffic hazard, the center poles were removed and the trolley wires were suspended from span wires attached to new poles at curbside.

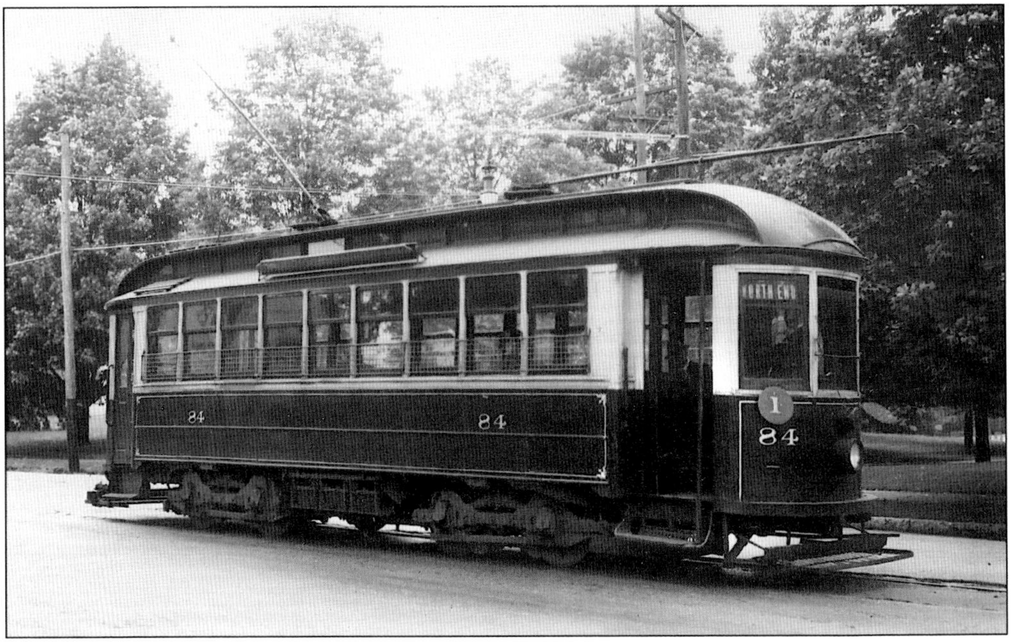

The rails on Elm Street were extended northward from Webster Street to Clarke Street in 1896 and then from Clarke Street to Carpenter Street in 1900. Number 84 is at Elm and Carpenter Streets in 1936.

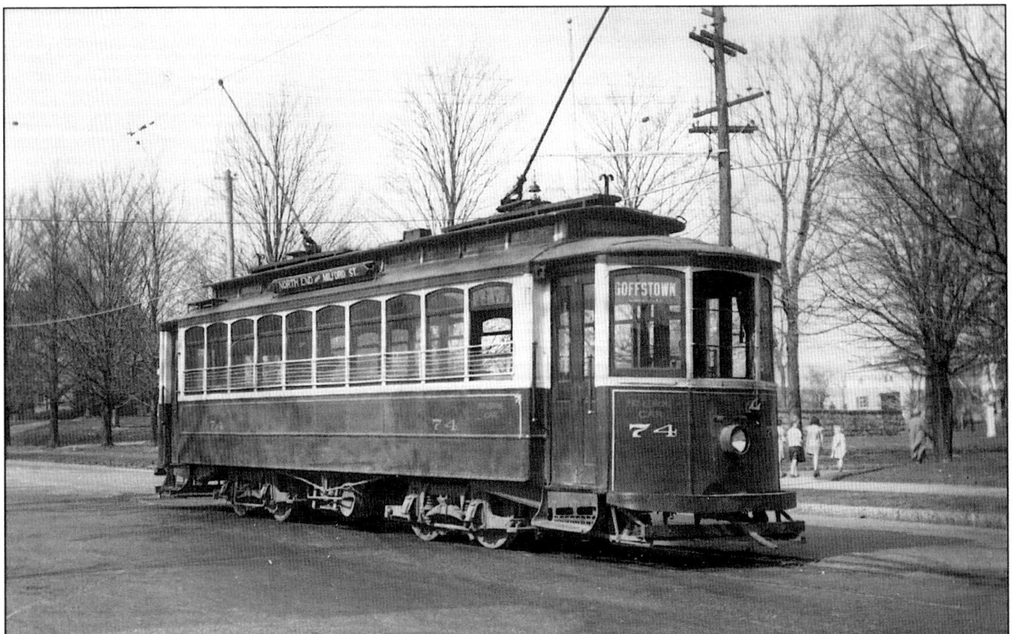

Goffstown cars started leaving from Elm and Carpenter Streets in Manchester's North End in November 1927 and continued to do so until January 8, 1938. The operator of No. 74 is changing ends (reversing direction) on April 28, 1936.

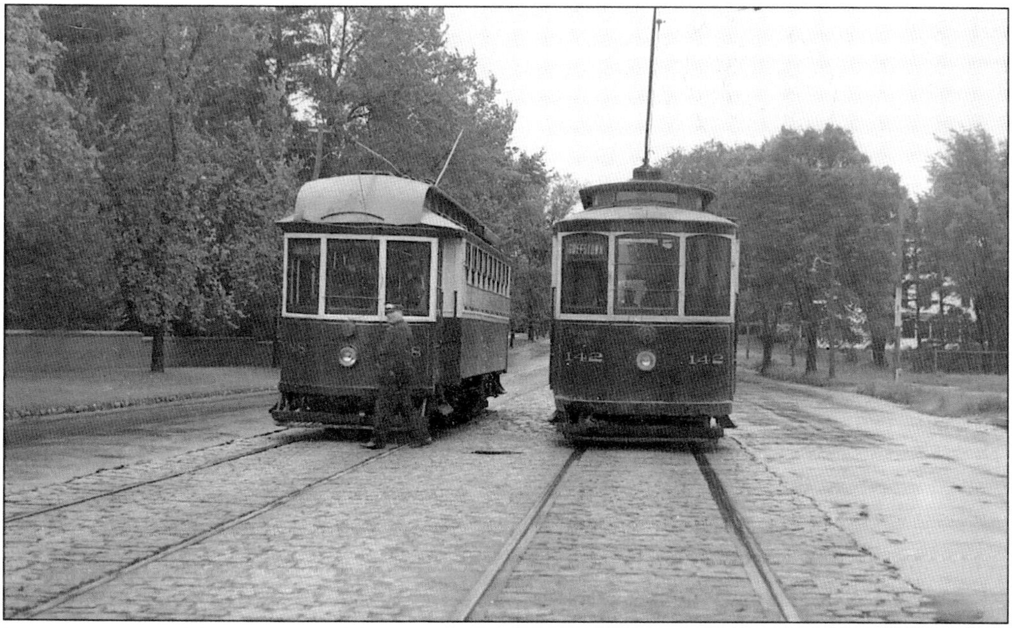

Meeting on the Elm Street double track immediately south of Clarke Street are Nos. 88 and 142, *c.* 1936. The latter is bound for Goffstown via West Manchester and Pinardville, while the former is en route to the North End terminus.

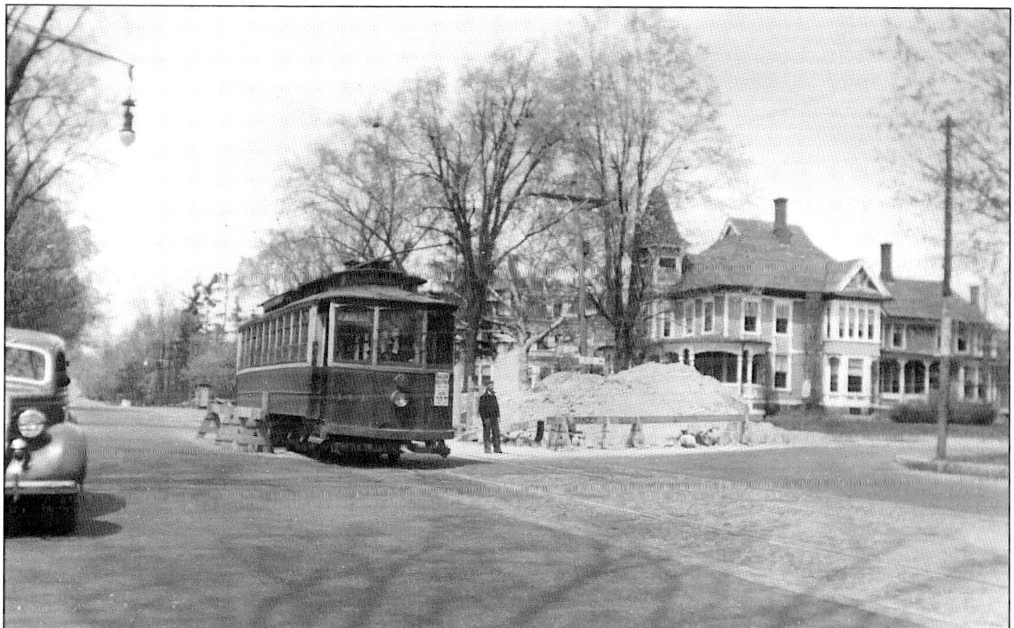

The end of trolley service in Manchester was only 13 days away on May 12, 1940, when Bill Maier snapped this view of No. 144 at Elm and Webster Streets. Note the 1935 Ford V-8 at the extreme left.

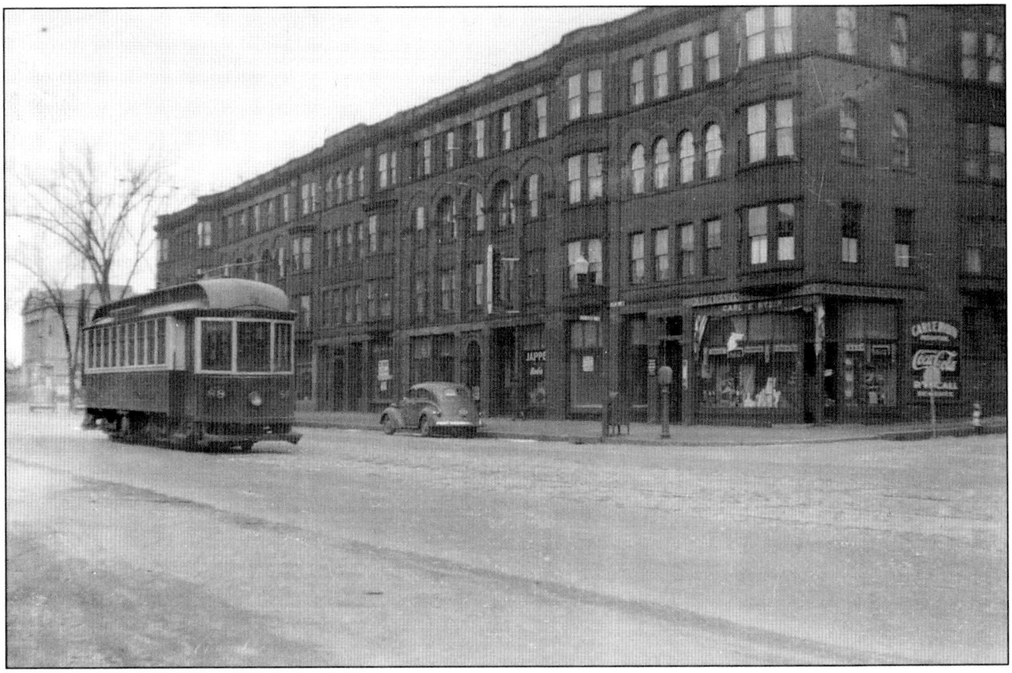

The Bedford Block is in the background in this March 8, 1939 view of No. 88 at Elm and Myrtle Streets. Although the streetcars are long gone, the brick building still stands; the ground floor is occupied by a number of business establishments.

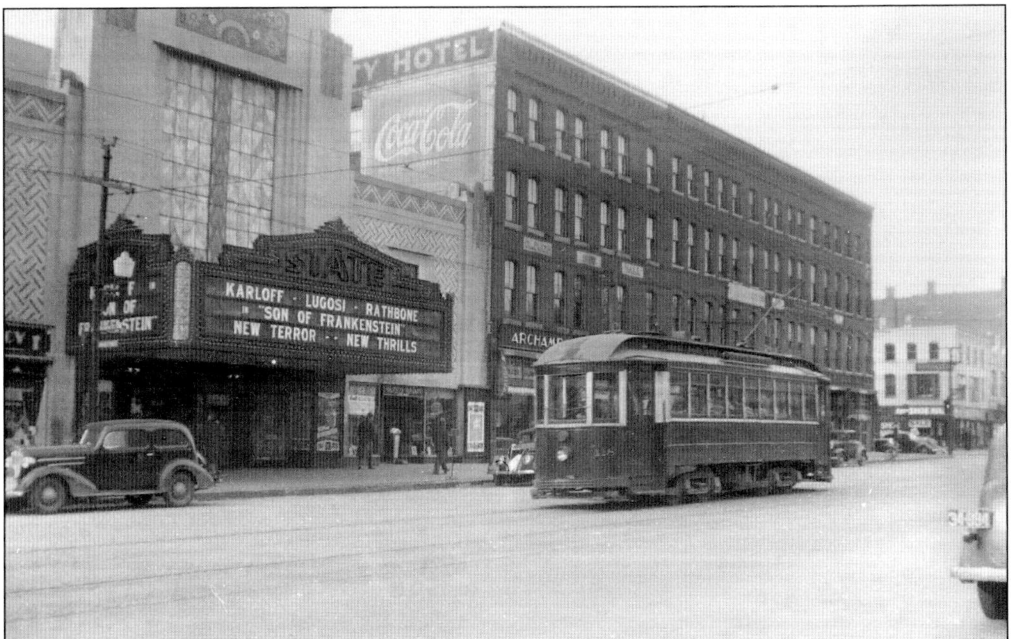

Son of Frankenstein, starring Boris Karloff, Bela Lugosi, and Basil Rathbone, was playing at the State Theater in this January 19, 1939 view of No. 118 heading south on Elm Street. Alas, the theater no longer stands.

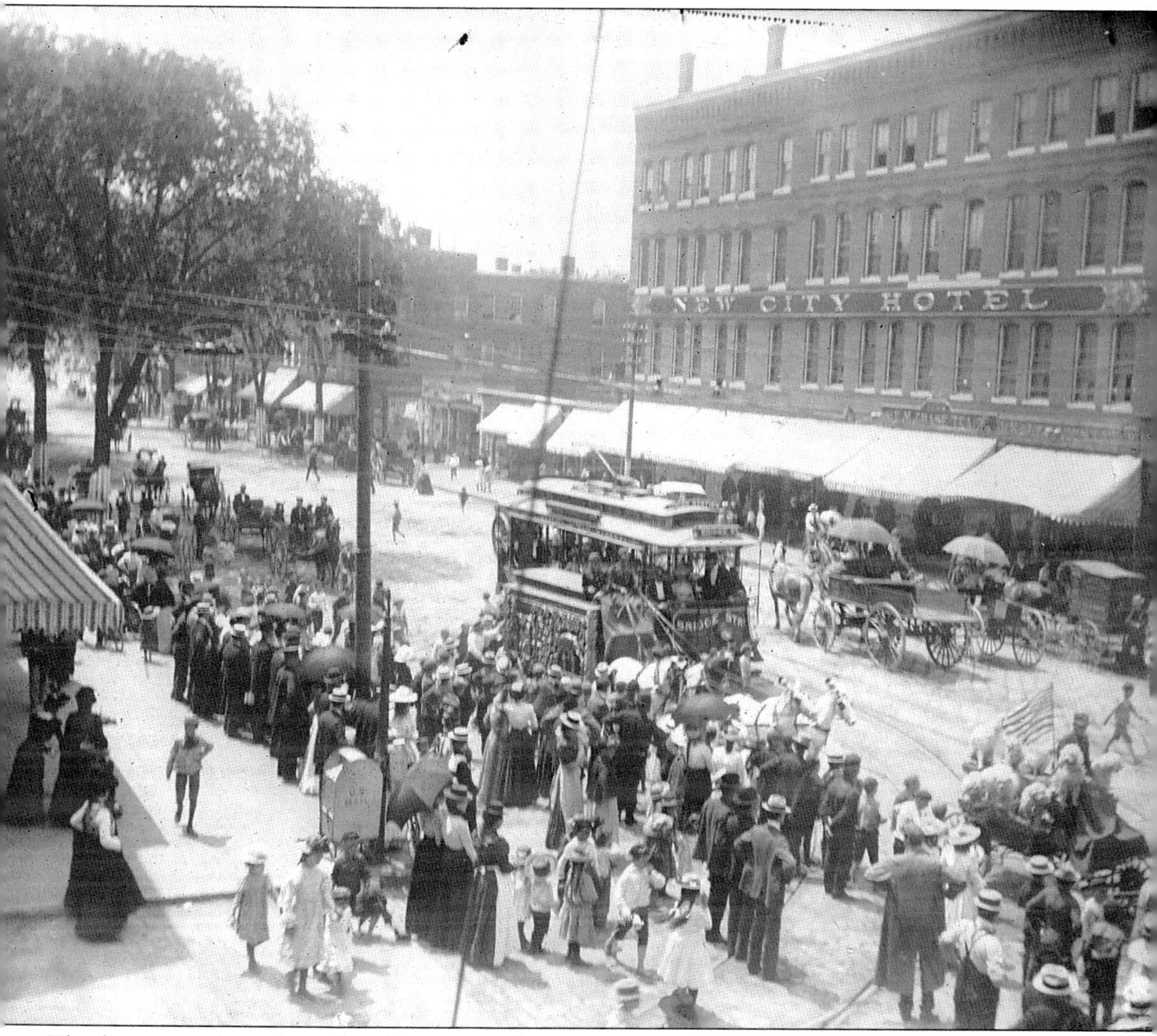

The large crowd on the sidewalk suggests that some sort of a celebration is in progress, as a Bridge Street open trolley heads north on Elm Street near the New City Hotel, a well-patronized hostelry c. 1895 when this photograph was taken. The hotel, which had retail stores at street level, was still in business when the trolley stopped running in 1940. (MHA.)

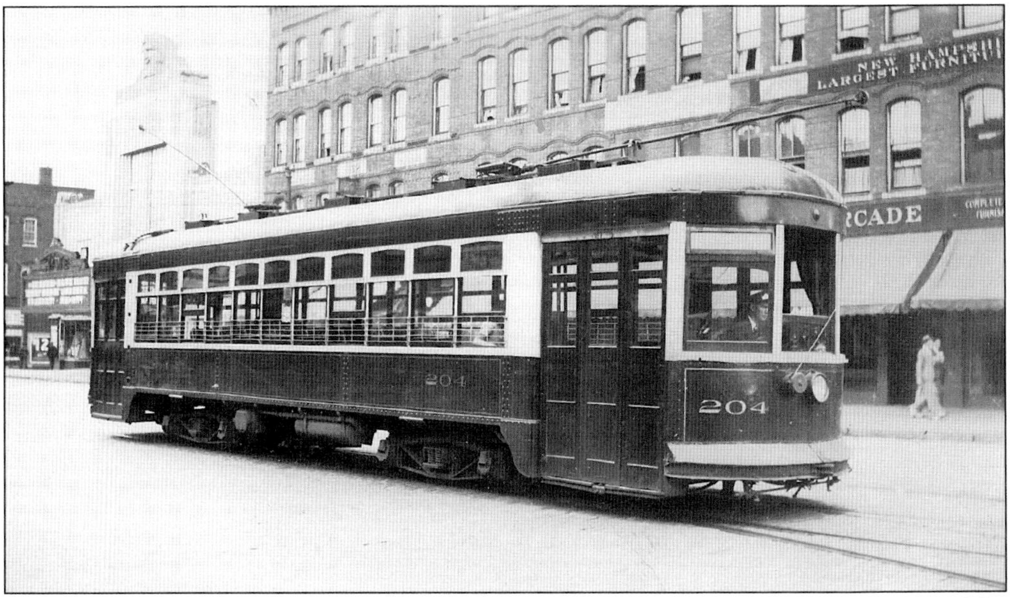

Turning from Elm Street onto Bridge Street on its way to Derryfield Park is No. 204, one of the four cars purchased secondhand in Muskegon, Michigan, in 1930. In the background is the E.M. Chase furniture store, then advertised as New England's largest.

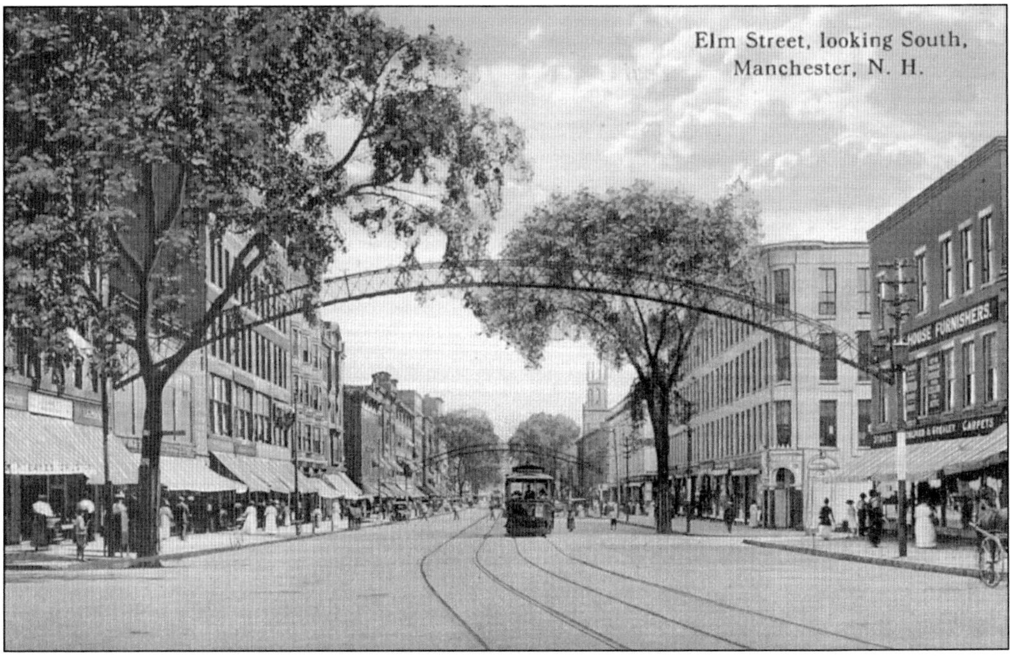

One of the ten streetlight arches erected in the Elm Street business district between Pearl Street and Lake Avenue in 1908 appears in this view looking south on Elm Street, *c.* 1910. All ten arches were removed *c.* 1919.

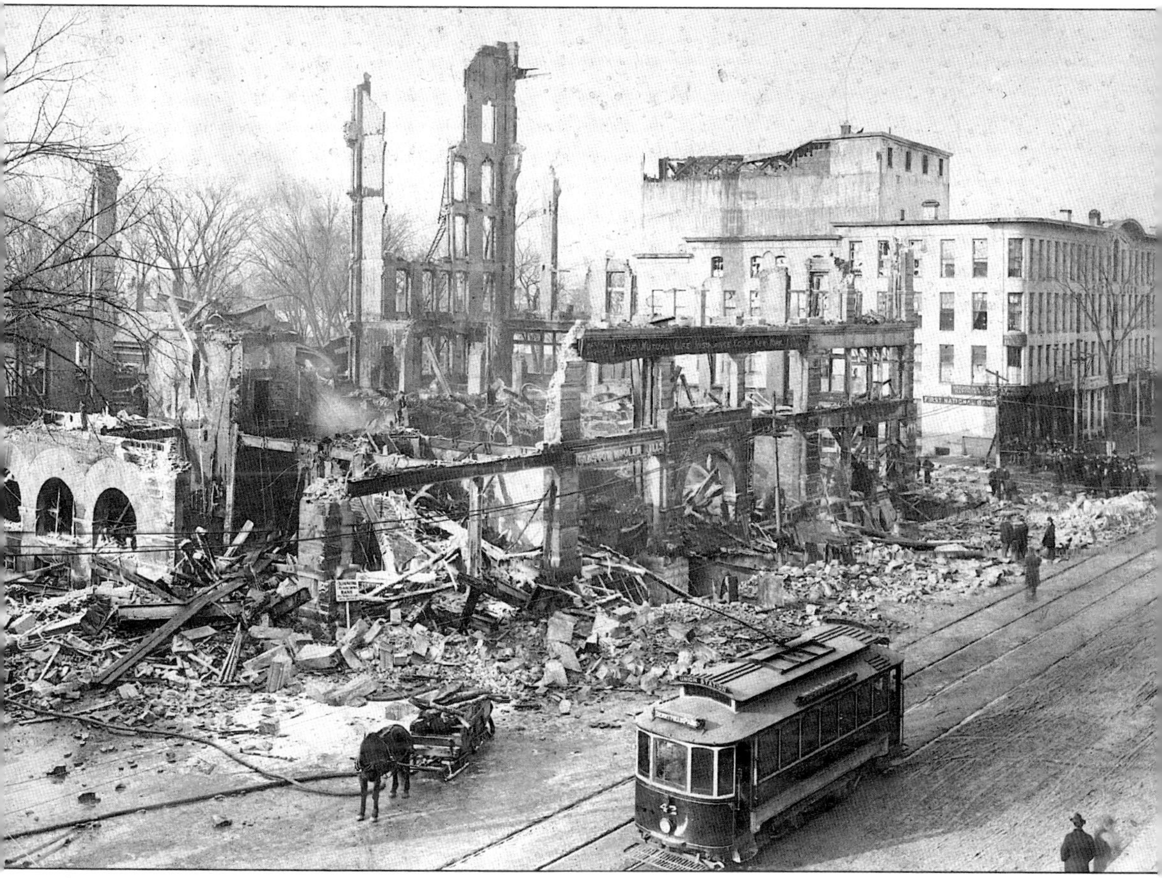

The ruins of the Kennard Block are still smoldering on June 15, 1902, as Car 42 heads north on Elm Street en route to Bridge Street and Derryfield Park. The block at 1008 Elm Street was soon rebuilt, only to be razed during the construction of the present Hampshire Plaza. In the background is the four-story Smyth Block, 1028–1048 Elm Street, which also was demolished when the plaza was created. There were stores on the first floor of both blocks and offices or apartments above.

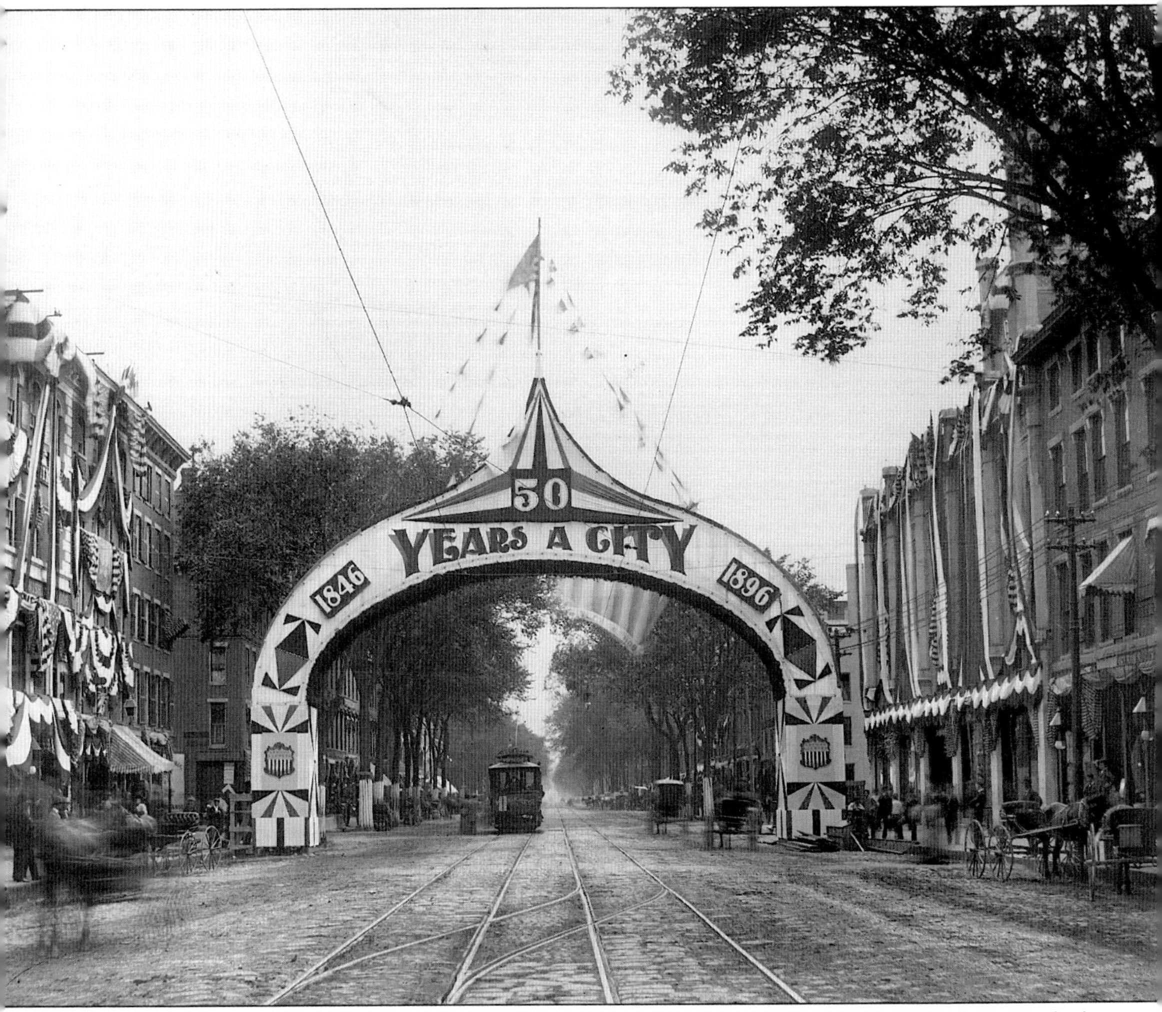

Manchester celebrated its semicentennial as a city in September 1896 and erected this ornamental arch across Elm Street at Manchester City Hall. The celebration lasted four days and many Queen City residents traveled by electric car to and from the various events. The trolley approaching the arch is headed for the North End, where the run terminated at Elm and Webster Streets. Note the cobblestone paving. (MHA.)

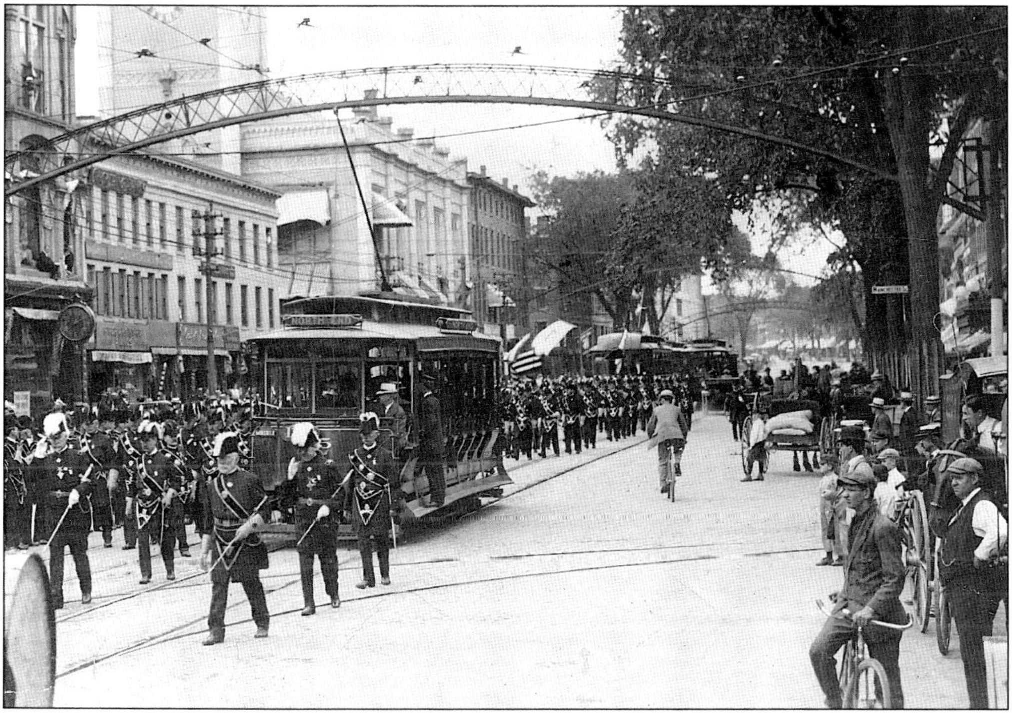

A Knights Templar parade delays trolley service on Elm Street near Manchester Street c. 1910. The open car in the foreground continued on to the North End after the procession passed.

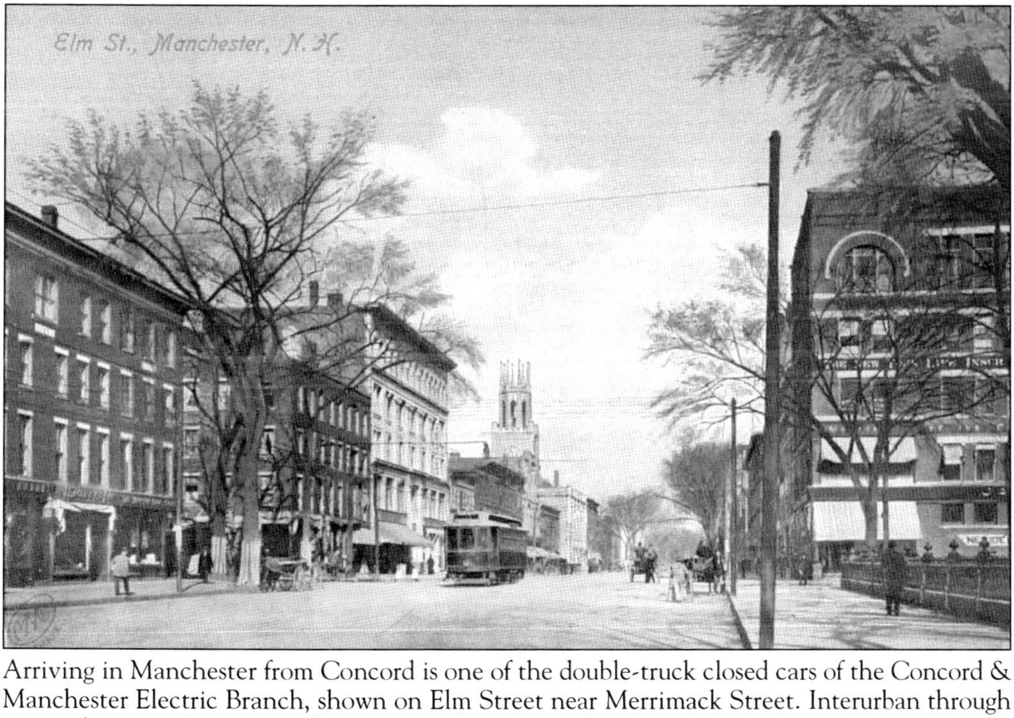

Arriving in Manchester from Concord is one of the double-truck closed cars of the Concord & Manchester Electric Branch, shown on Elm Street near Merrimack Street. Interurban through service between Concord and Manchester began in February 1903.

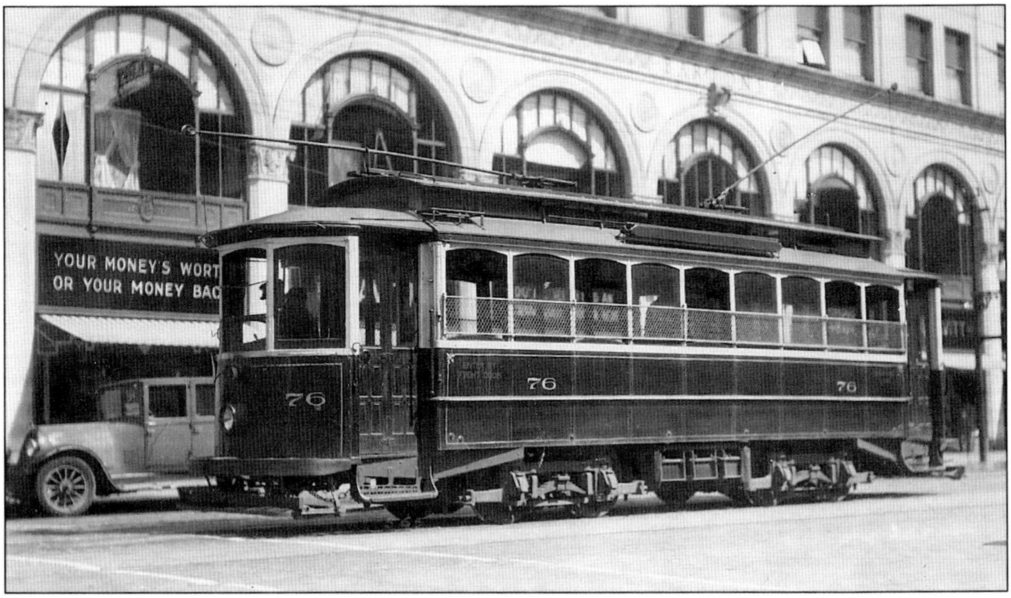

Northbound No. 79 passes the Leavitt Company department store, at 855 Elm Street between Manchester and Hanover Streets, *c.* 1932. Leavitt's is no longer in business. Its former site is occupied by part of the complex of Citizens Bank.

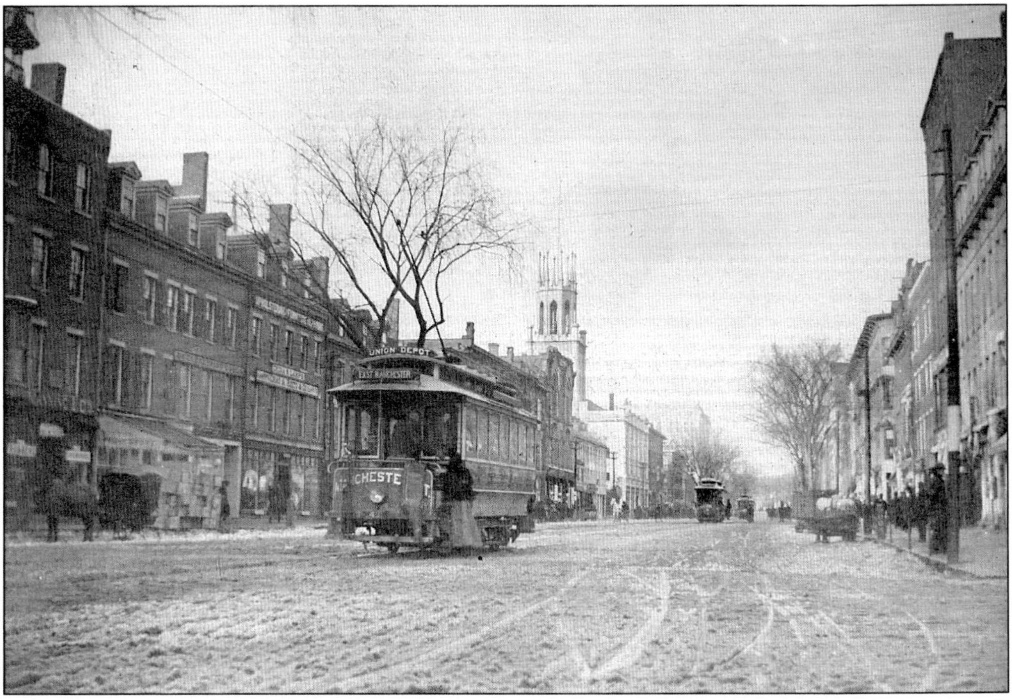

Elm Street is covered with snow from curb to curb, as a North End-bound trolley stops to pick up a woman passenger immediately north of Merrimack Street prior to 1900.

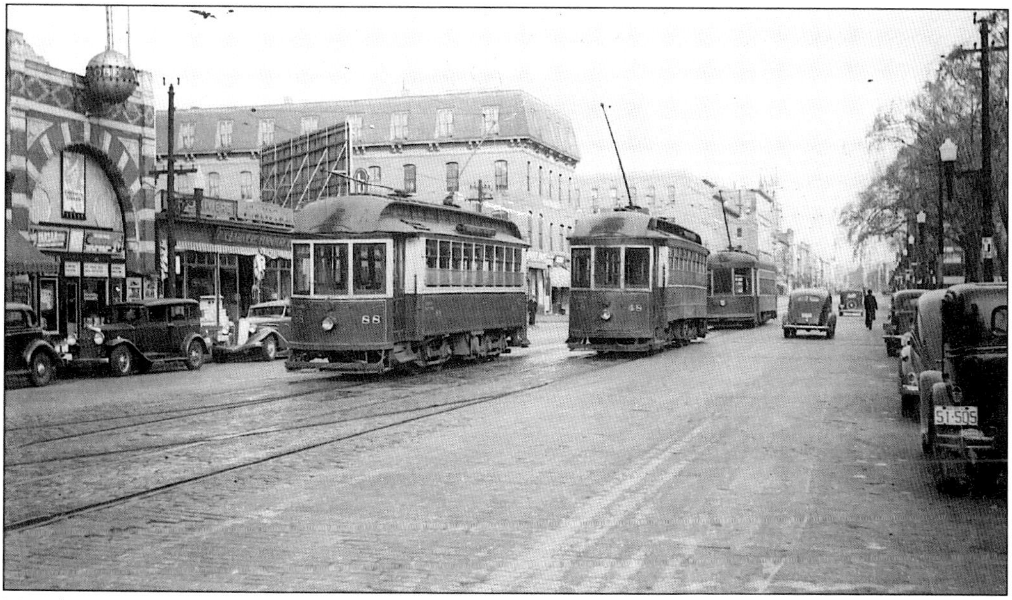

Numbers 88, 48, and 200 are on Elm Street near the now-long-gone Globe Theater on October 22, 1939. Behind No. 88 is the Prout Block at the intersection of Elm and West Central Streets.

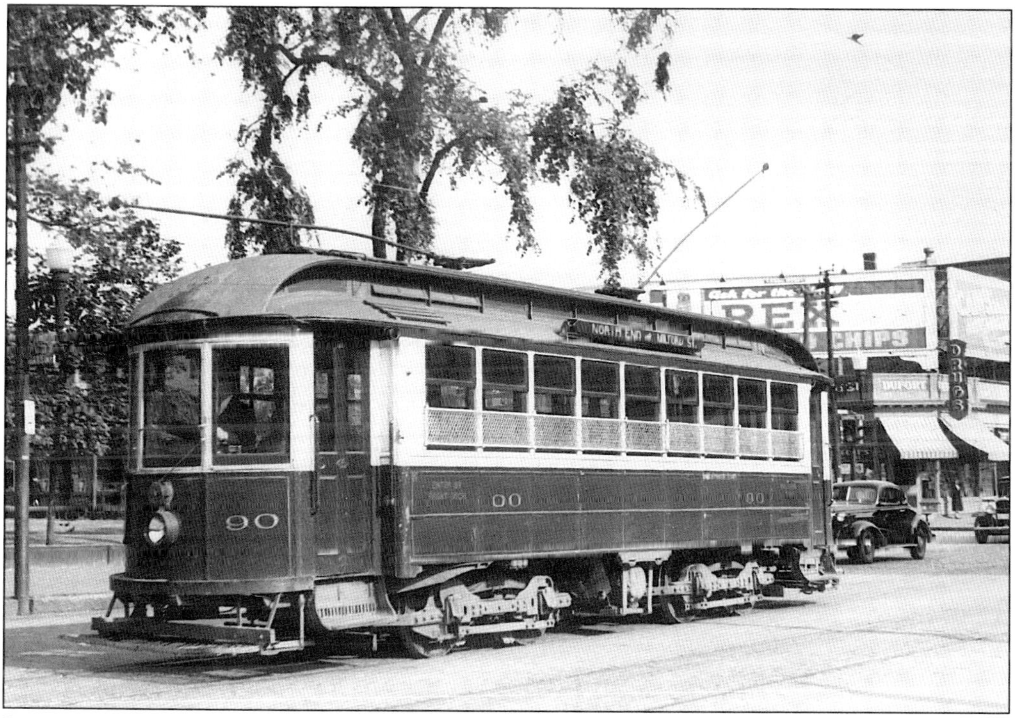

Passing Merrimack Common on Elm Street between Central and Merrimack Streets is No. 90, headed for the North End in June 1939. Behind the trolley is Dufort's Drug Store, on the site of the present George's Apparel Inc.

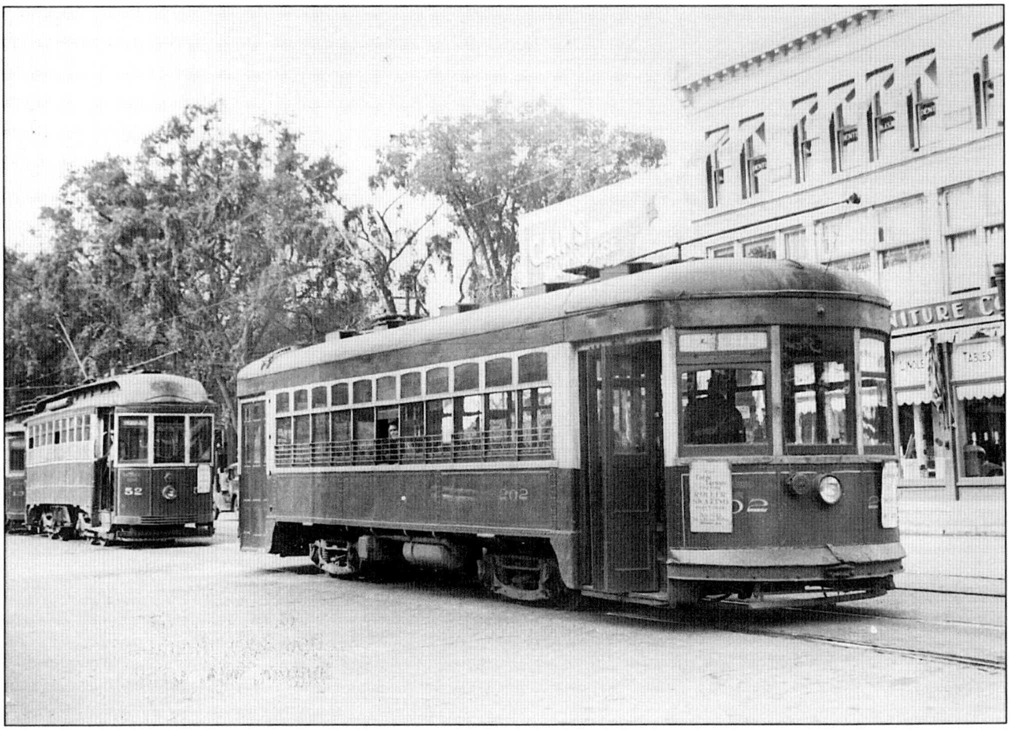

Cars on all routes of the Manchester Street Railway connected at the intersection of Elm, Central, and West Central Streets, a point officially identified as the Transfer Station. Numbers 202 and 52 were photographed in June 1939.

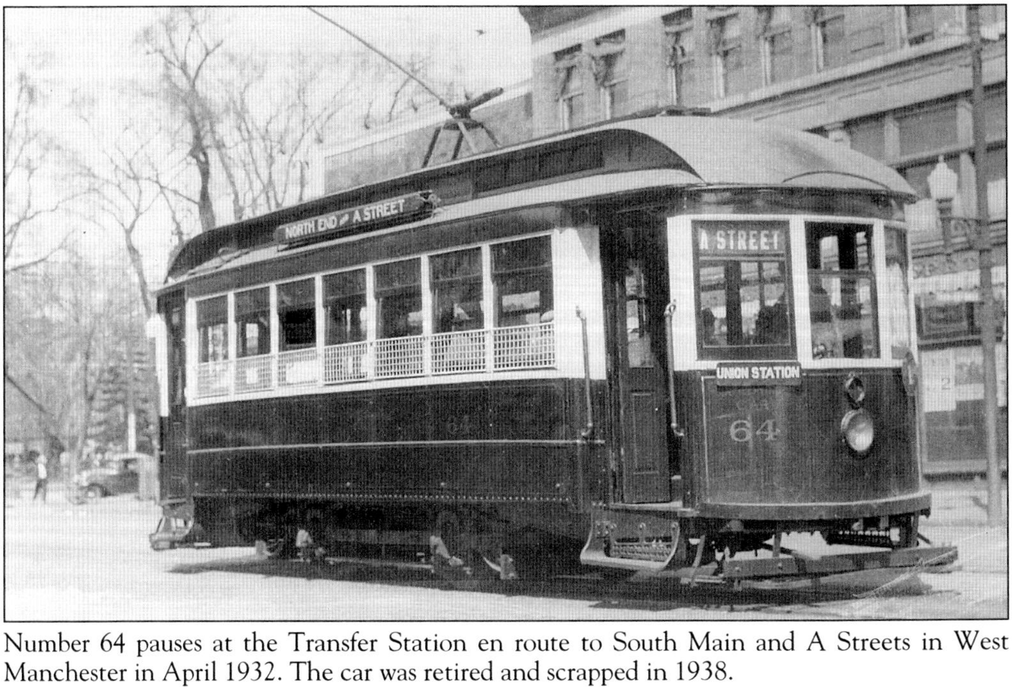

Number 64 pauses at the Transfer Station en route to South Main and A Streets in West Manchester in April 1932. The car was retired and scrapped in 1938.

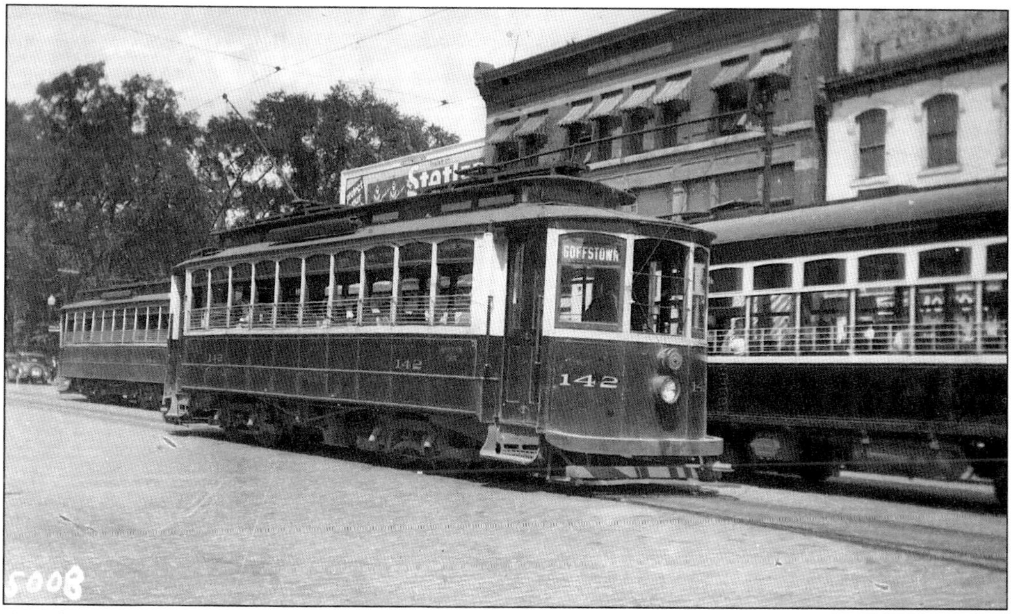

Another view at the Transfer Station shows No. 142 displaying Goffstown on its destination sign on July 8, 1935. Behind it is one of the 200-series cars on its way to Derryfield Park.

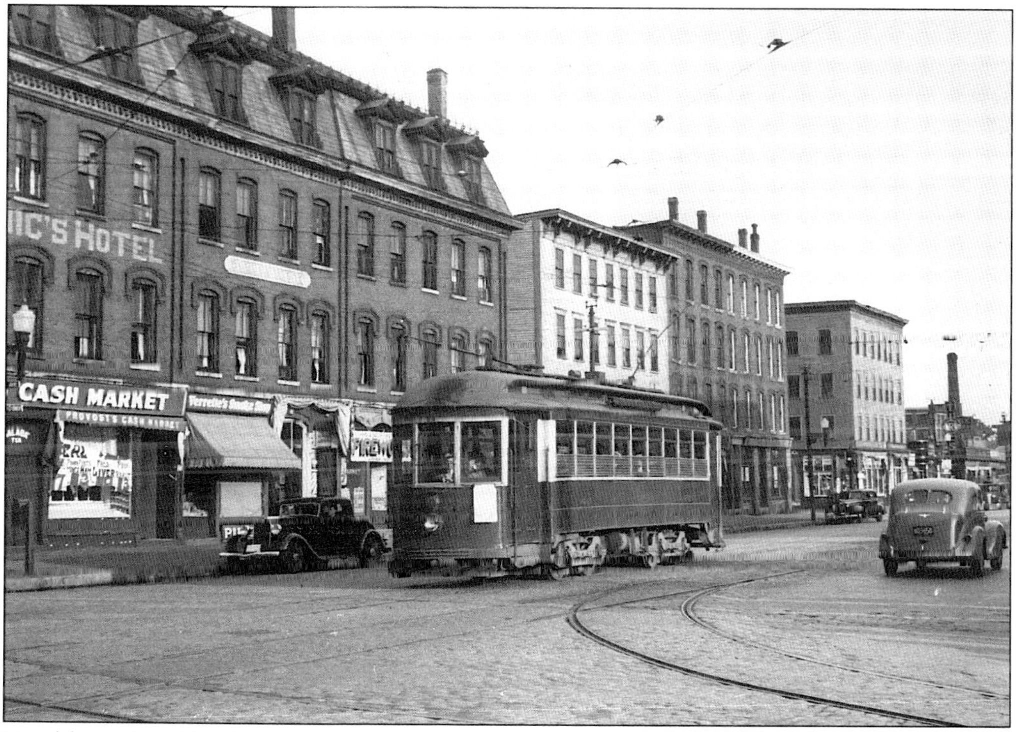

Northbound on Elm Street at Lake Avenue in June 1939 is No. 58. All of the buildings to the left and right of the trolley were razed in conjunction with an urban renewal project, which produced the complex now occupied in part by Staples Office Superstore.

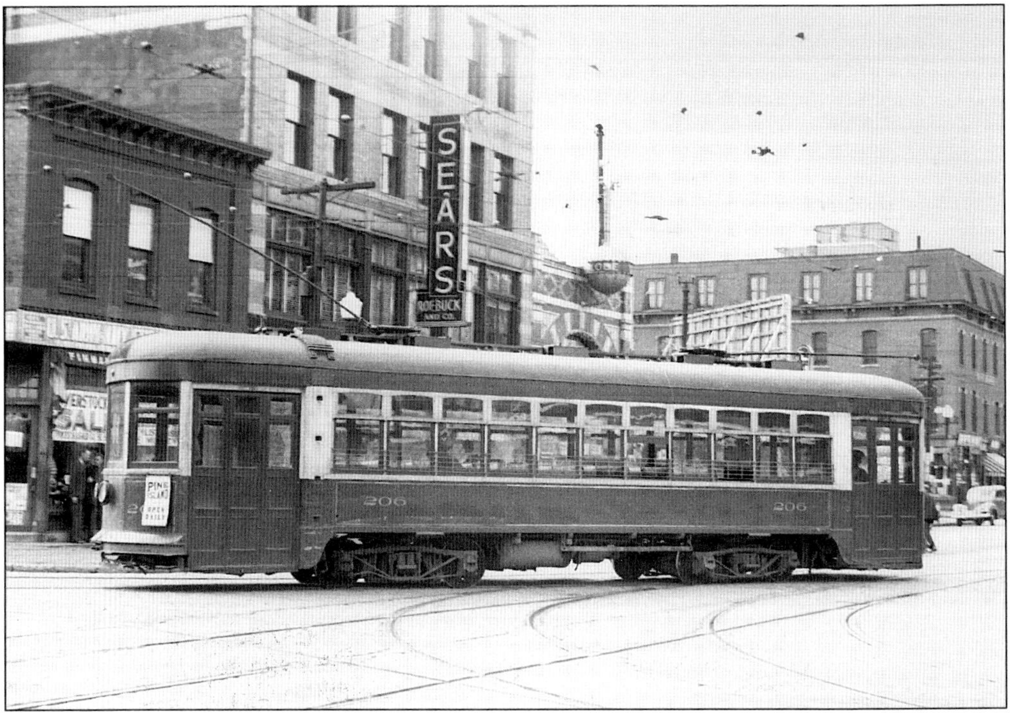

Turning onto Elm Street from Traction Street in June 1939 is No. 206, running on the Notre Dame–Derryfield Park route. The Sears, Roebuck & Company store was then at 652 Elm Street.

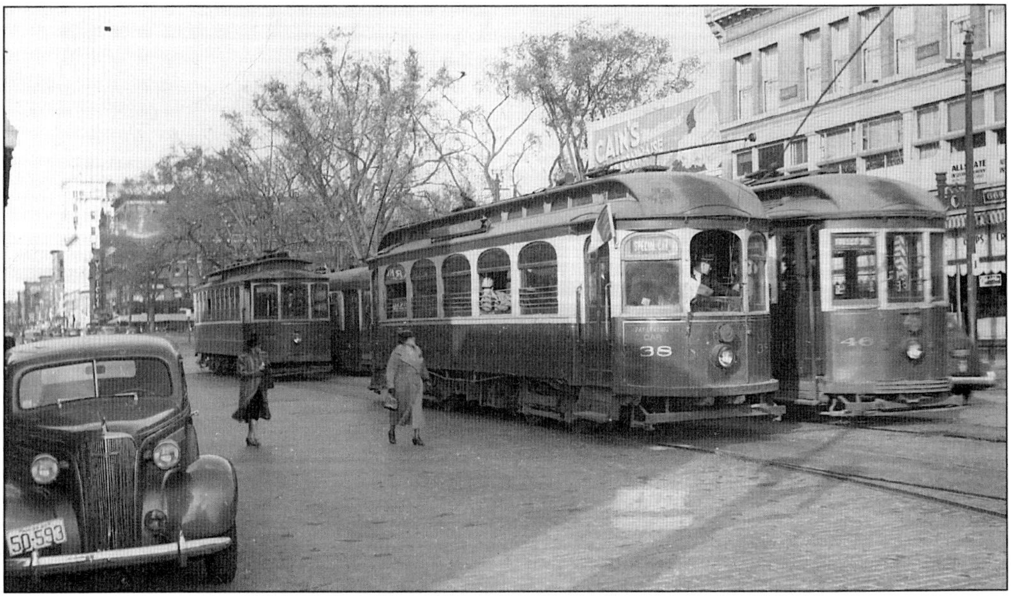

Rapid No. 38 is carrying a charter party, as it pauses on Elm Street near the Transfer Station on October 22, 1939. Beside it is No. 46, and behind it is No. 138.

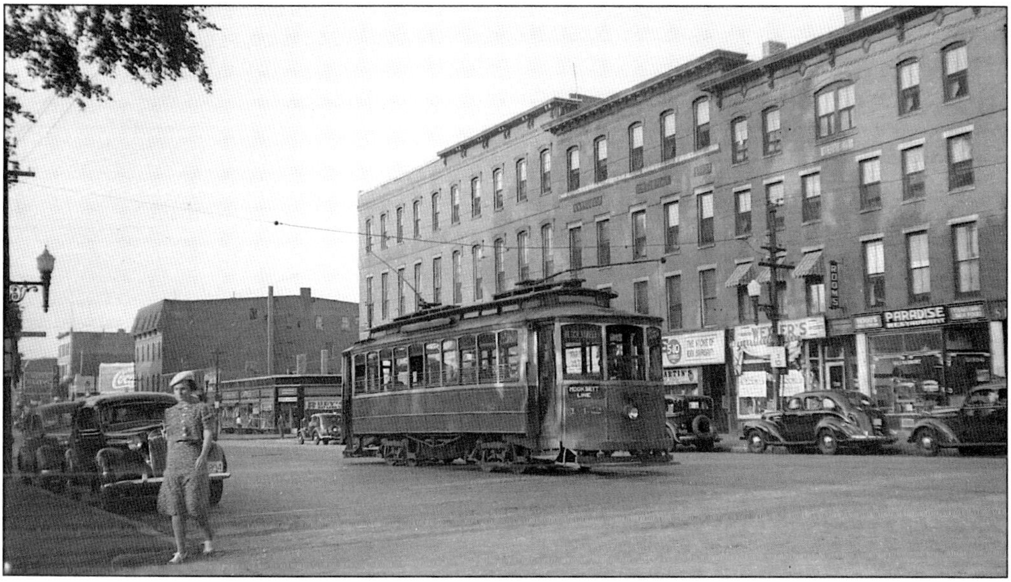

A Hooksett Line sign is displayed on the dasher of No. 142 heading north on Elm Street, between Pleasant and West Merrimack Street, in June 1939.

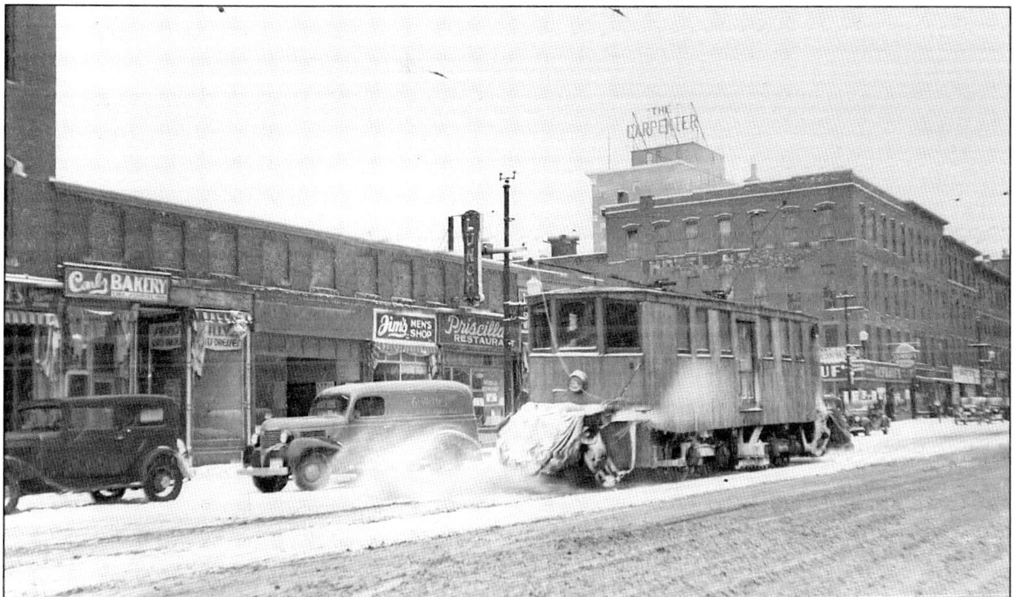

Snow sweeper X-2 clears the tracks on Elm Street south of Pleasant Street after a light storm on January 11, 1940. Looming above the sweeper is the top of the Carpenter hotel on Franklin Street.

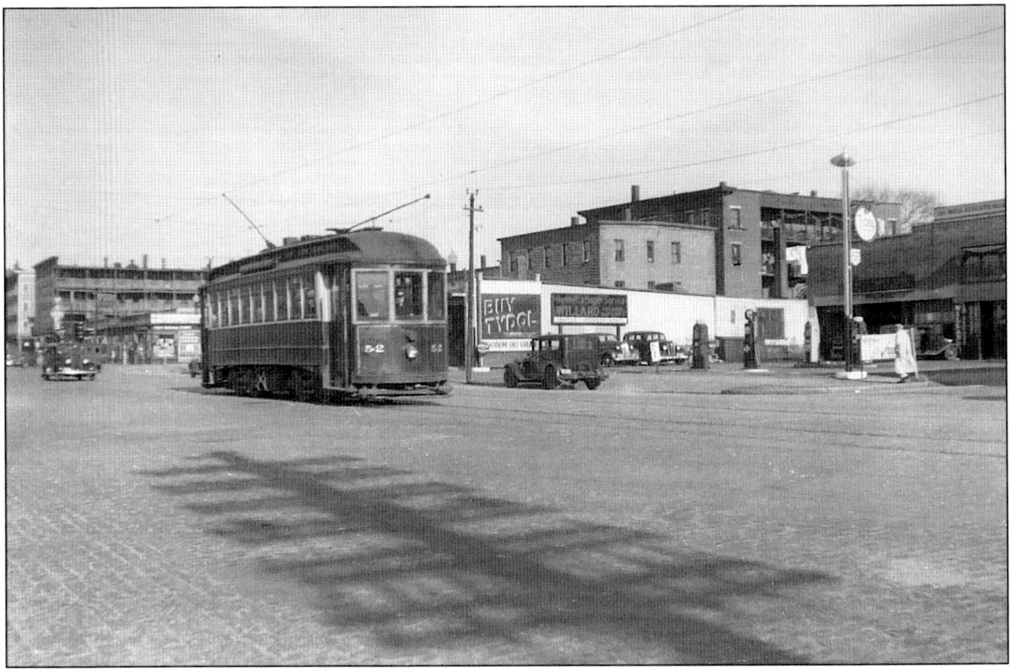

Southbound Valley Street car No. 52 is on Elm Street at Auburn Street on December 13, 1938. The intersection certainly looks a lot different today.

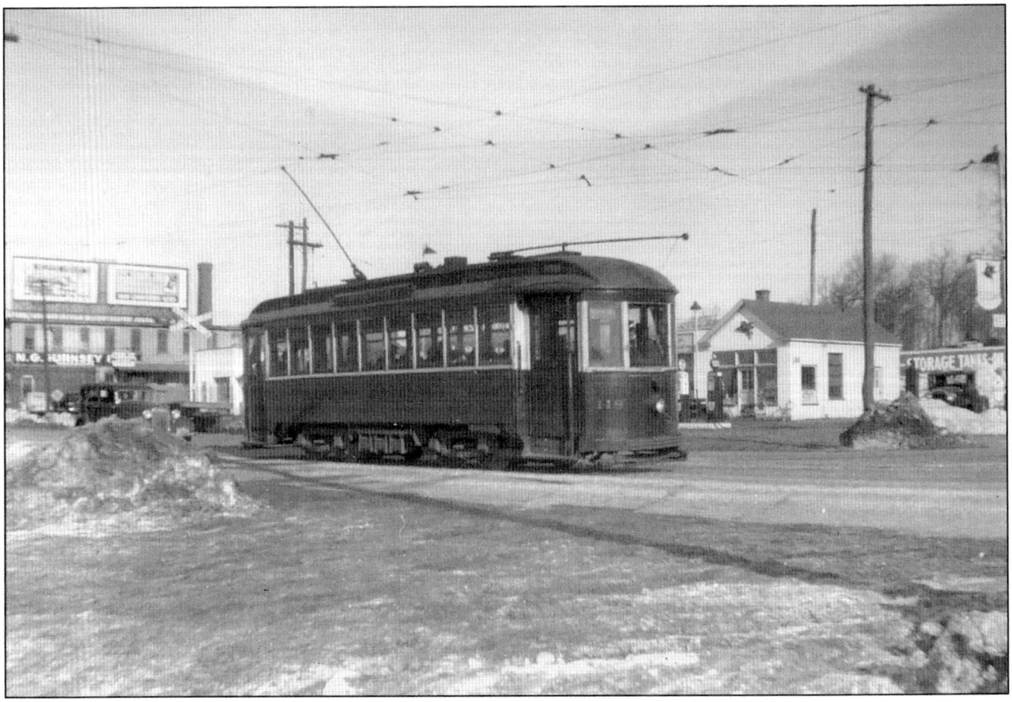

Having just crossed a Boston & Maine industrial spur track, No. 118 is on Elm Street at Valley Street on August 14, 1939. The Triangle Credit Union building now occupies the site of the gasoline station at the right.

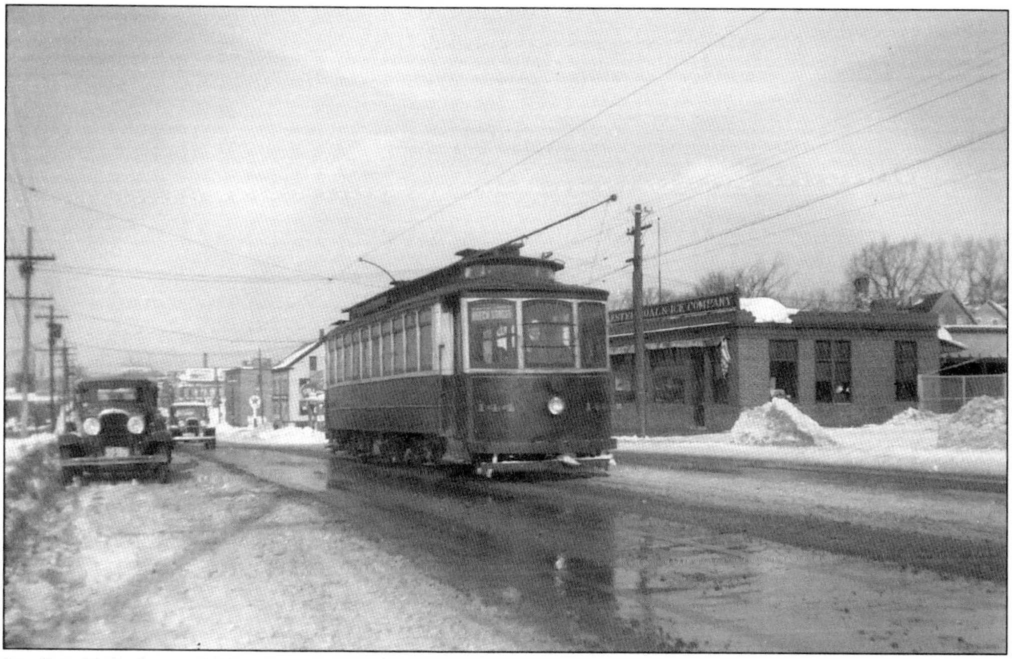

Goffe's Falls-bound No. 144 is on Elm Street near Hayward Street in 1939. At the right is the Manchester Coal & Ice Company at 159 Elm Street, now the headquarters of the Dead River Company, fuel oil dealers.

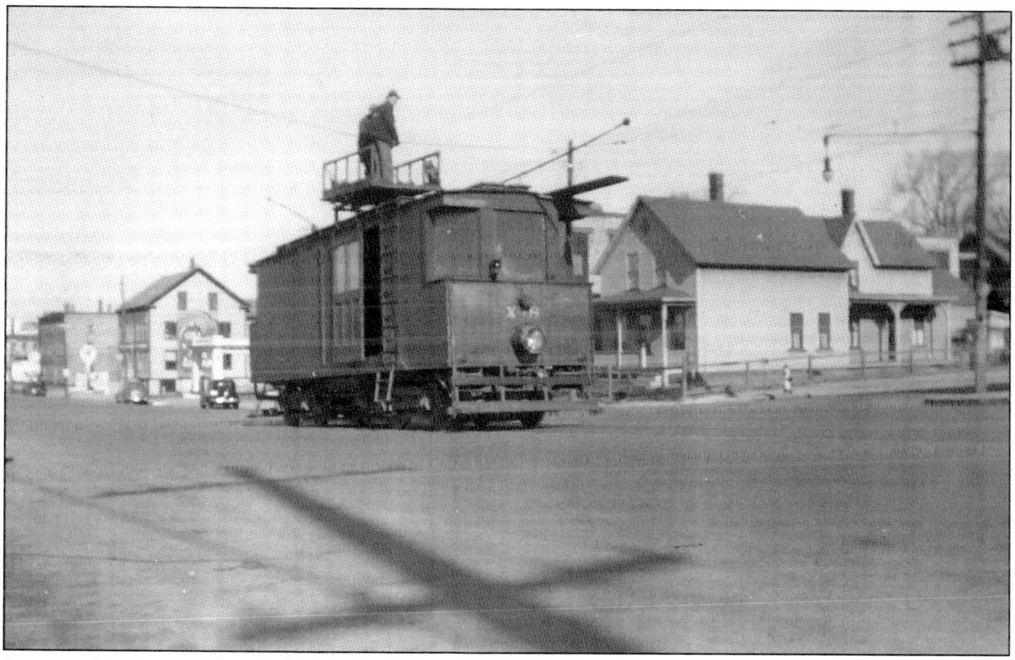

Line car X-18 is at Elm and Hayward Streets as its crew replaces a stretch of trolley wire over the southbound track on November 14, 1939, just a few months prior to the end of trolley service.

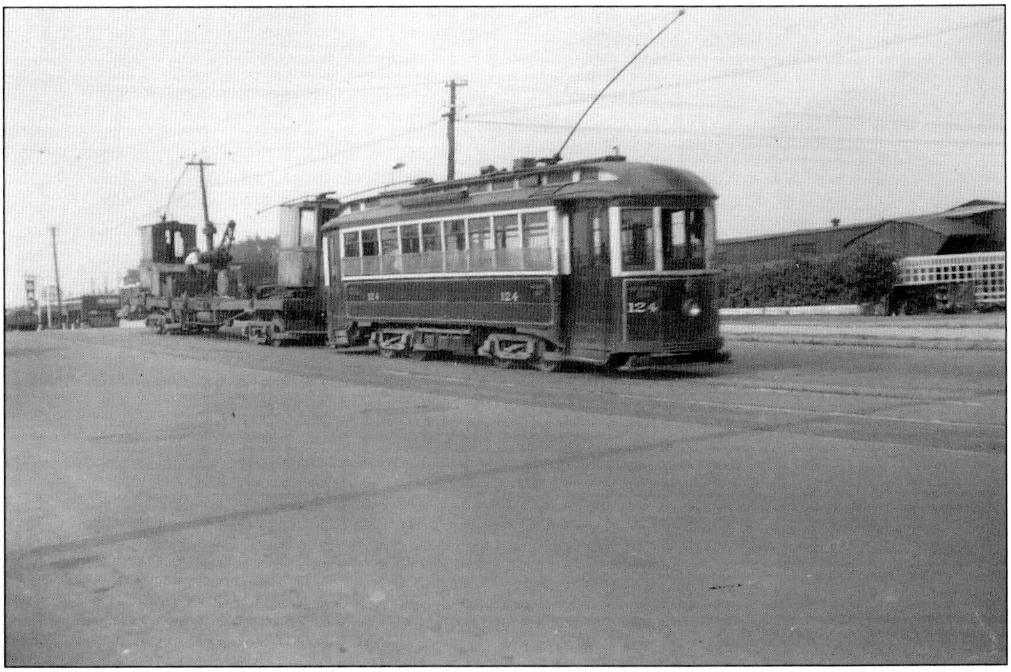

A disabled No. 124 is towed by a motor flat at the so-called "Dry Bridge," where Elm Street crossed the Manchester–Lawrence Branch of the Boston & Maine Railroad.

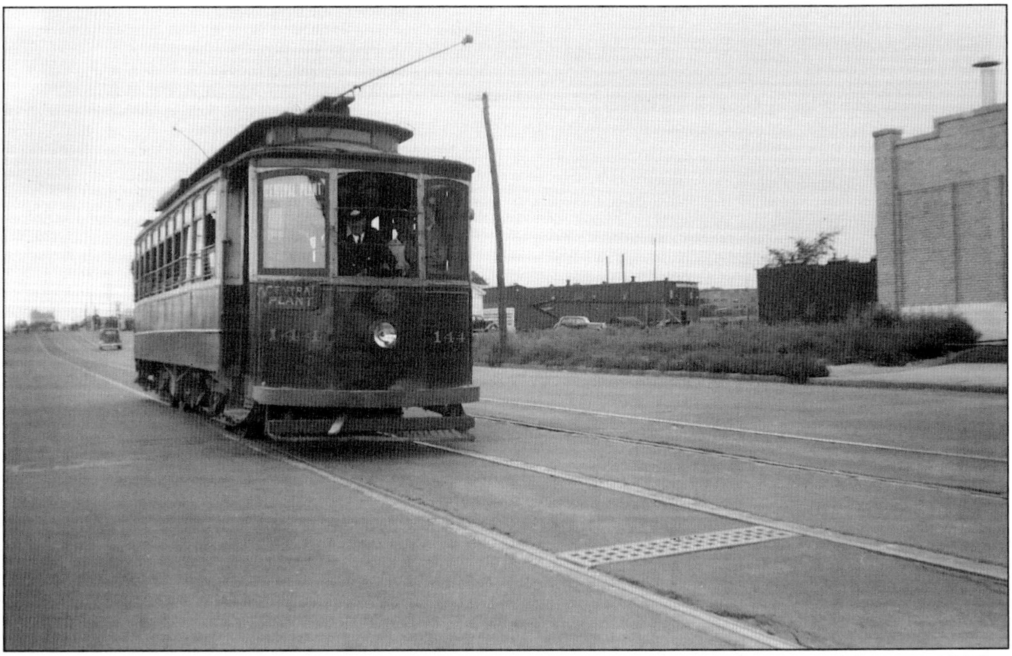

No. 144 passes the Cote Brothers Inc. bakery, now known as the Sunbeam Building, at 87 Elm Street, north of Queen City Avenue on August 27, 1939.

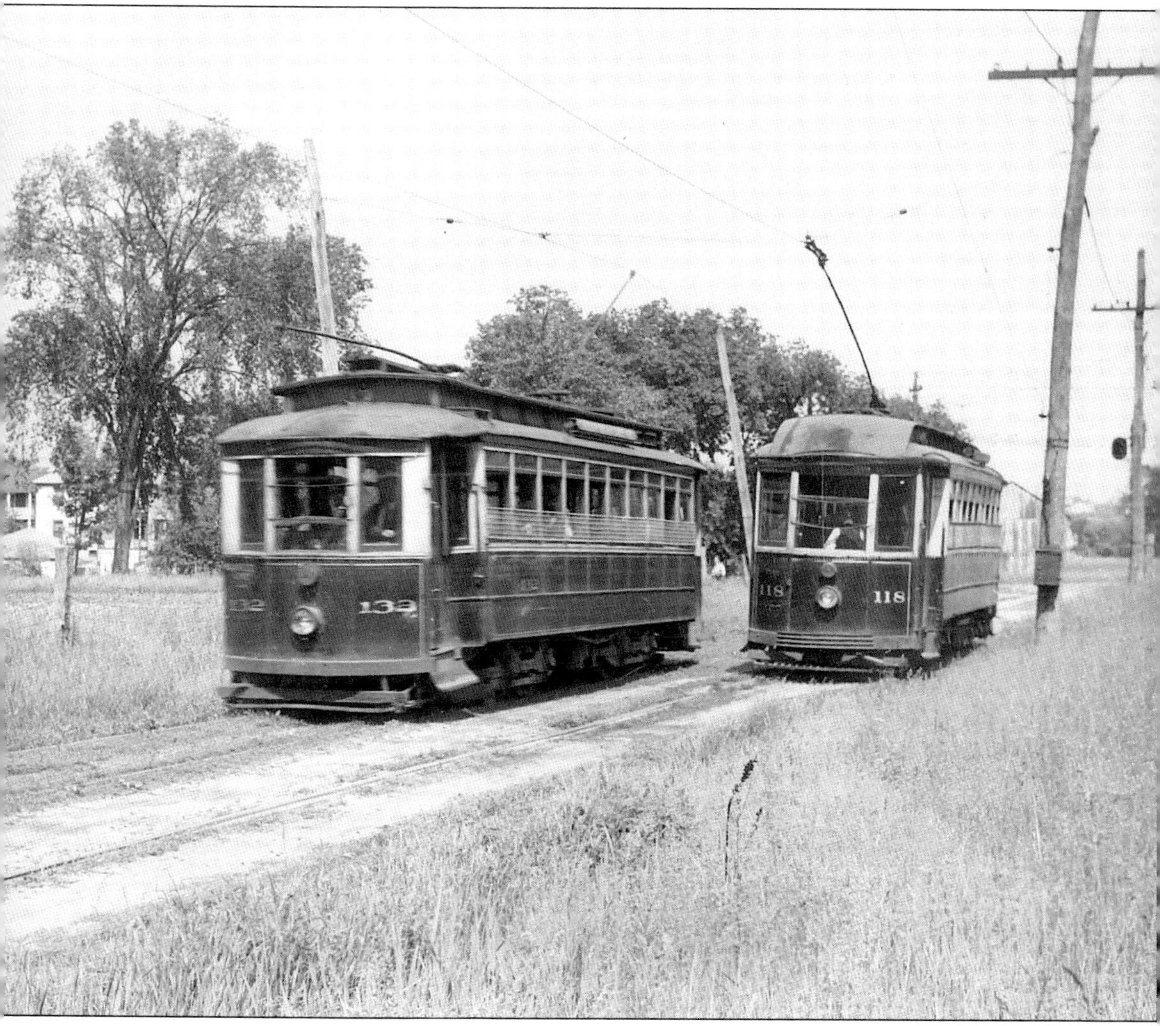

Cars No. 132 and No. 118 meet on the private right-of-way between South Elm Street and Calef Road on June 12, 1938. Wyoming Avenue is now situated on the old trolley roadbed. The turnout shown was also known as Central Plant, as it was within convenient walking distance of the central plant of the International Shoe Company off Queen Avenue. The signal on the pole at the far right protected the single track of Calef Road.

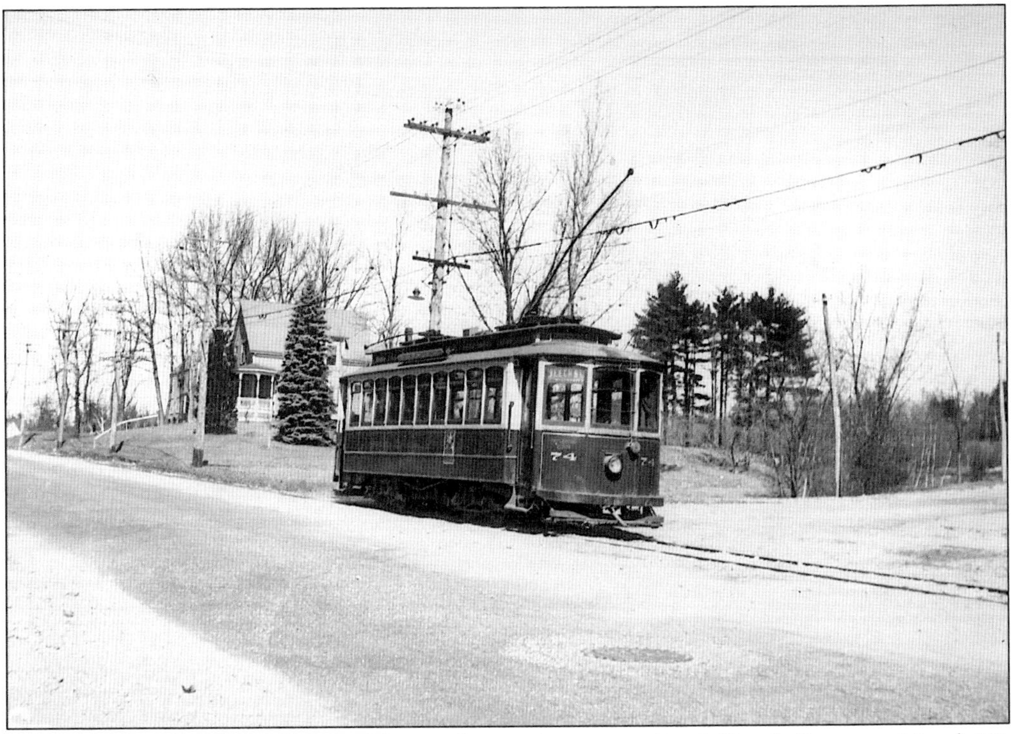

Returning from Goffe's Falls, No. 74 is on Brown Avenue at South Beech Street on March 29, 1937. Interstate 293 now crosses the avenue just south of this intersection.

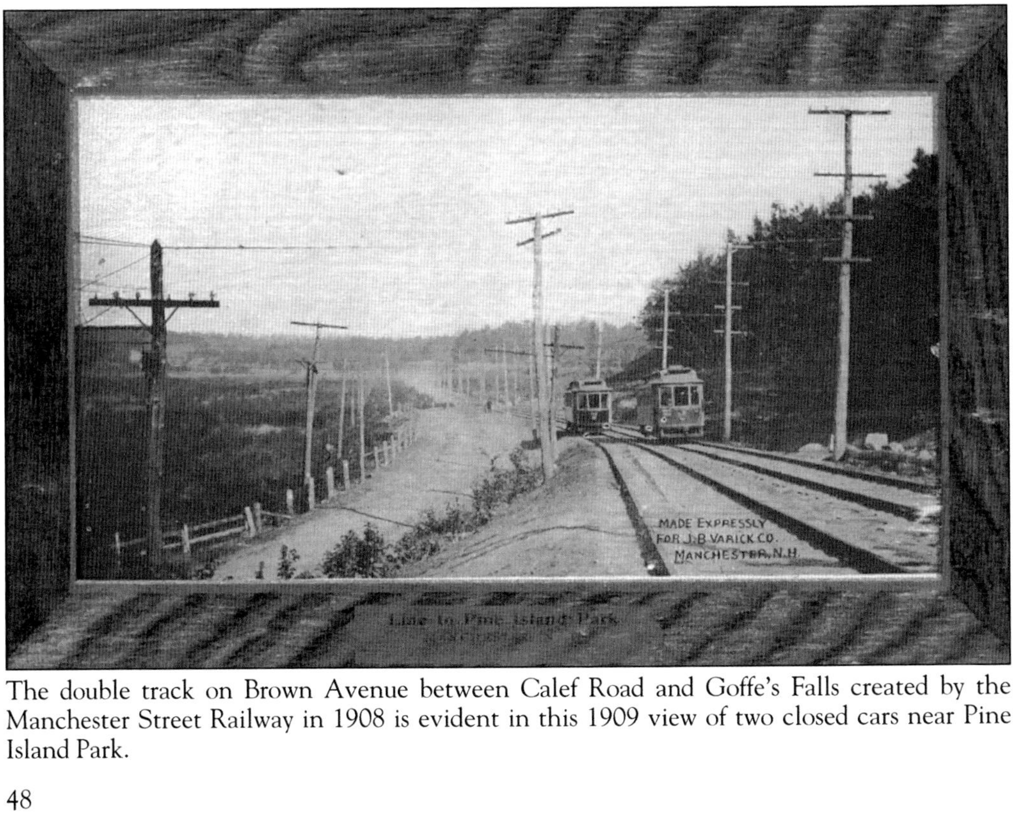

The double track on Brown Avenue between Calef Road and Goffe's Falls created by the Manchester Street Railway in 1908 is evident in this 1909 view of two closed cars near Pine Island Park.

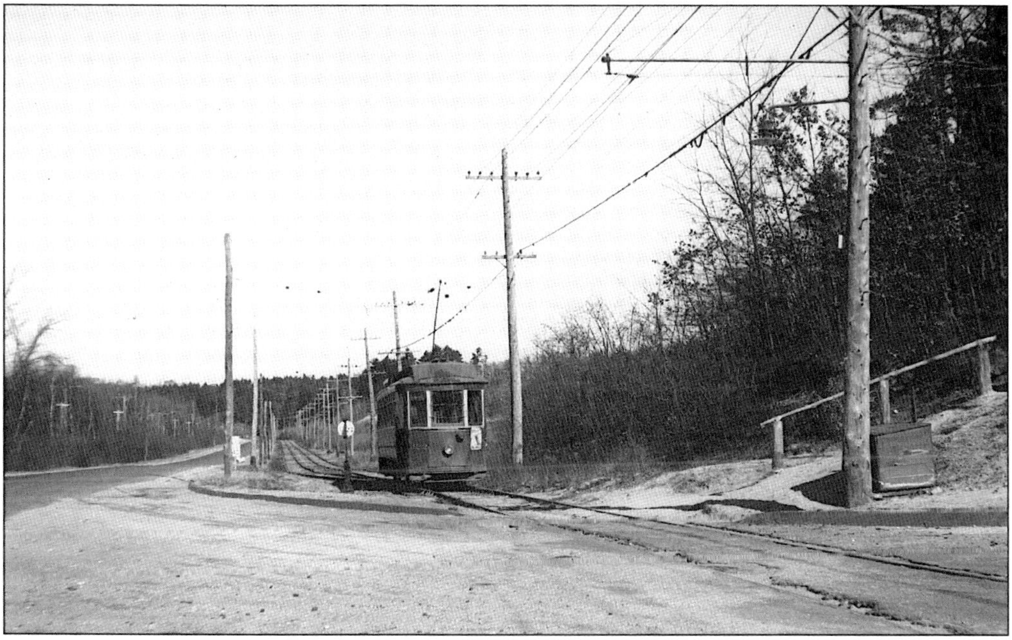

After crossing what was then known as Pine Island Road, No. 122 runs northerly beside Brown Avenue en route from Goffe's Falls to downtown Manchester on February 15, 1938.

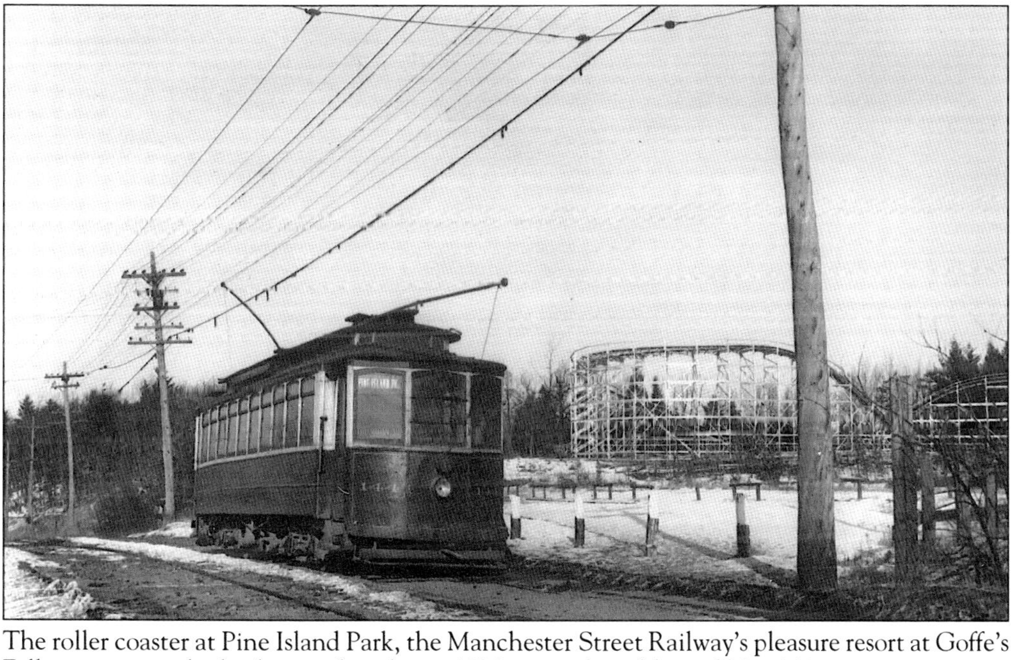

The roller coaster at Pine Island Park, the Manchester Street Railway's pleasure resort at Goffe's Falls, appears in the background in this *c.* 1938 view of southbound No. 144.

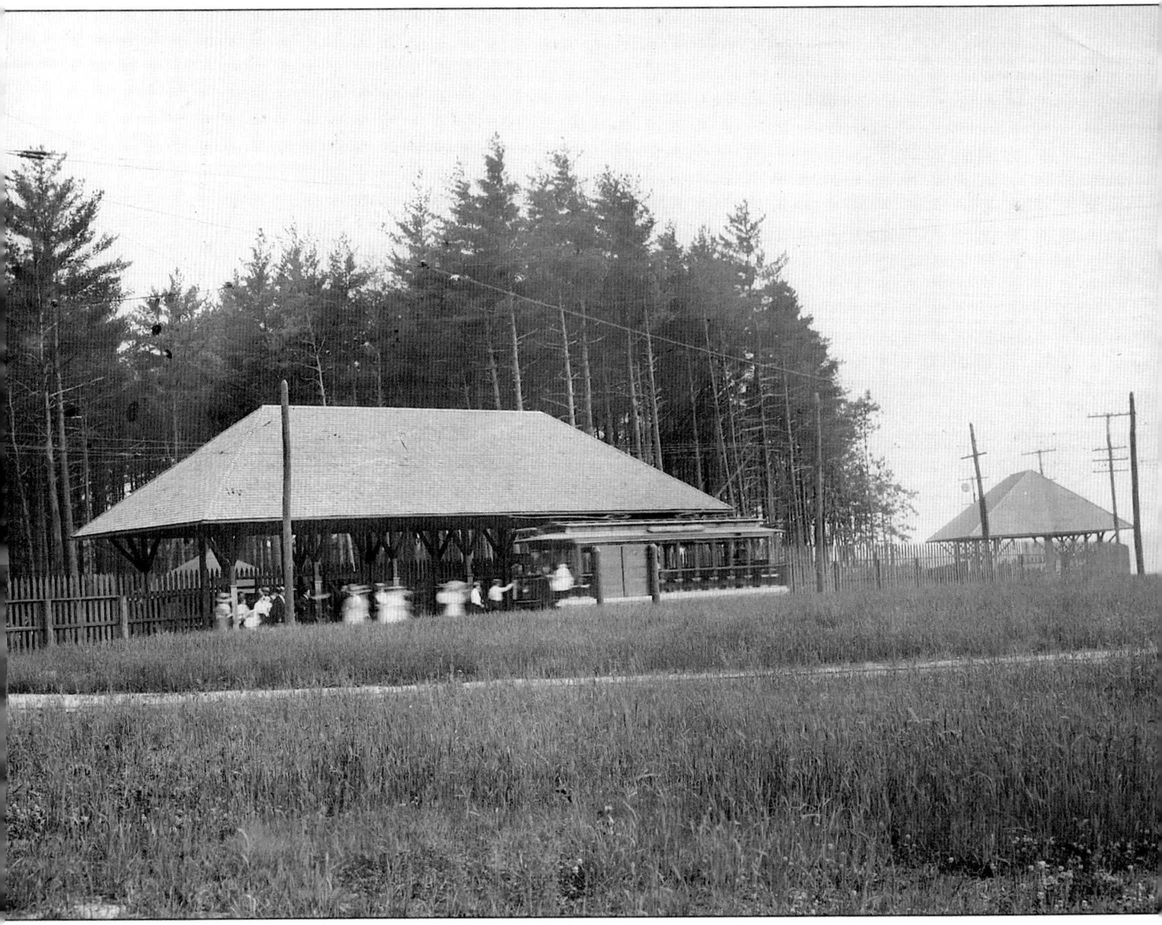

Formally opened to the public on August 3, 1902, Pine Island Park immediately became a mecca for Manchester residents, from the late spring until the early fall. By the 1908 season, a trolley loop and a waiting station, known as the Upper Landing, had been built at the main entrance to the resort. Much of the park property is now occupied by the headquarters of Anthem Blue Cross and Blue Shield.

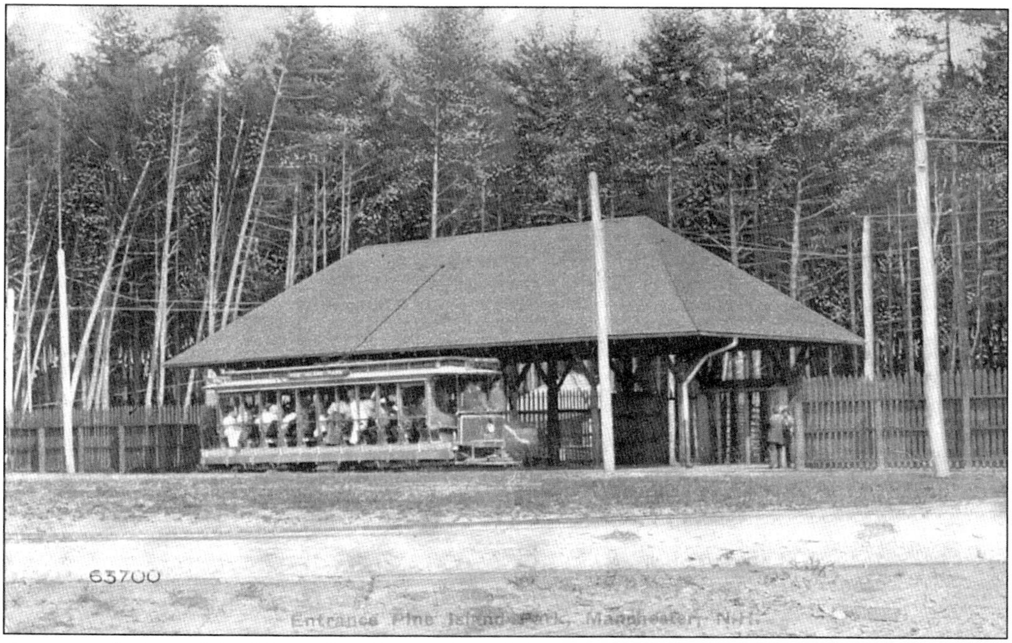

A postcard view of the Upper Landing at Pine Island Park shows a 13-bench open trolley fully loaded and ready to leave for downtown Manchester. For many summers on both weekdays and Sundays, cars were run every 15 minutes between Manchester City Hall and the resort.

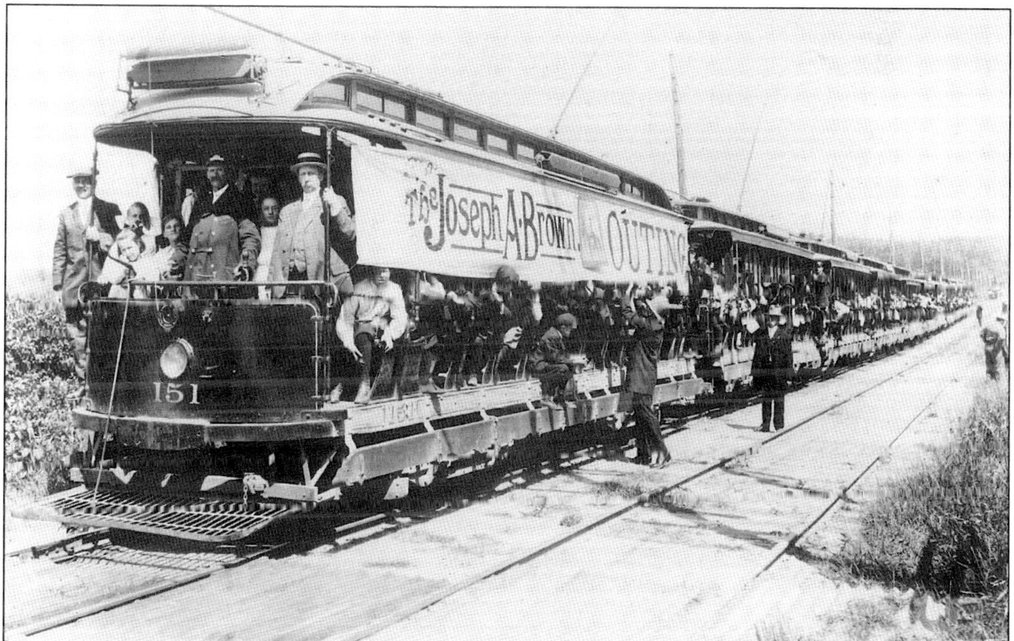

Beginning in 1907, Pine Island Park was the scene of the annual Joseph A. Brown outing for the poor children of Manchester. The youngsters traveled to the park in open cars, a long string of which was photographed on the Brown Avenue double track.

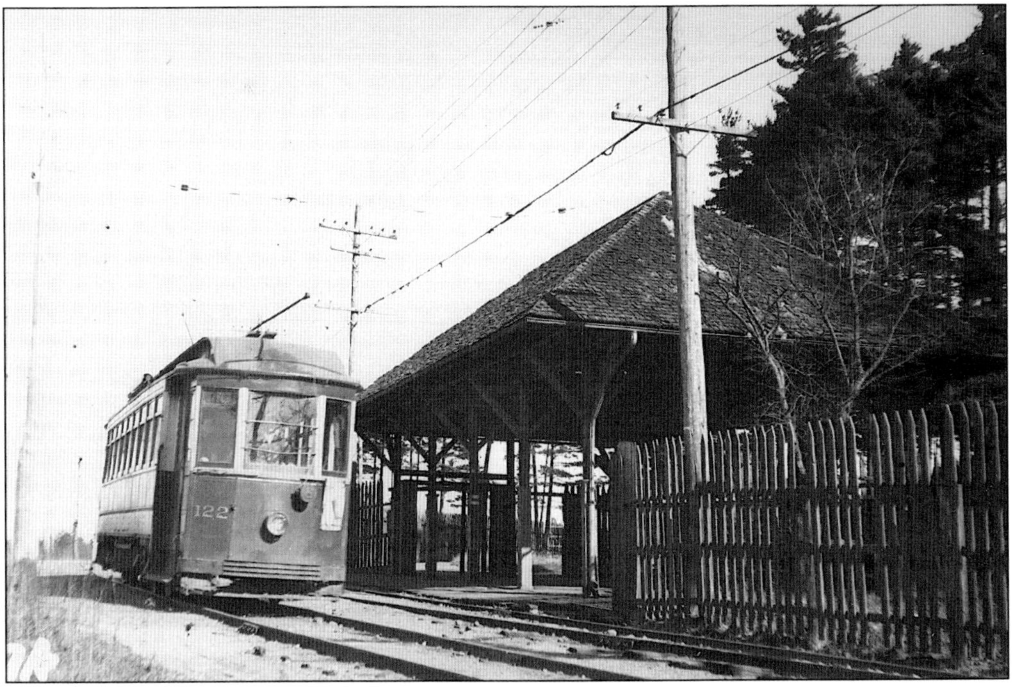

The so-called Lower Landing at Pine Island Park is passed by No. 122 on February 15, 1938. During that year, the resort opened for the season on the last Monday in April and closed prematurely due to the New England hurricane of September 21.

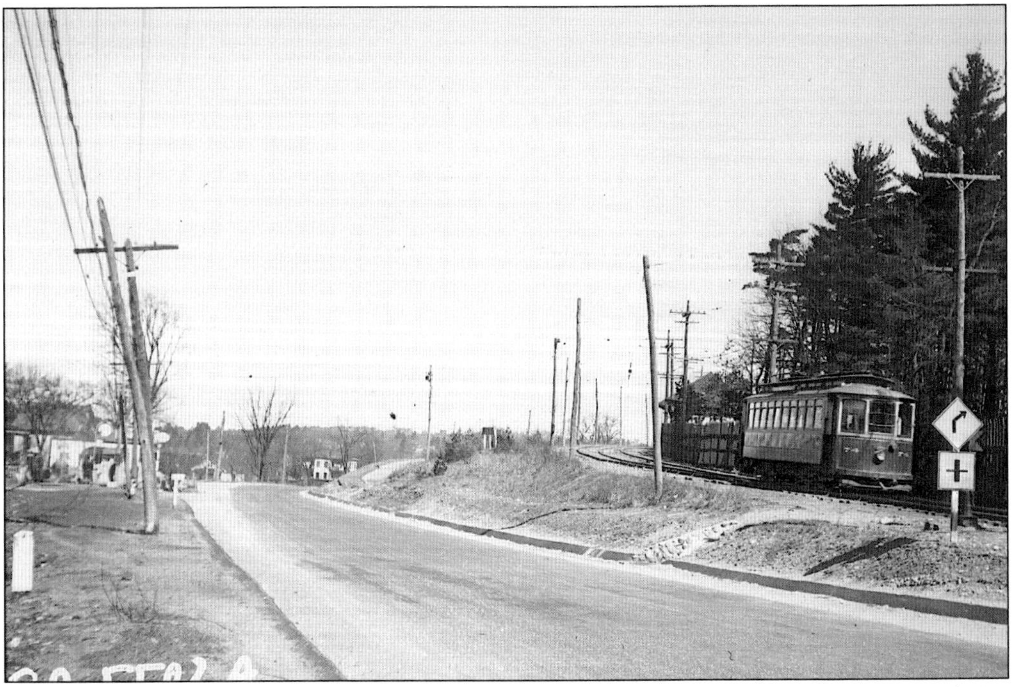

Leaving Pine Island Park, No. 74 is en route to the end of the line at Goffe's Falls on March 29, 1937. At this time Goffe's Falls trolleys were run half-hourly all year long.

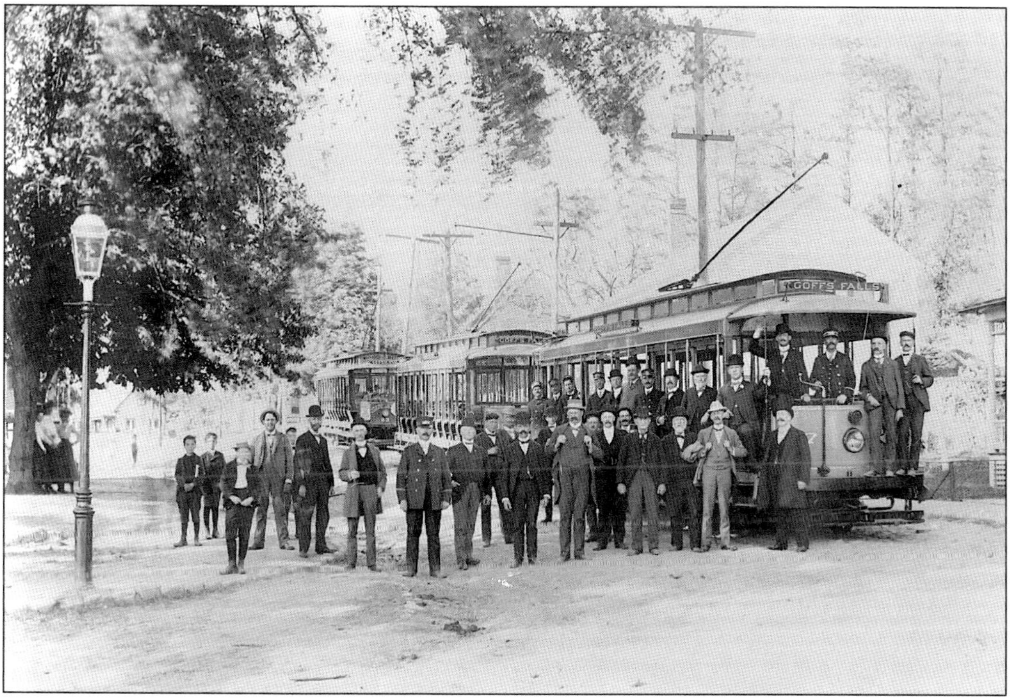

Passengers pose for the photographer after the arrival of the very first trolleys from Manchester City Hall to Goffe's Falls on June 10, 1901. Regular service commenced the same day. Cars initially ran every 15 minutes, and a 5¢ fare was charged.

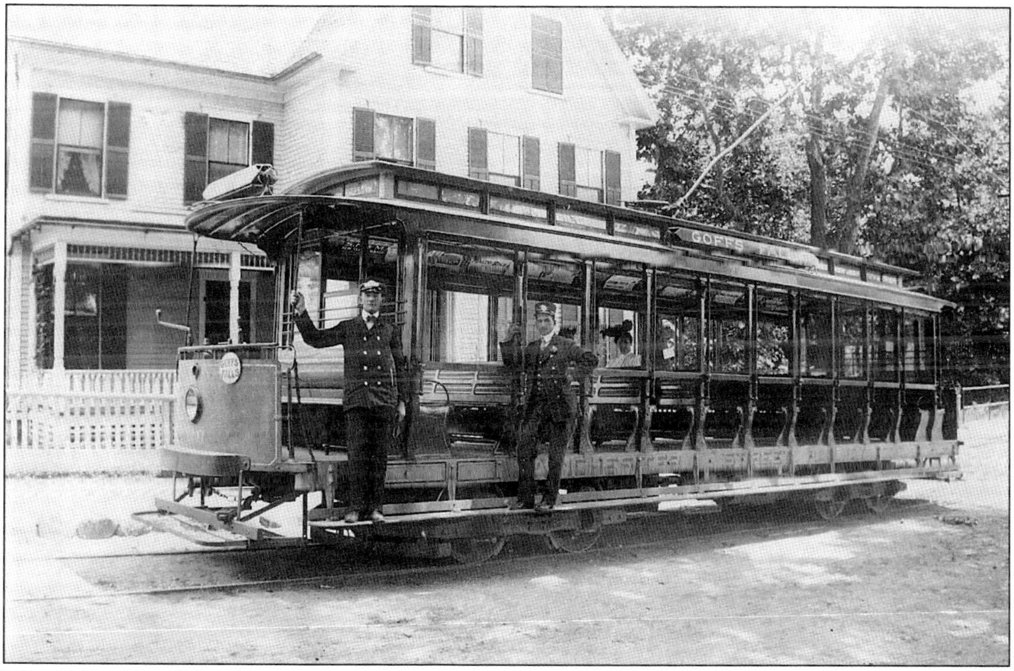

The Cohas Brook bridge on Brown Avenue was the original terminus of the Goffe's Falls line in 1901. Here is a 13-bench open about to leave for downtown Manchester.

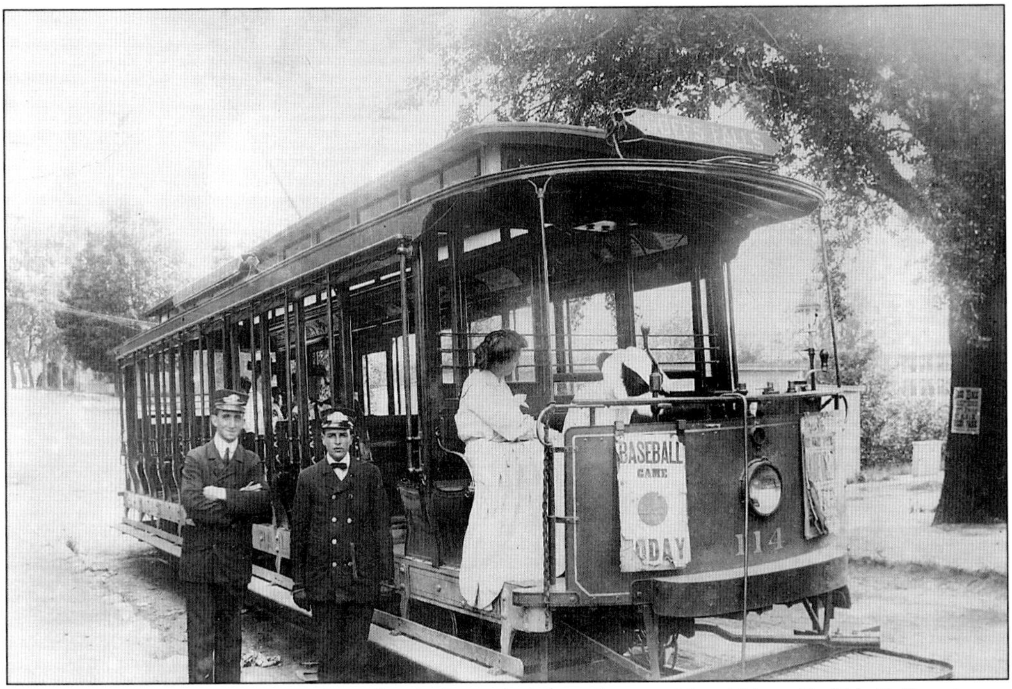

Advertising signs are displayed on the dasher of 13-bench open No. 111 at Goffe's Falls prior to 1906. Two women passengers occupy the coveted front seat behind the motorman.

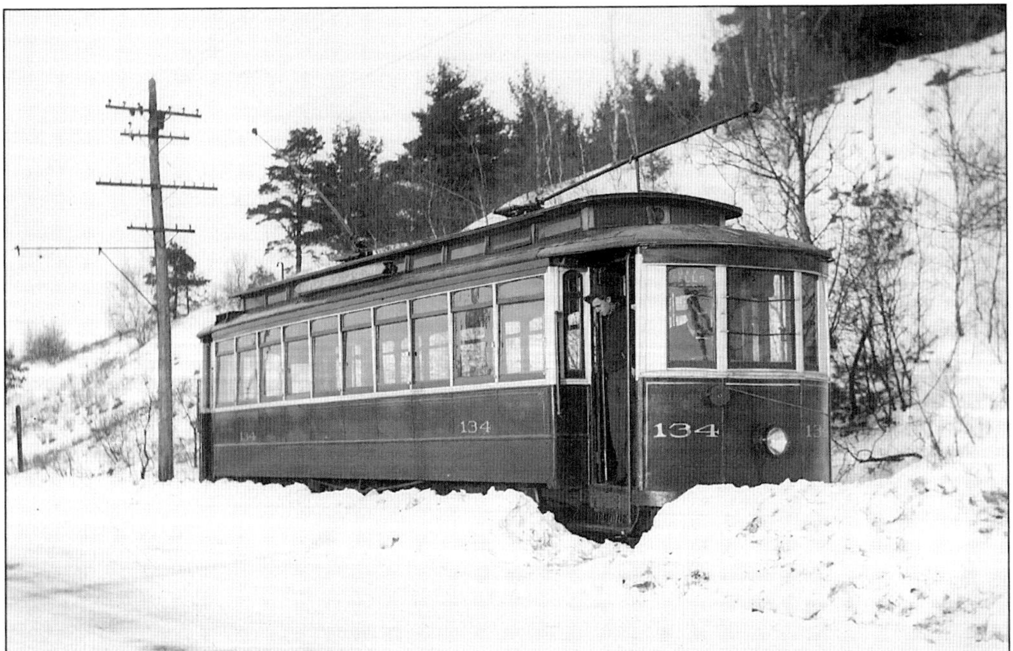

The terminus of the Goffe's Falls line after 1937 was on Brown Avenue, near the present St. Francis Assisi Church. Number 124 was snapped at that point on January 2, 1938, after a heavy snowstorm.

Four

BRANCH LINES

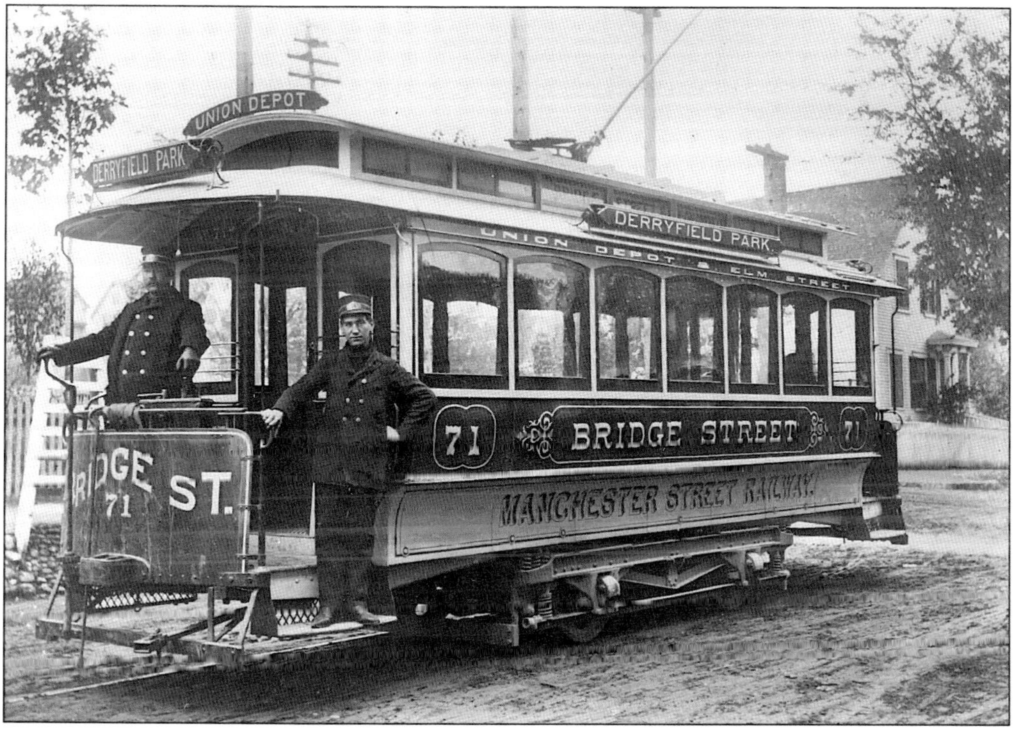

Resplendent in its original bright red exterior livery, Laconia-built No. 71 is at Bridge and Belmont Streets, on the westerly fringes of Derryfield Park, in 1895. The Bridge Street tracks were extended westward to Highland Street, near the main entrance to the park, in 1903. For the next 37 years, through trolleys were run between that point and Kelley Street in McGregorville. This locale was officially identified as Notre Dame in 1917 in belated recognition of the then predominant French Canadian population of the area.

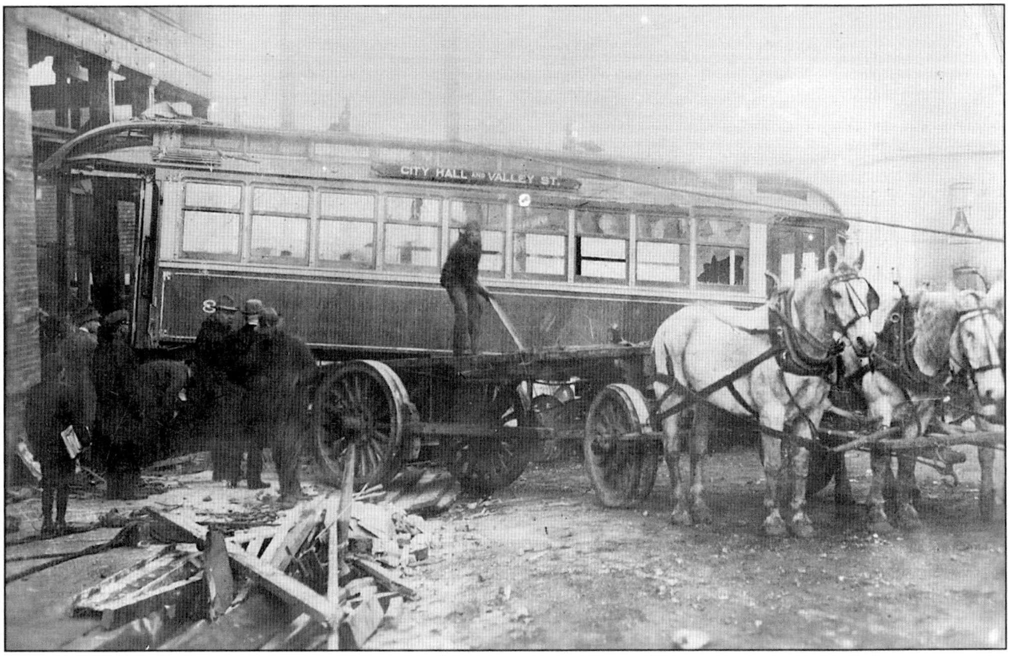

After a wild ride down Bridge Street from Derryfield Park, No. 82 left the rails and crashed into the E.M. Chase furniture store at Elm and Bridge Streets on October 28, 1912. Fortunately, there were no passengers in the trolley and no customers in the store.

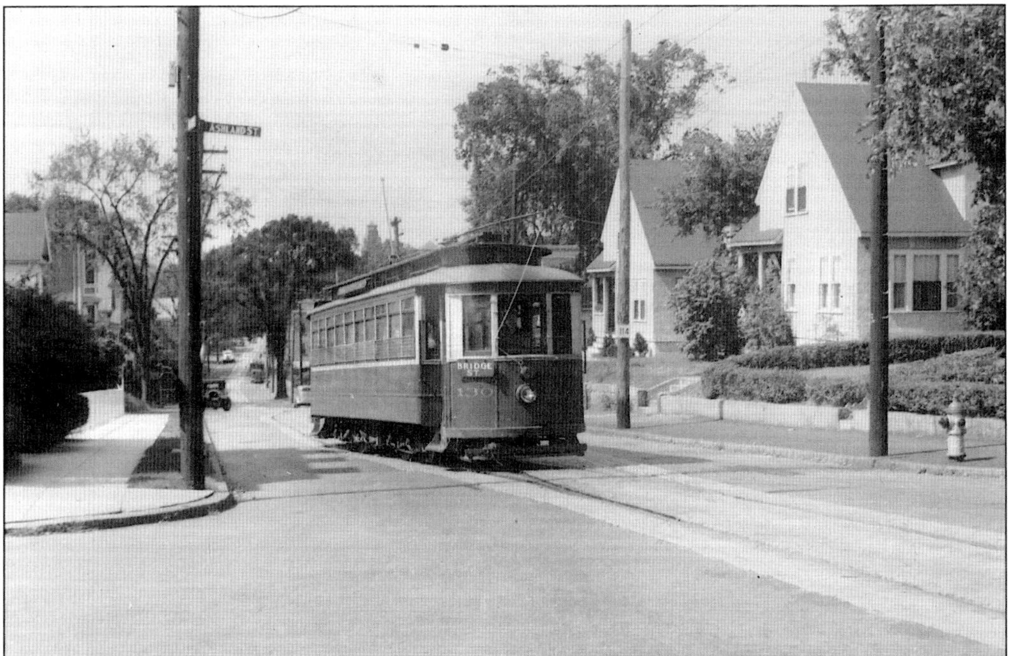

Outbound on Bridge Street, No. 130 passes Ashland Street on its way to Derryfield Park, *c.* 1938. In those days 20-minute service was offered between the park and Notre Dame.

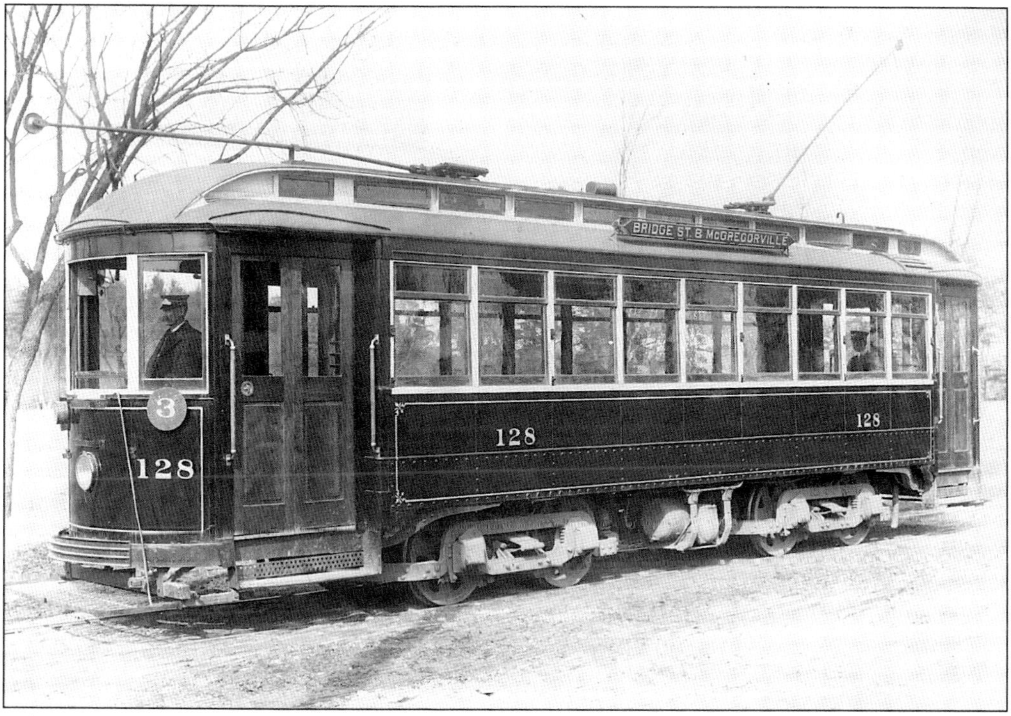

When cars 118–128 were purchased in 1912, they were originally assigned to the Derryfield Park–McGregorville line, which had been identified as Route 3 in 1910. Car No. 128 is at Bridge and Highland Streets.

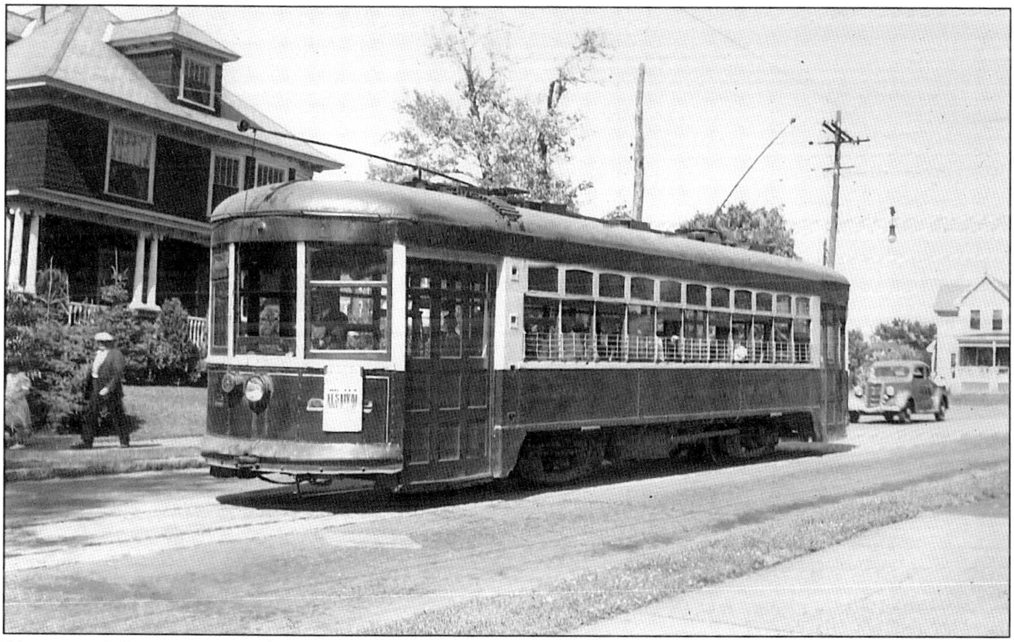

Shown is No. 202 at Bridge and Highland Streets on July 10, 1937. It operated regularly on the Derryfield Park–Notre Dame route for nearly a decade.

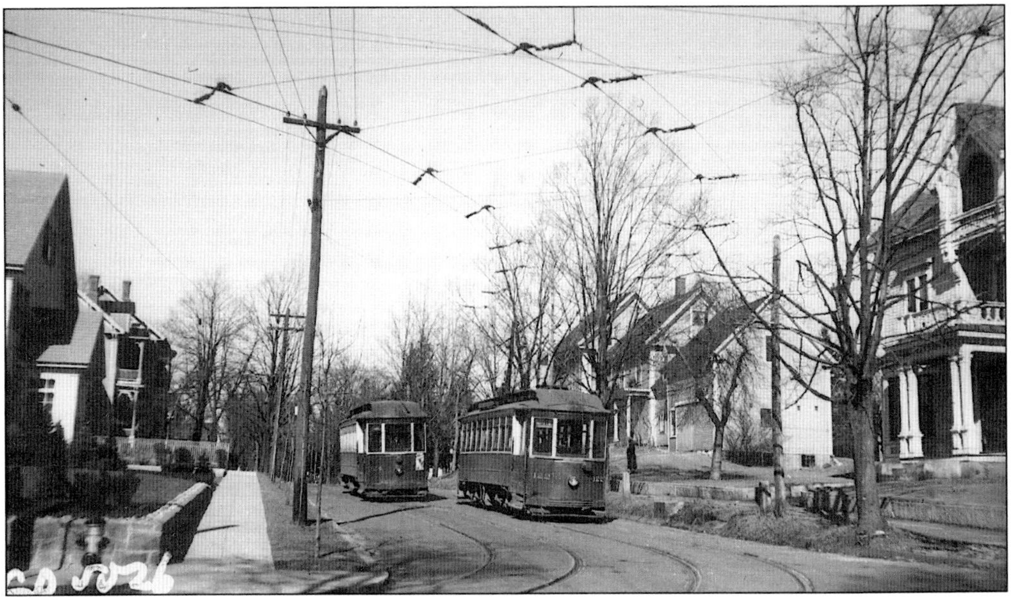

Branching from the Bridge Street route was the Beech Street line, which extended northward along Beech to Webster Street and out Hooksett Road to the Hooksett boundary. Cars No. 124 and No. 122 meet at Bridge and Beech Streets on February 15, 1938.

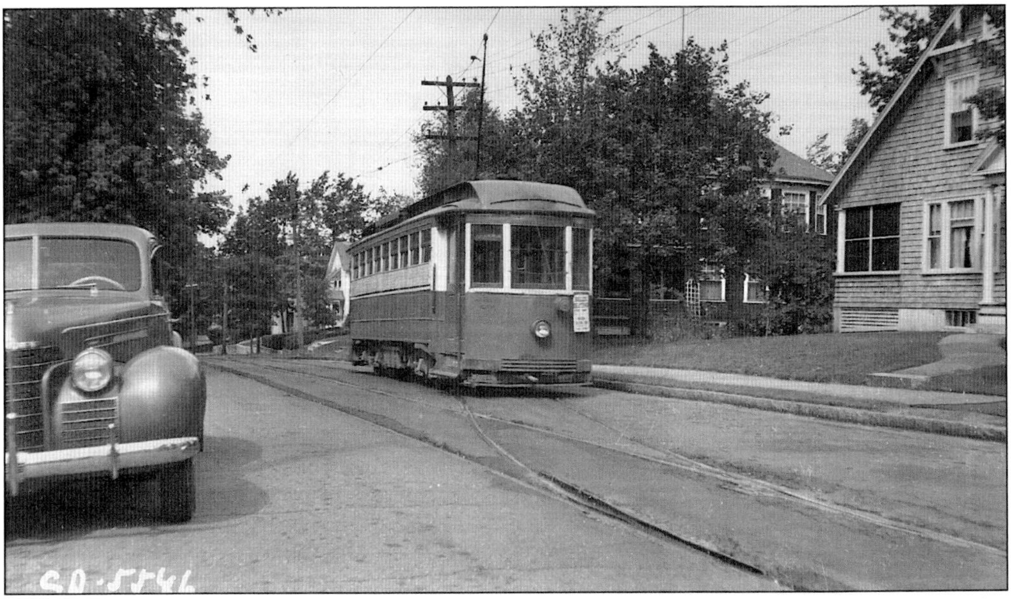

The sole turnout on Beech Street was situated between Sagamore and Webster Streets. Charles A. Duncan snapped this view of No. 122 in September 1939, when trolleys were run half-hourly between Goffe's Falls and Webster Street.

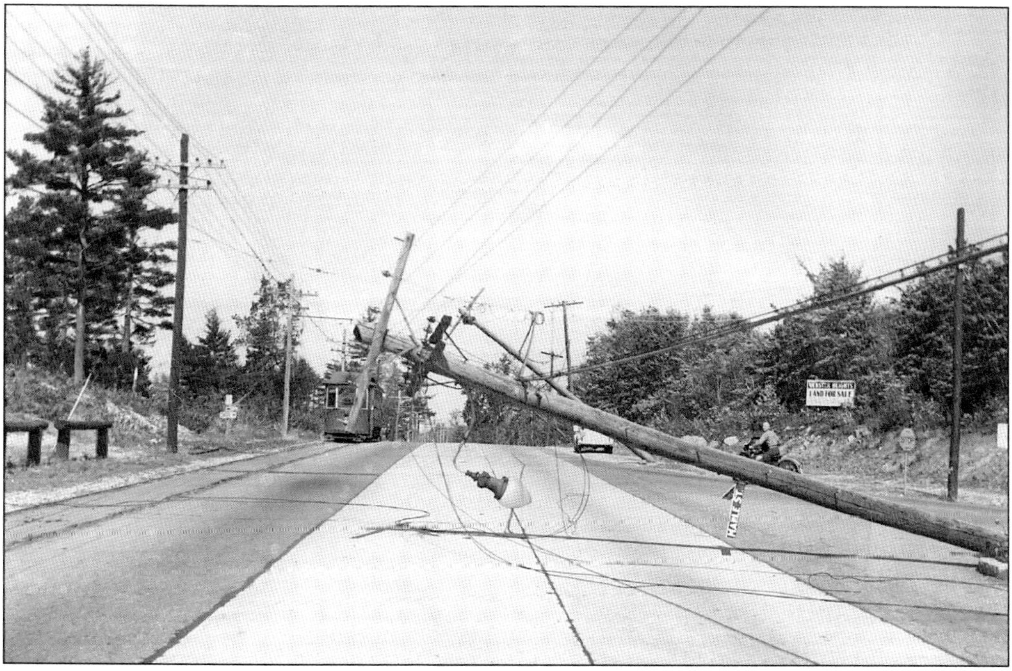

Probably struck and felled by an automobile, a utility pole hangs over Hooksett Road at Maple Street in the 1930s, as a trolley headed for downtown Manchester approaches. The commercial development of the east side of Hooksett Road was still many years away.

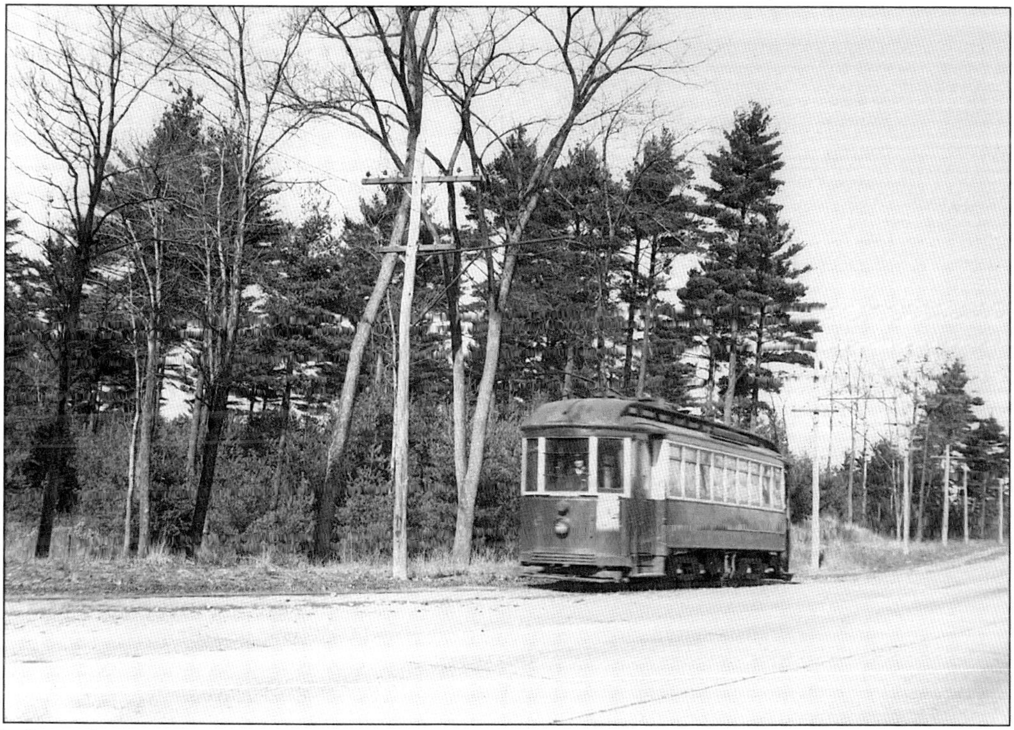

Inbound No. 122, en route from the Hooksett line to downtown Manchester and Goffe's Falls, passes Livingston Park on February 15, 1938.

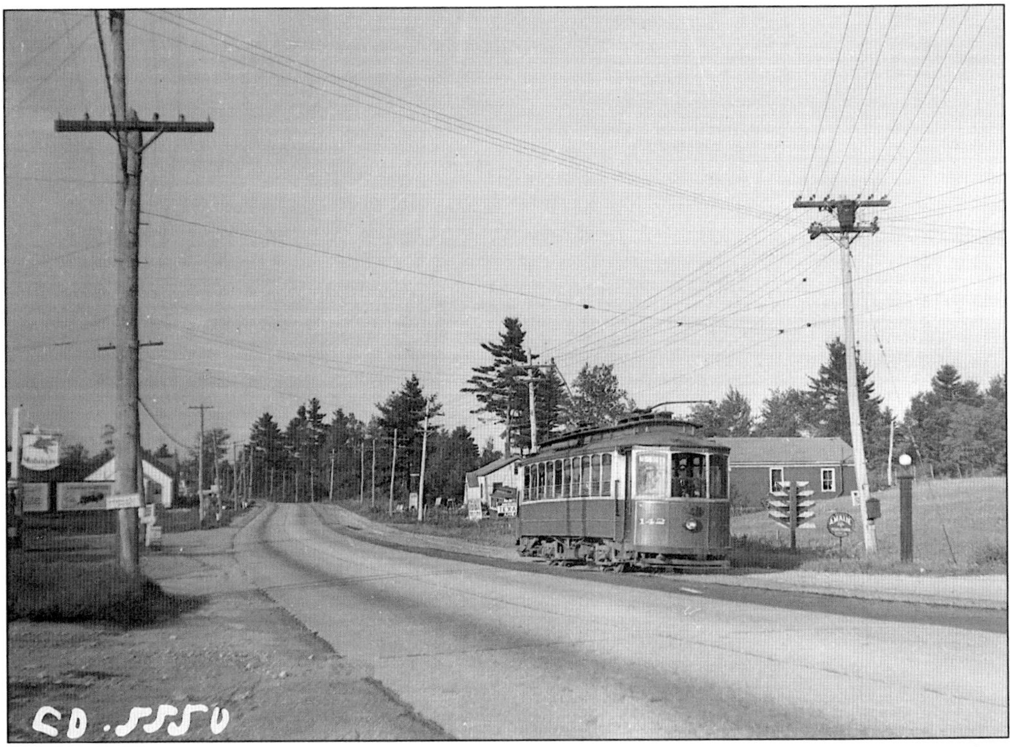

Approaching the Hooksett town line, No. 142 runs along the west side of Hooksett Road in September 1939. Hourly service was then given between Goffe's Falls and the Hooksett line.

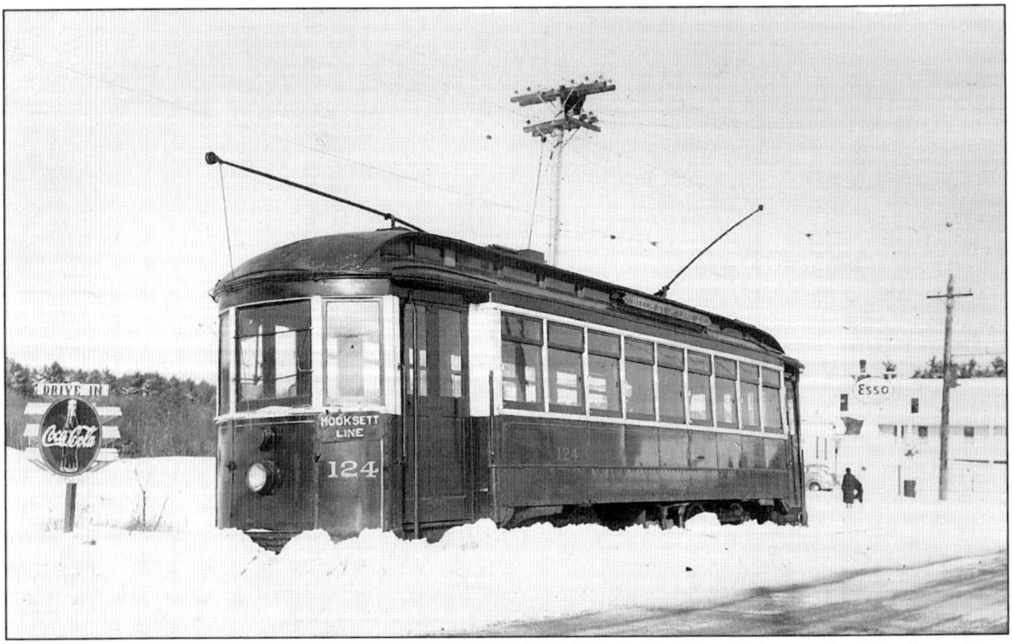

Preparing to return to downtown Manchester and Goffe's Falls, No. 124 is at the Hooksett line on January 2, 1938. From 1903 to 1933, this point was the junction of the Manchester Street Railway and the Concord & Manchester Electric Branch.

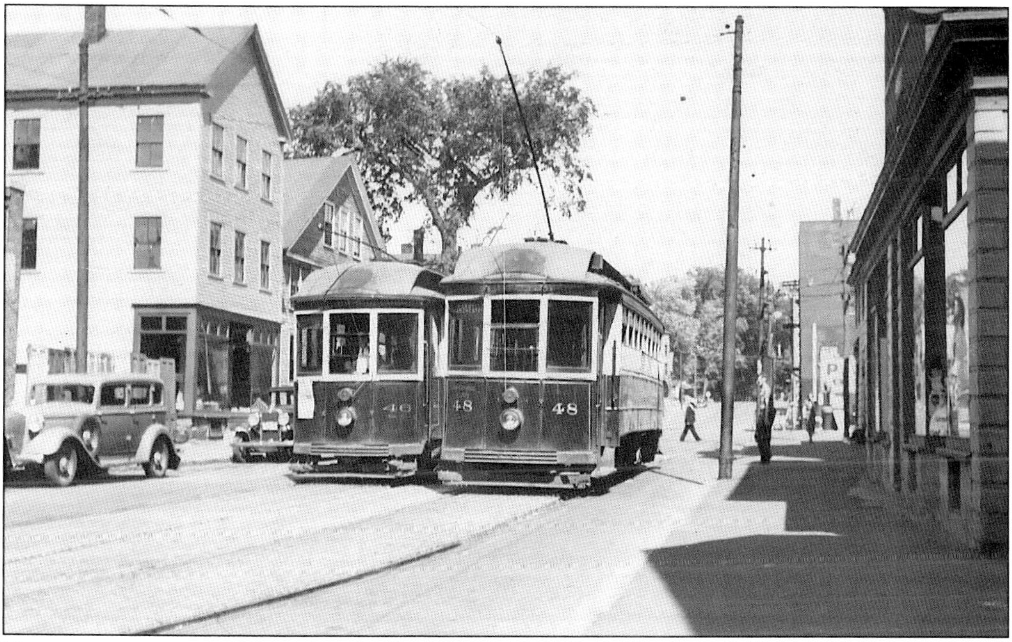

Horsecar service was inaugurated on Manchester and Hall Streets in 1885, and the line was electrified 10 years later. Here, Nos. 46 and 48 meet on the Manchester Street turnout, near Chestnut Street, on July 10, 1937.

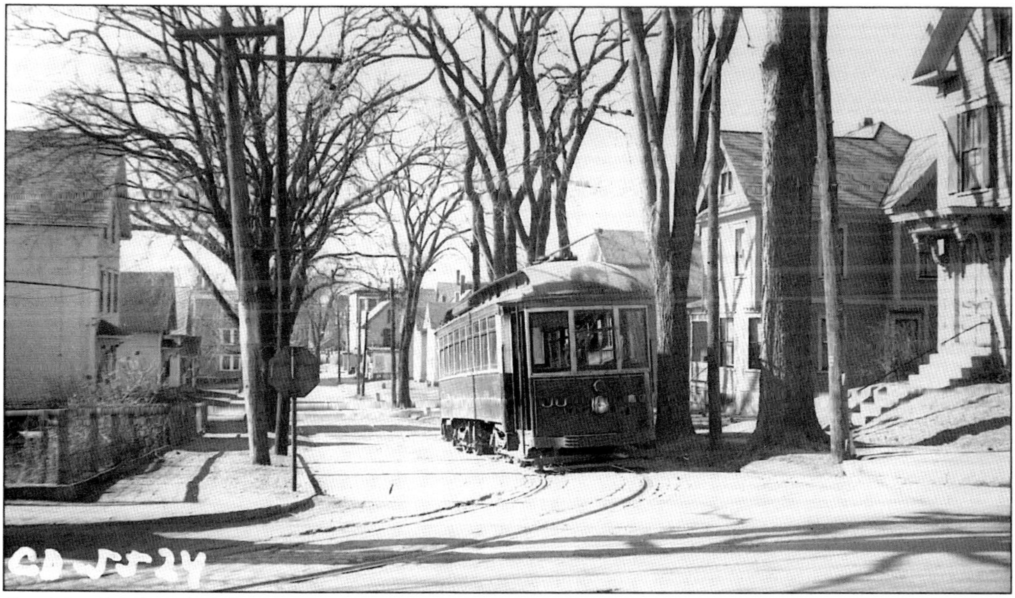

Car No. 56, headed for the East Manchester depot, halts for a stop sign at the intersection of Manchester and Hall Streets on February 15, 1938.

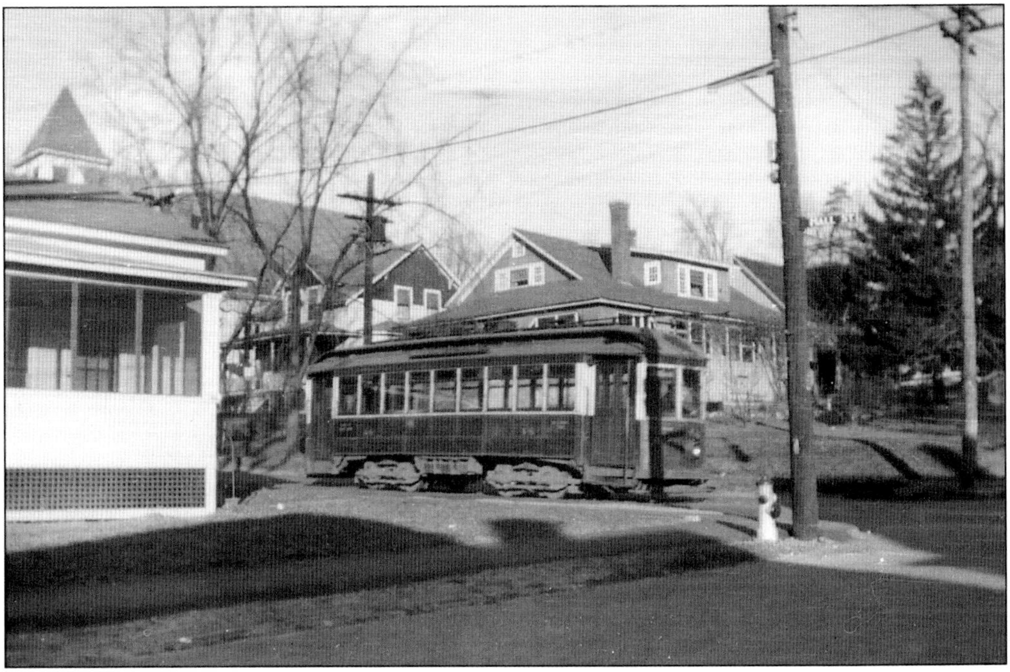

Car No. 48 passes through a thickly settled neighborhood on Hall Street at Laurel Street on November 30, 1939. The first snow of the season had yet to fall.

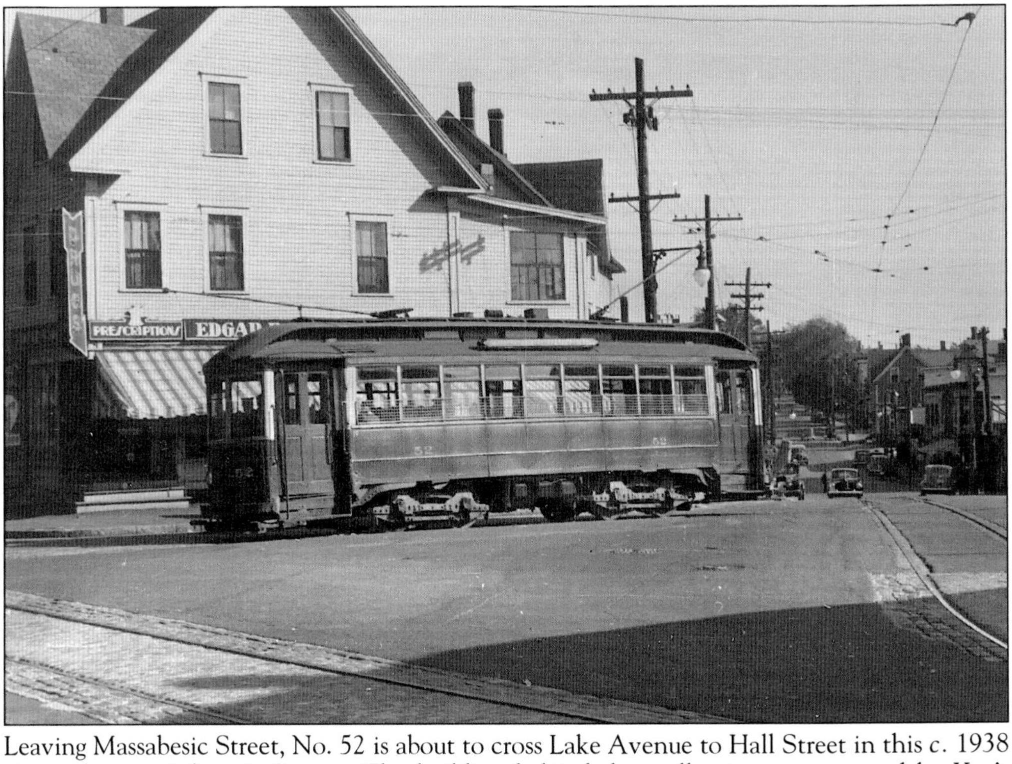

Leaving Massabesic Street, No. 52 is about to cross Lake Avenue to Hall Street in this *c.* 1938 view taken at Gilman's Corner. The building behind the trolley is now occupied by Kay's Bakery, 443 Lake Avenue.

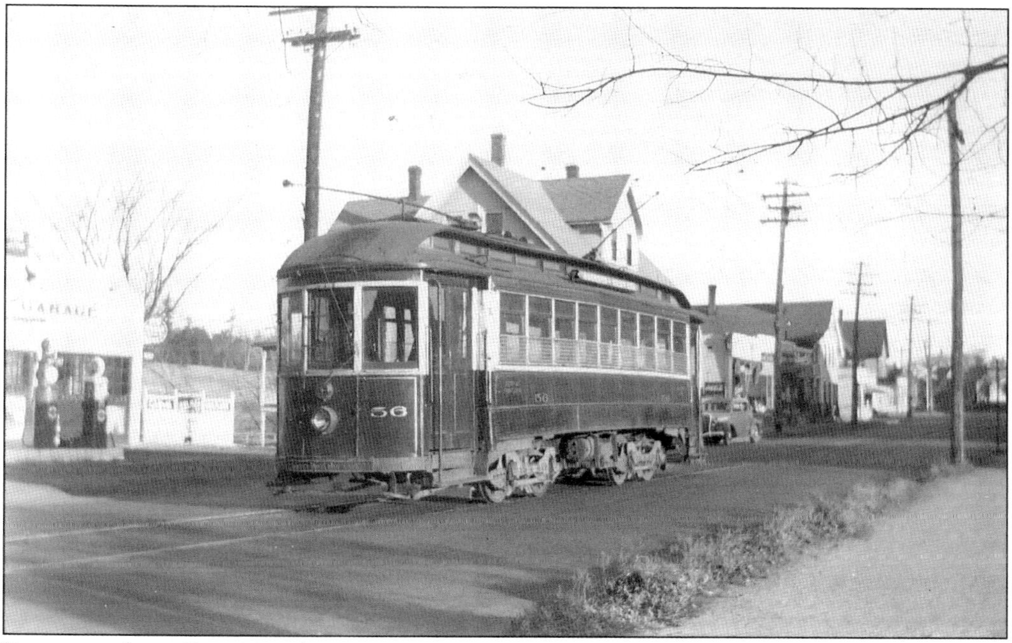

Returning from East Manchester, No. 98 is on Massabesic Street near Belmont Street on November 12, 1939. The Massabesic Street Garage is at the far left.

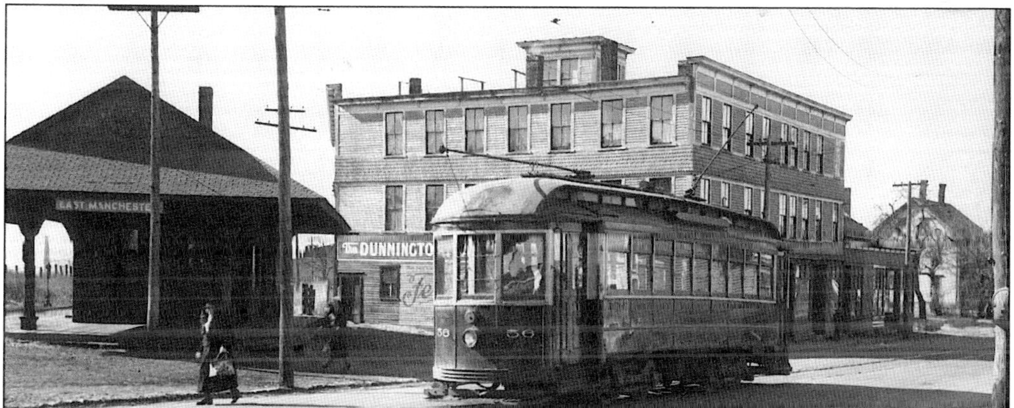

The Massabesic Street track ended at the East Manchester depot of the Boston & Maine Railroad, which appears at the left of No. 56 on February 15, 1938. The railroad station was razed many years ago, but the building behind the trolley still stands.

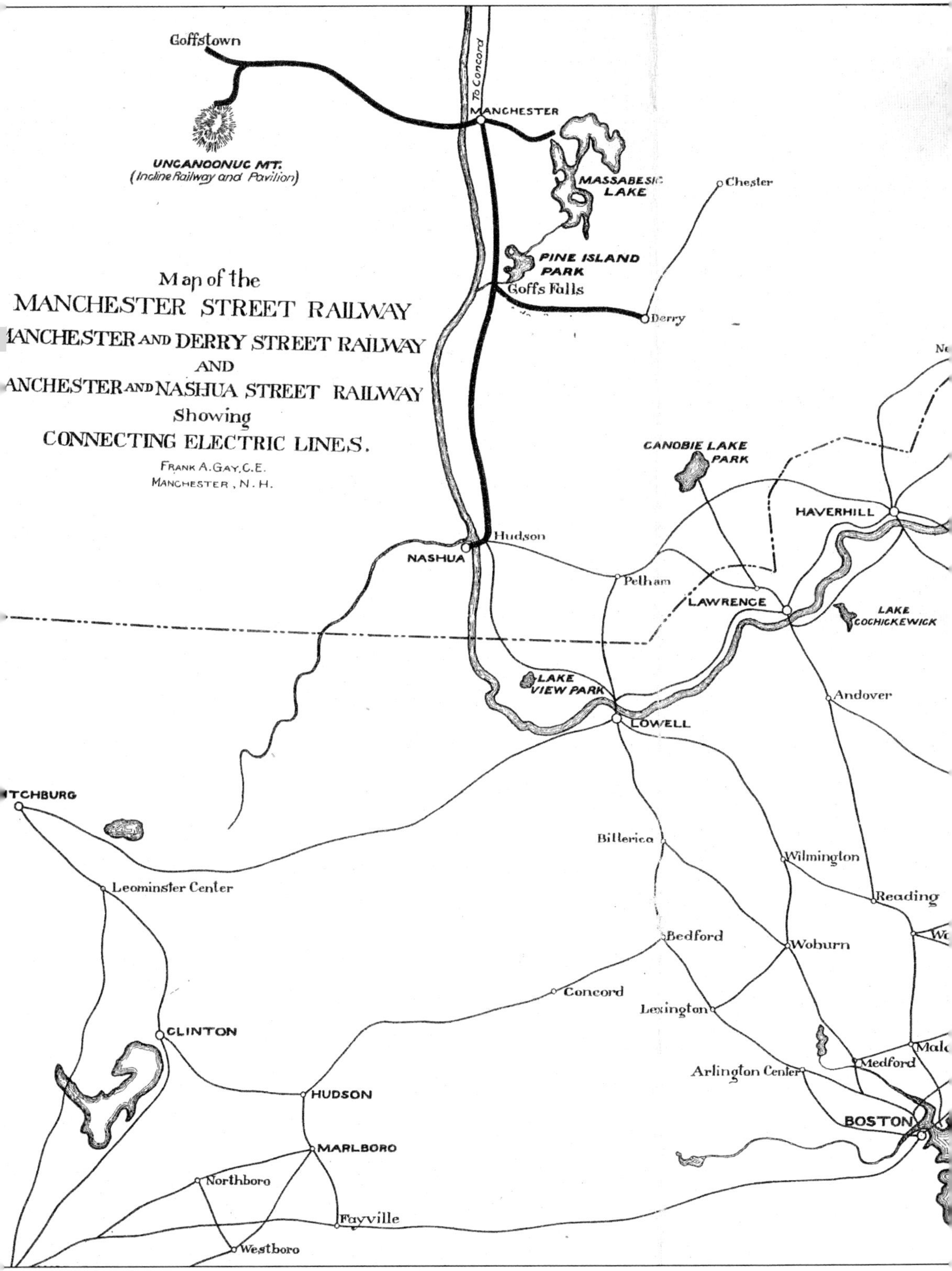
Map of the
MANCHESTER STREET RAILWAY
[M]ANCHESTER AND DERRY STREET RAILWAY
AND
[M]ANCHESTER AND NASHUA STREET RAILWAY
Showing
CONNECTING ELECTRIC LINES.
FRANK A. GAY, C.E.
MANCHESTER, N.H.
Goffstown
UNCANOONUC MT.
(Incline Railway and Pavilion)
To Concord
MANCHESTER
MASSABESIC LAKE
Chester
PINE ISLAND PARK
Goffs Falls
Derry
CANOBIE LAKE PARK
HAVERHILL
Hudson
NASHUA
Pelham
LAWRENCE
LAKE COCHICKEWICK
LAKE VIEW PARK
Andover
LOWELL
TCHBURG
Billerica
Wilmington
Leominster Center
Reading
Bedford
Woburn
Concord
Lexington
CLINTON
Medford
Arlington Center
HUDSON
BOSTON
MARLBORO
Northboro
Fayville
Westboro

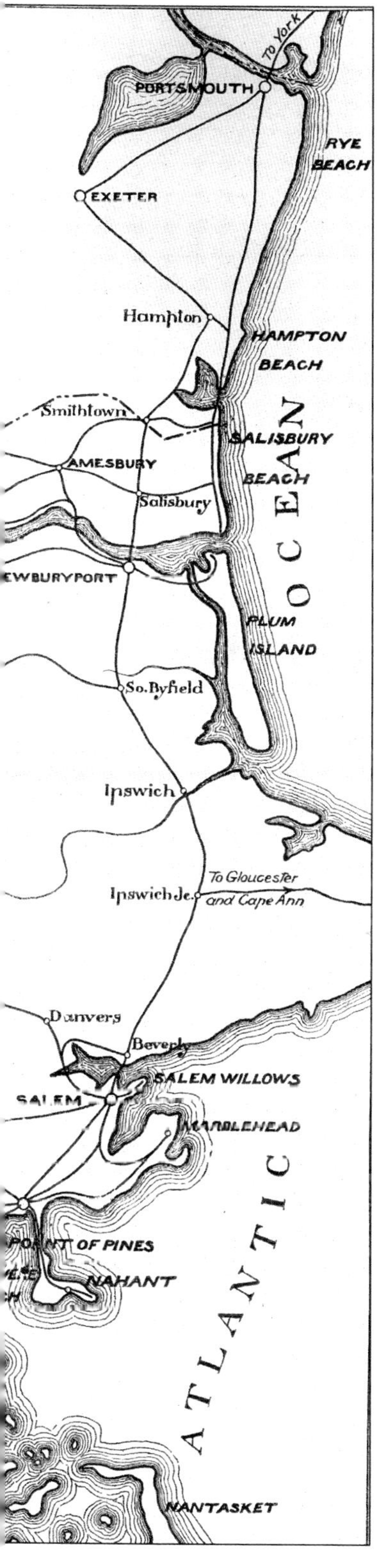

Southeastern New Hampshire and northeastern Massachusetts trolley lines, which connected with the Manchester Traction, Light, & Power Company system after January 1, 1908, are shown on this map. The map appeared in one of the trolley guides issued by the Manchester Traction, Light, & Power Company between 1907 and 1921. As is readily apparent, many trips from the Queen City were possible and one was to Boston, 58 miles, via Nashua and Lowell. The running time was four hours—considerably more than that via the Boston & Maine Railroad—and involved numerous car changes.

A popular destination for many Queen City residents was Canobie Lake Park in Salem, and at least one excursion was run from Manchester to Hampton Beach on the coast. From this resort one could ride by trolley to Portsmouth and after taking a ferry across the Piscataqua River into Maine, continue on to such sites as Portland, Lewiston, Augusta, and Waterville.

Trolley service between Nashua and Lowell ended in 1920 and by mid-1924, after the abandonment of the line from Hudson to Canobie Lake Park, the only possible electric car trips from the Queen City were those to Goffstown, Concord, Nashua, and Derry. The Derry and Nashua routes were abandoned in 1926 and 1931, respectively; trolley service to Concord ended in 1933, and the last cars from Manchester to Goffstown ran in 1938.

Yes, the trolley era was great while it lasted!

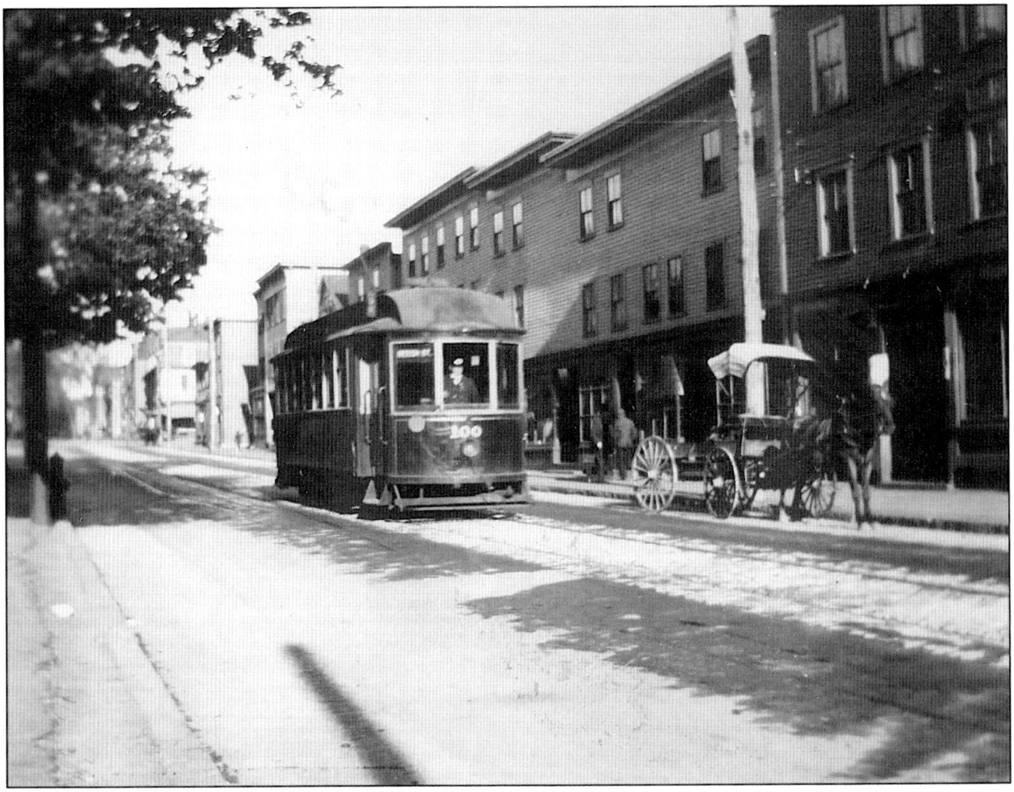

Merrimack Common, now Veterans Memorial Park, is at the left in this *c.* 1910 view. Car No. 100 runs westward on Central Street toward Elm Street and the Transfer Station.

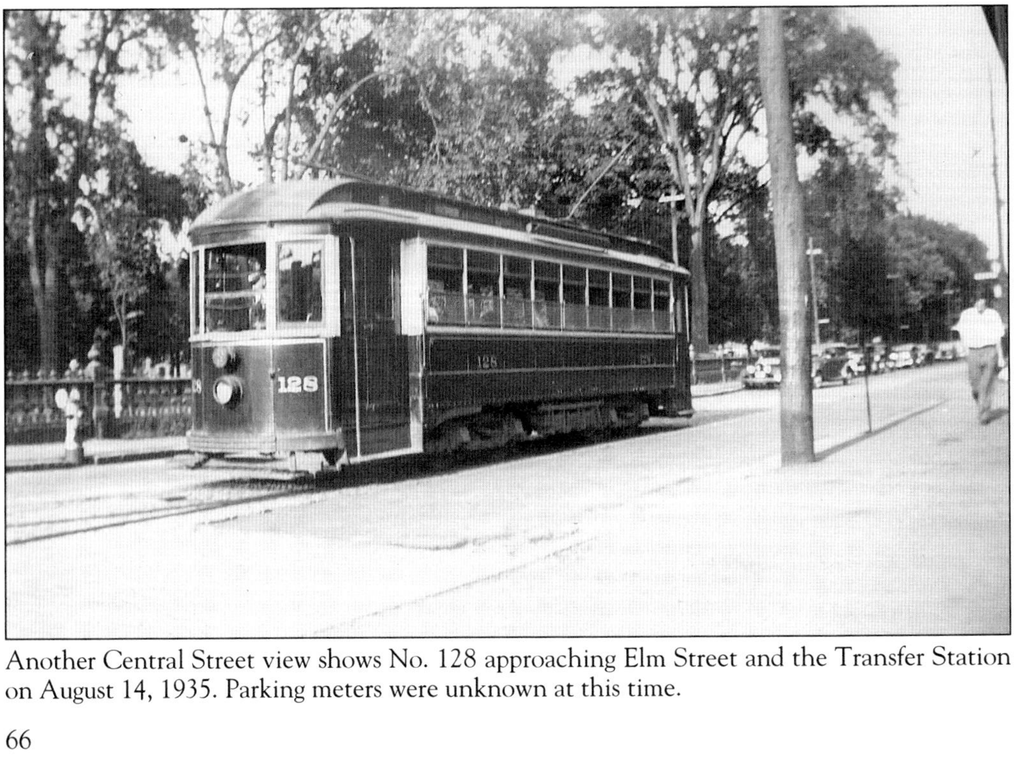

Another Central Street view shows No. 128 approaching Elm Street and the Transfer Station on August 14, 1935. Parking meters were unknown at this time.

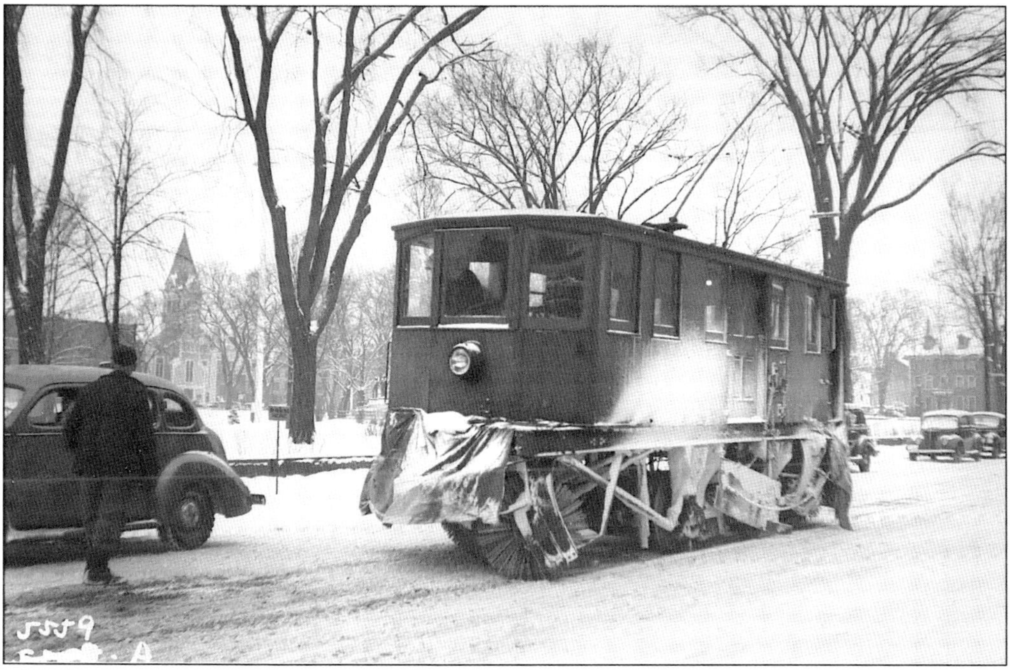

This four-wheel snow sweeper was purchased secondhand in 1928 and is shown here in action on Central Street on January 11, 1940. It was junked before the end of the year.

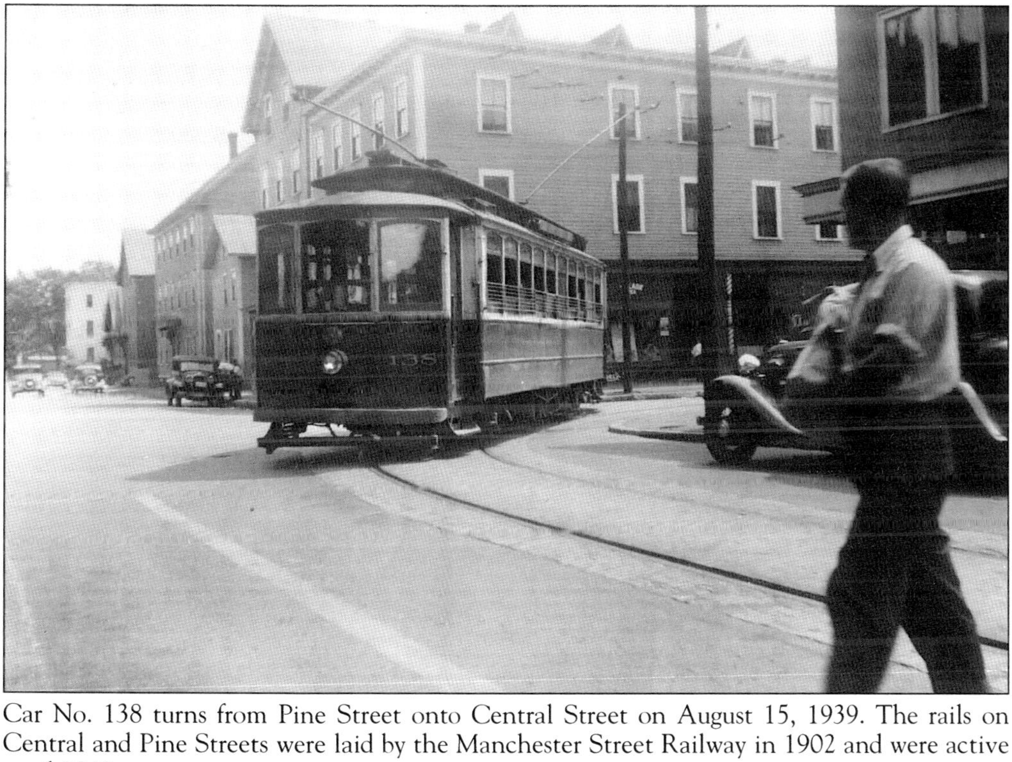

Car No. 138 turns from Pine Street onto Central Street on August 15, 1939. The rails on Central and Pine Streets were laid by the Manchester Street Railway in 1902 and were active until 1940.

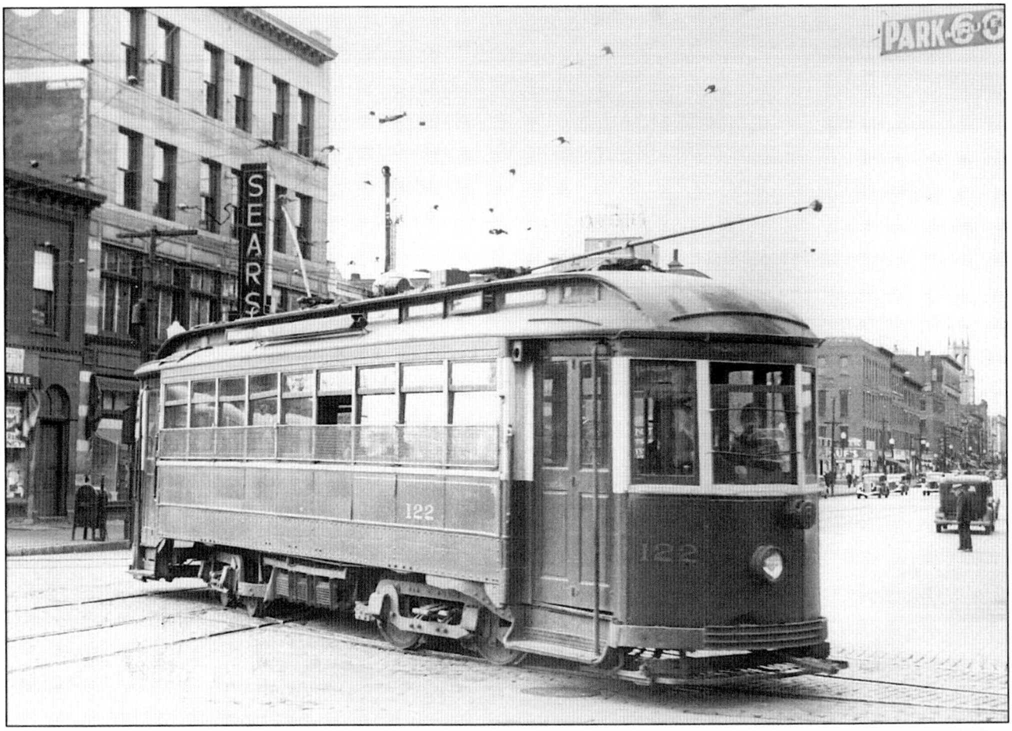

Massabesic Lake was the destination of No. 122, photographed at the intersection of Elm Street and Lake Avenue in June 1939. Less than a year later, trolley service in Manchester was history.

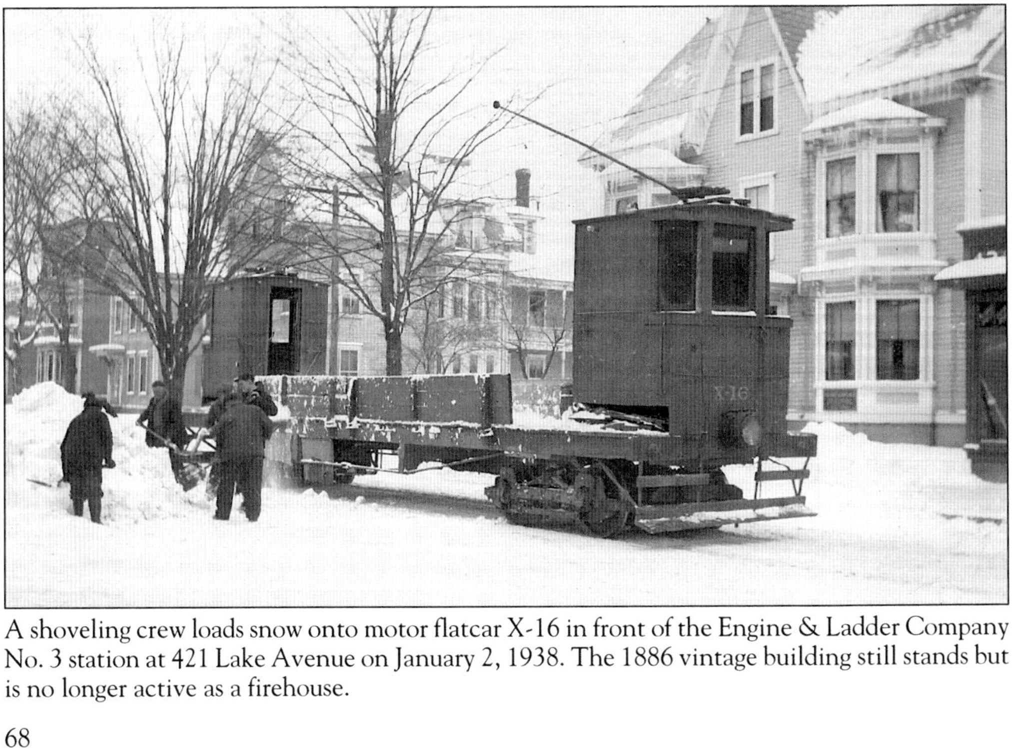

A shoveling crew loads snow onto motor flatcar X-16 in front of the Engine & Ladder Company No. 3 station at 421 Lake Avenue on January 2, 1938. The 1886 vintage building still stands but is no longer active as a firehouse.

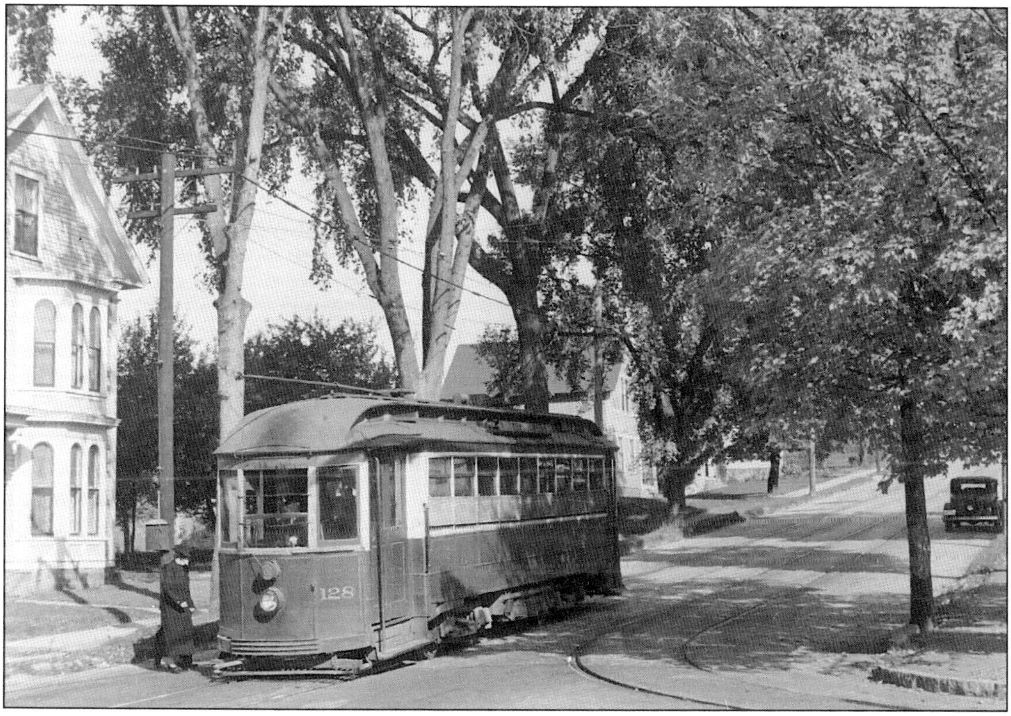

Returning from Massabesic Lake, No. 128 stops to pick up a passenger on Lake Avenue at Cass Street, *c.* 1938. At one time, there was double track all the way from this point to the lake terminus. The area covered by the double track was known as the Trolley Block.

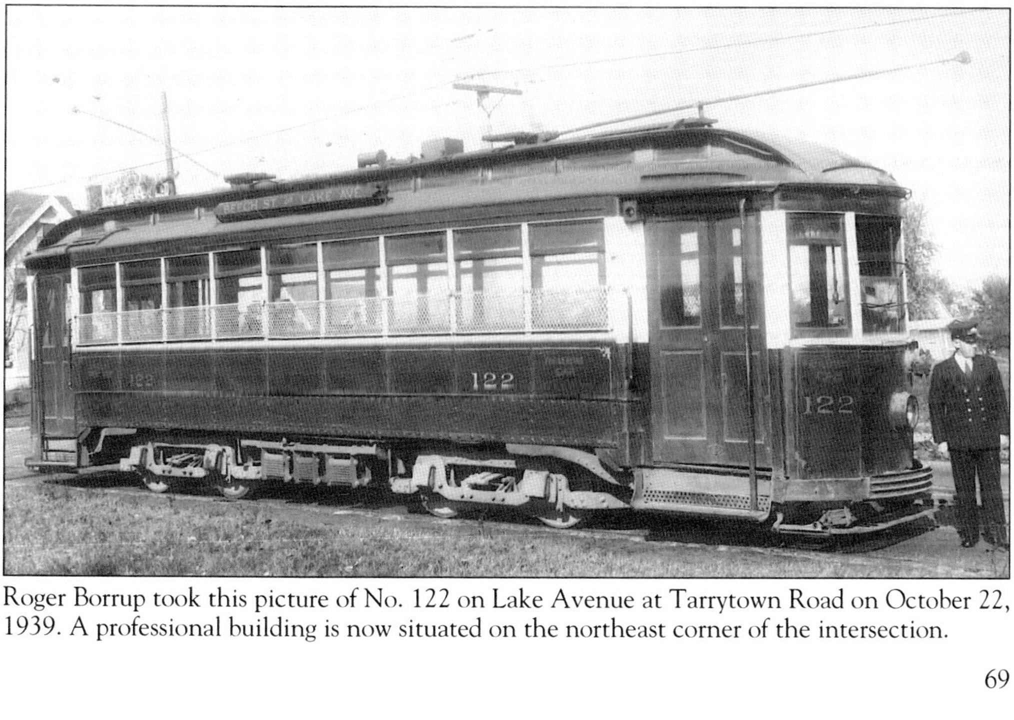

Roger Borrup took this picture of No. 122 on Lake Avenue at Tarrytown Road on October 22, 1939. A professional building is now situated on the northeast corner of the intersection.

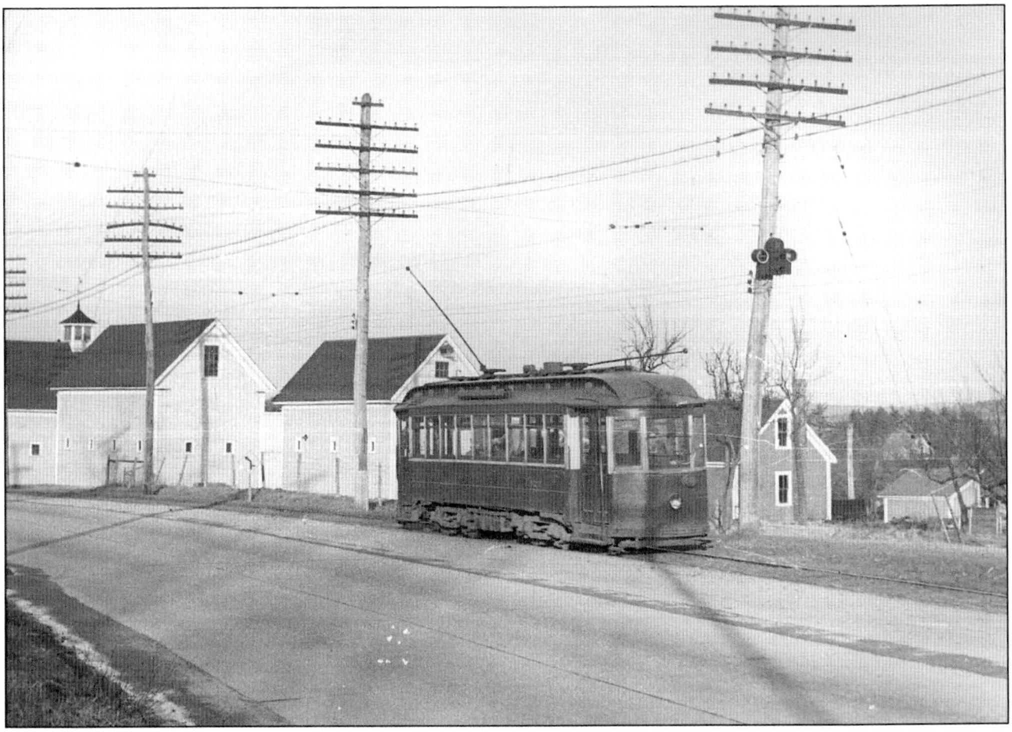

A new state highway built in 1928 is in the foreground, as inbound No. 122 runs along Hanover Street near the Candia Road intersection on April 14, 1940.

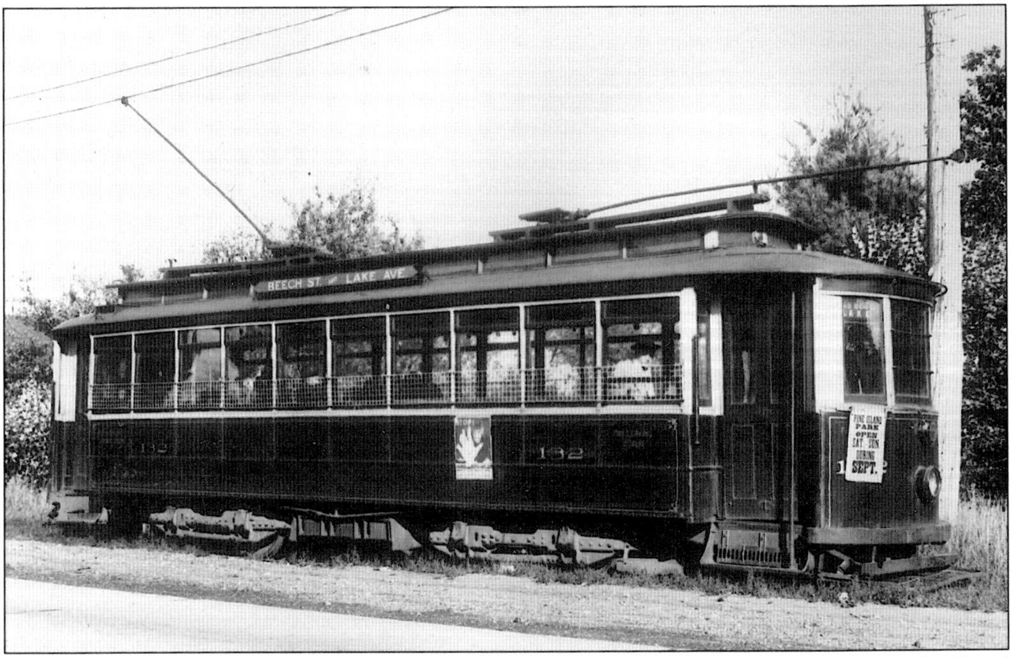

An advertising sign for Pine Island Park is displayed on the dasher of No. 142 on Candia Road on October 22, 1939. The trolley is returning from Massabesic Lake.

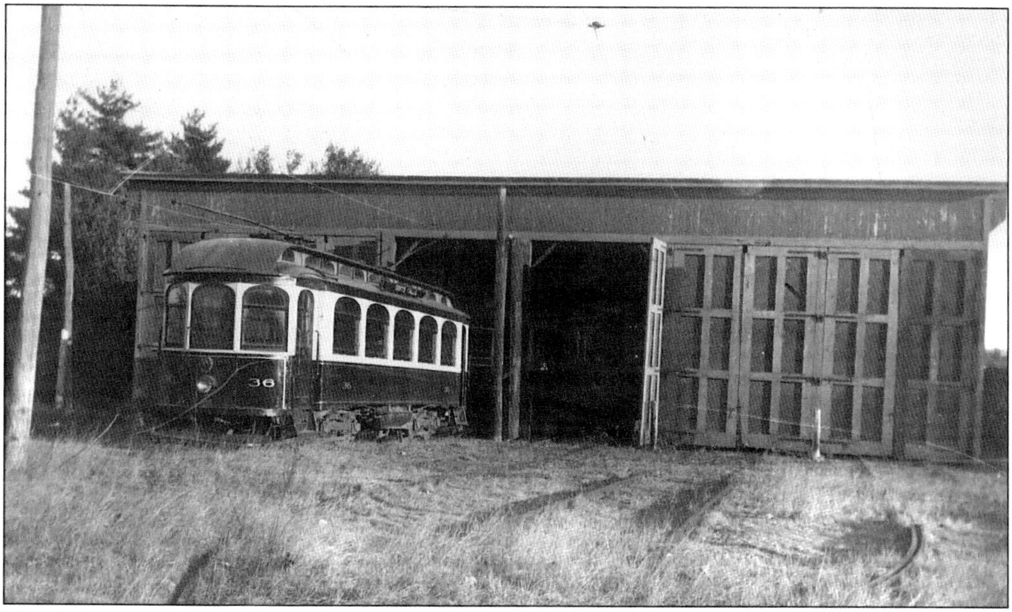

The Lake carbarn of the Manchester Street Railway, erected in 1902 on the south side of Candia Road, was used for the storage of inactive trolleys until 1938. The building still stands as part of the R.C. Hazelton Company complex.

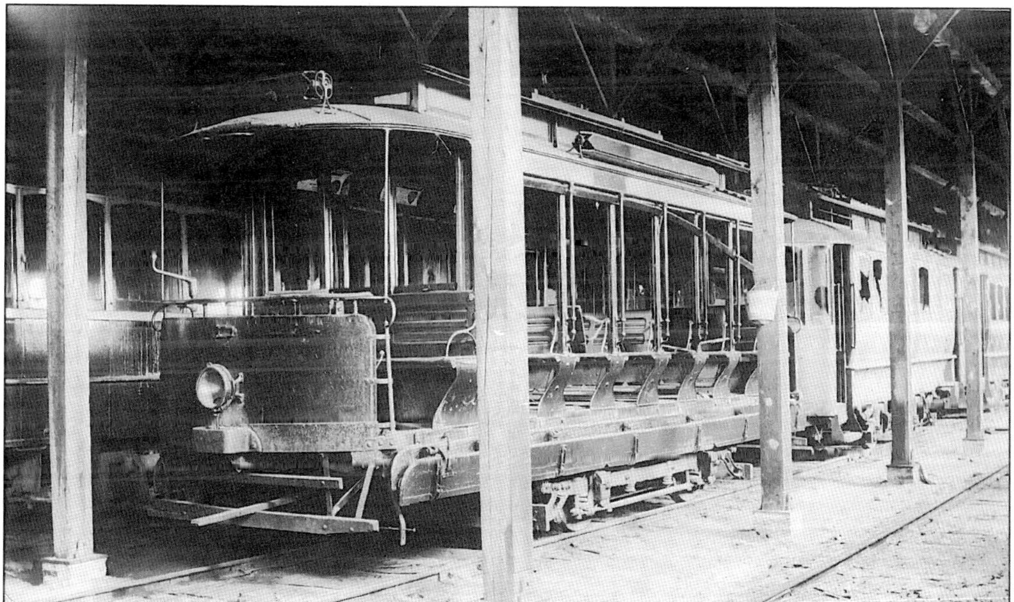

Two of the Manchester Street Railway's first trolleys, a nine-bench open and a 20-foot, one-inch closed car, are inside the Lake carbarn in this *c.* 1934 view. All cars stored in the building were scrapped in 1936.

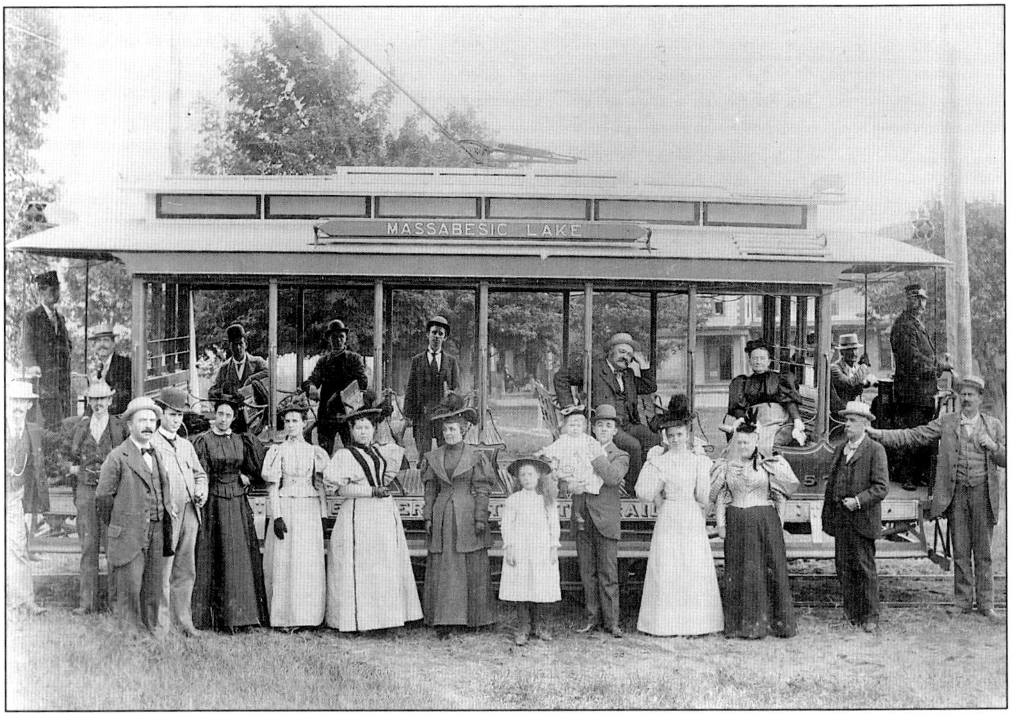

Nine-bench open No. 57 made the first trial trip from downtown Manchester to Massabesic Lake on the afternoon of Saturday, August 4, 1895. Regular service began the next morning, and cars ran every ten minutes.

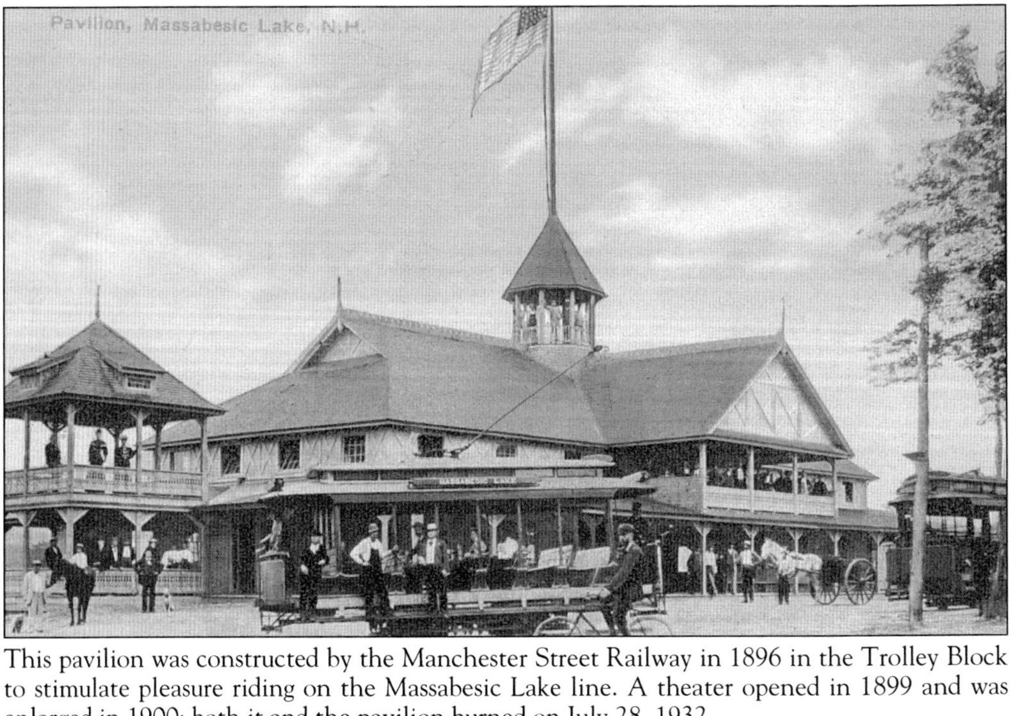

This pavilion was constructed by the Manchester Street Railway in 1896 in the Trolley Block to stimulate pleasure riding on the Massabesic Lake line. A theater opened in 1899 and was enlarged in 1900; both it and the pavilion burned on July 28, 1932.

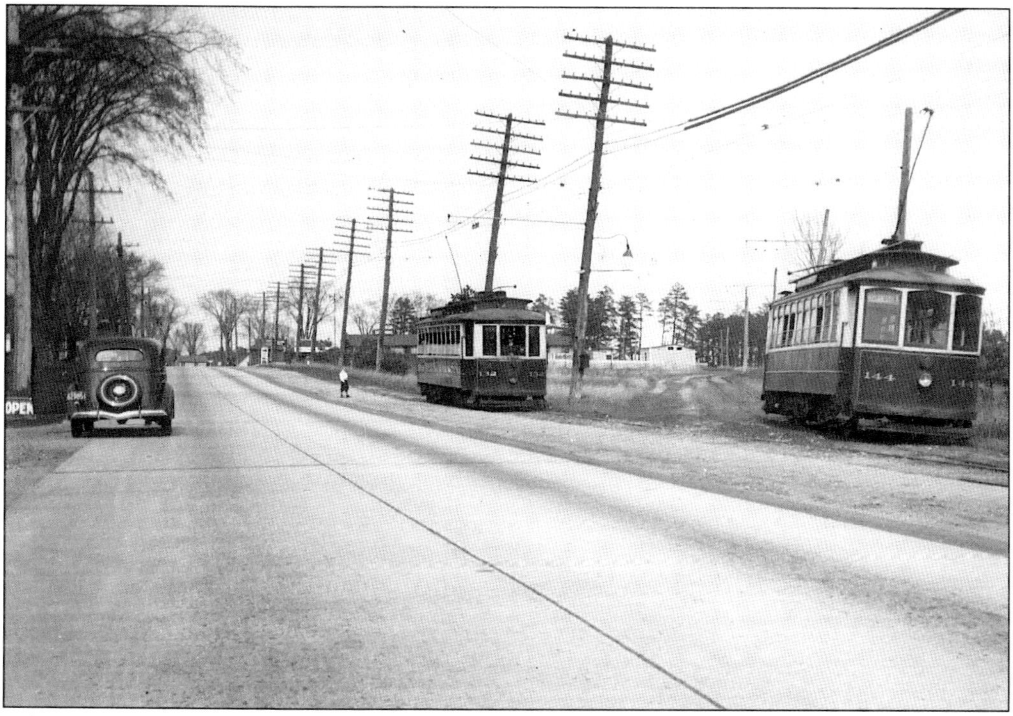

A loop constructed in the Trolley Block in 1895 survived until 1940. This April 28, 1936 view shows No. 144 entering the loop and inbound No. 132 on Candia Road.

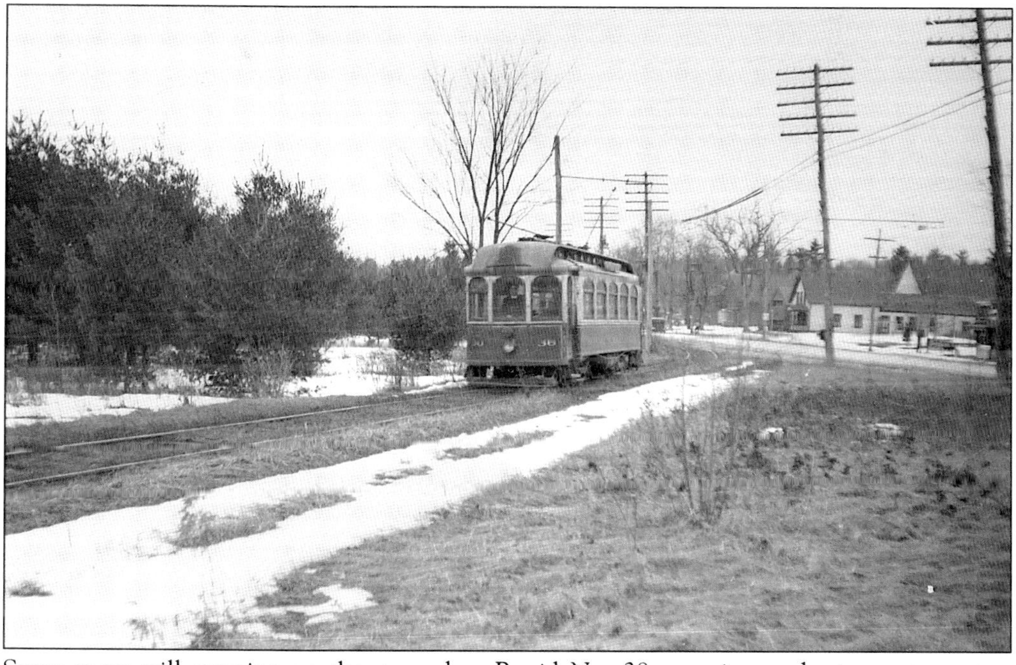

Some snow still remains on the ground as Rapid No. 38, carrying a charter party, enters the Massabesic Lake loop on March 19, 1940. Cars such as this one appeared only rarely on the line.

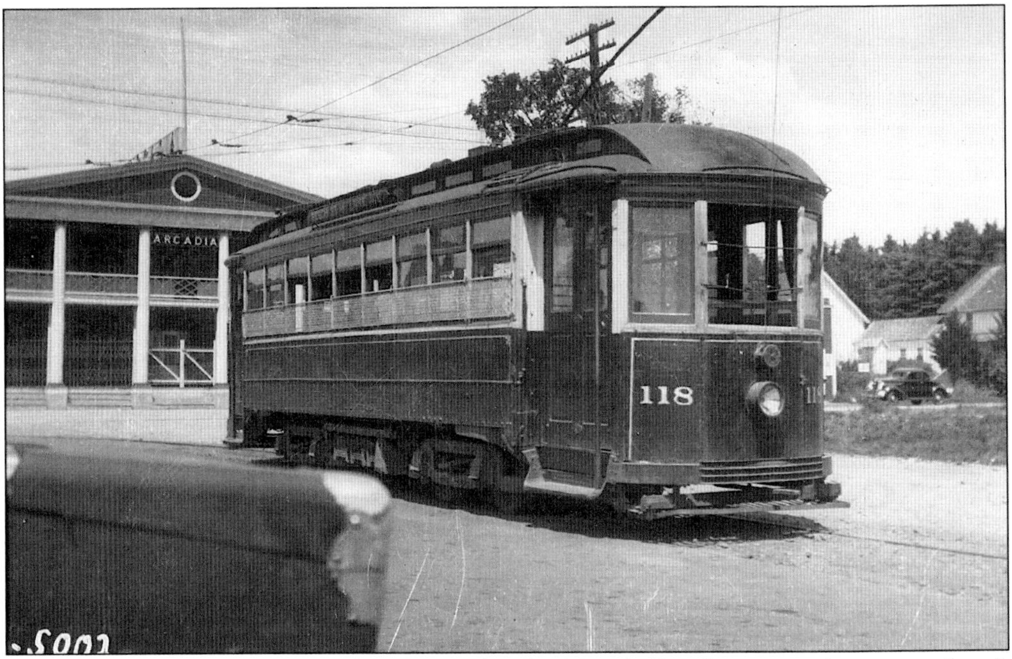

The Arcadia ballroom was erected on the north side of Candia Road, opposite the street railway's pavilion and theater, in 1914. It appears in the background, as No. 118 leaves the trolley loop on August 8, 1935.

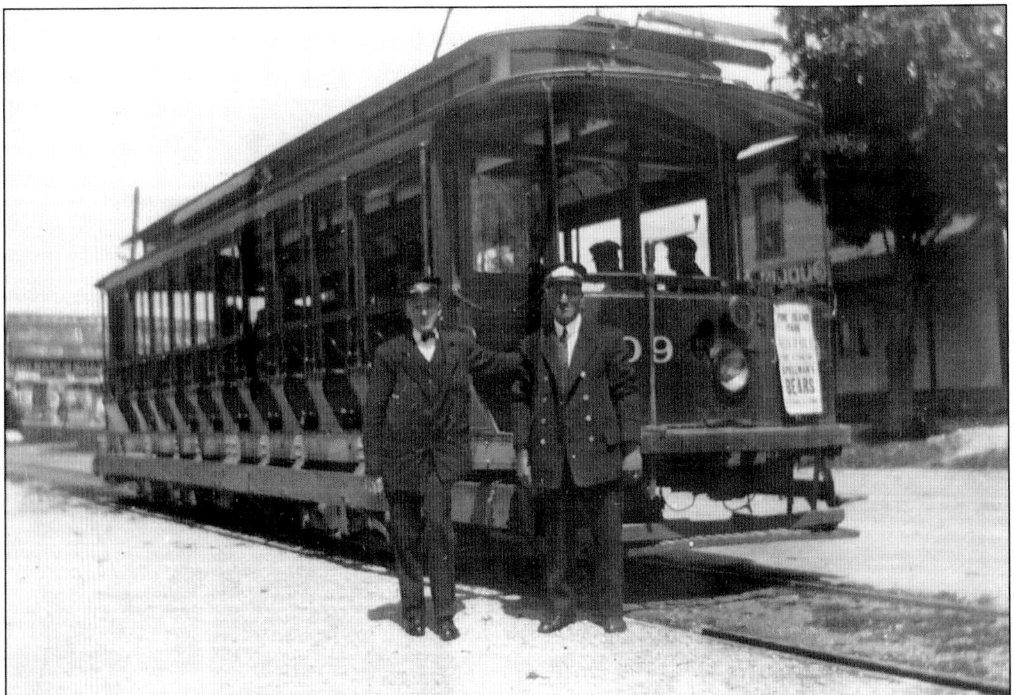

A motorman and conductor pose for a photographer, as 13-bench open No. 109, built in 1900, prepares to leave the Massabesic Lake loop *c.* 1910. All regular open-car operation on this route ended in the mid-1920s.

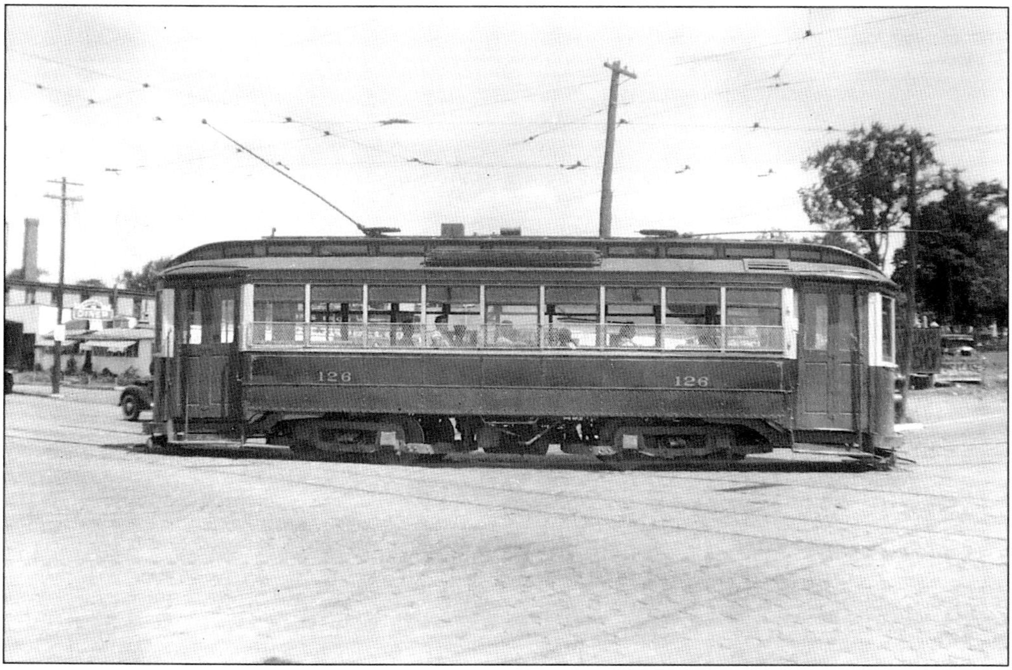

Turning from Elm Street onto Valley Street on August 14, 1939, is No. 116, built by the Laconia Car Company in 1912. Cars of this type originally had longitudinal seats accommodating 40 passengers, with 5-foot-wide aisles that provided plenty of room for standees.

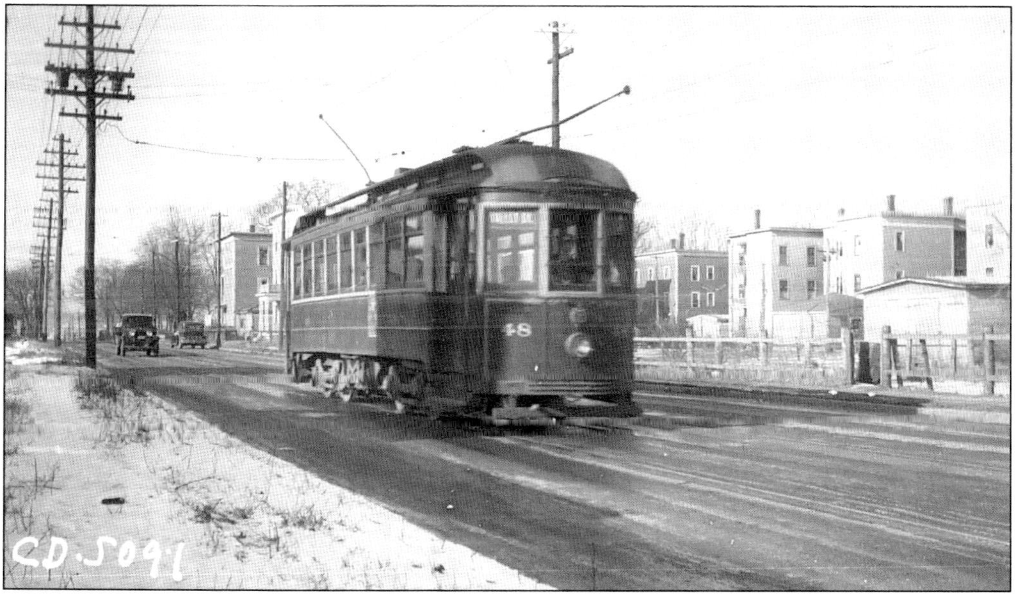

Outbound on Valley Street between Union and Beech Streets is No. 48 on January 13, 1937. Twenty-minute service was provided at this time on the Valley Street route, which was one of the busiest in the Queen City.

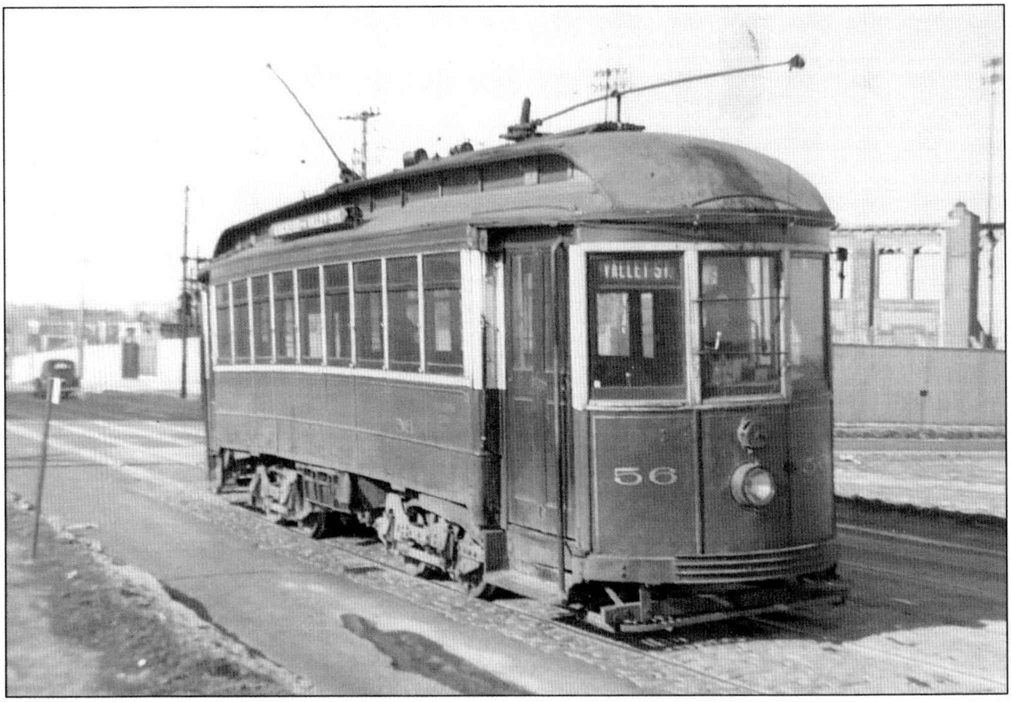

Passing the present Gill Stadium is No. 56 on January 28, 1940. When football or baseball games were played at the stadium, formerly known as Athletic Field, many extra cars were needed on the Valley Street line to carry large numbers of spectators.

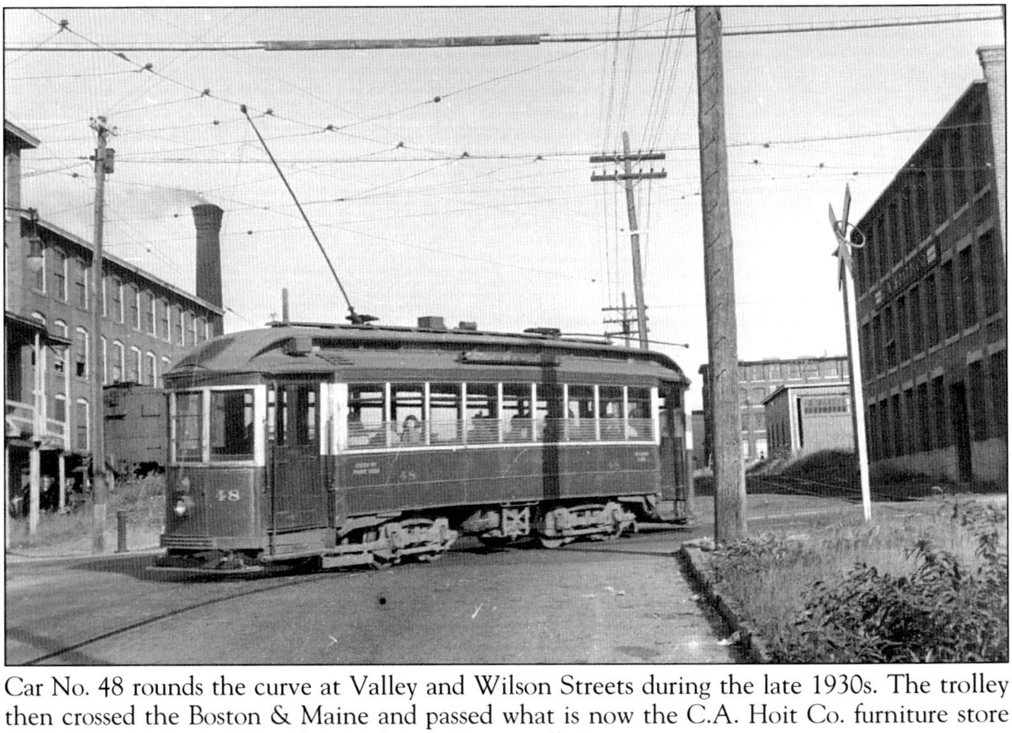

Car No. 48 rounds the curve at Valley and Wilson Streets during the late 1930s. The trolley then crossed the Boston & Maine and passed what is now the C.A. Hoit Co. furniture store before continuing southward on Wilson to Somerville Street.

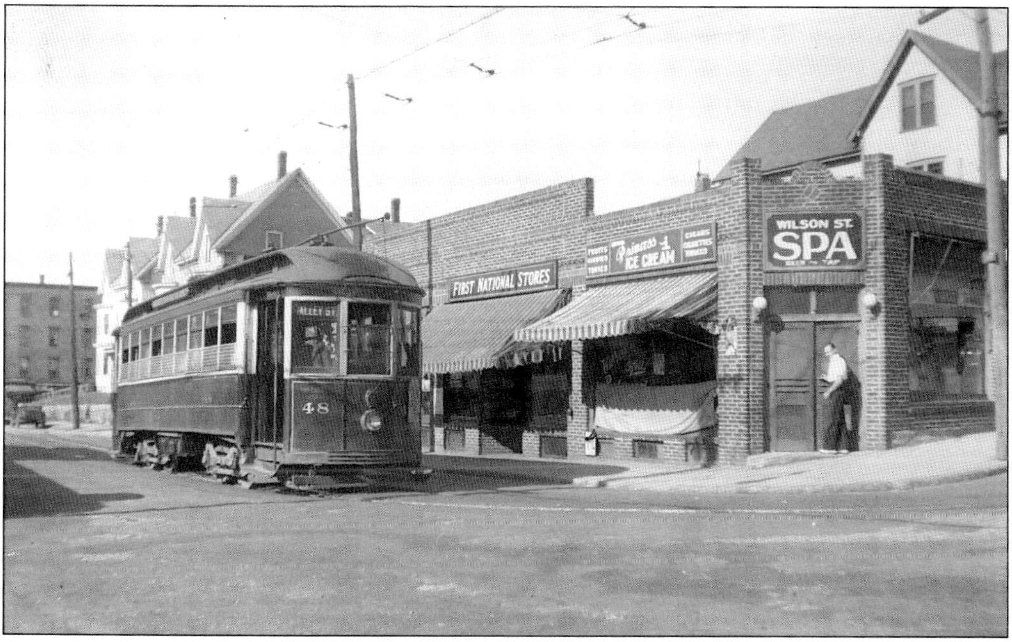

A neighborhood First National Store and the Wilson Street Spa are at the right, as No. 48 starts to turn from Wilson Street onto Somerville Street on July 31, 1938.

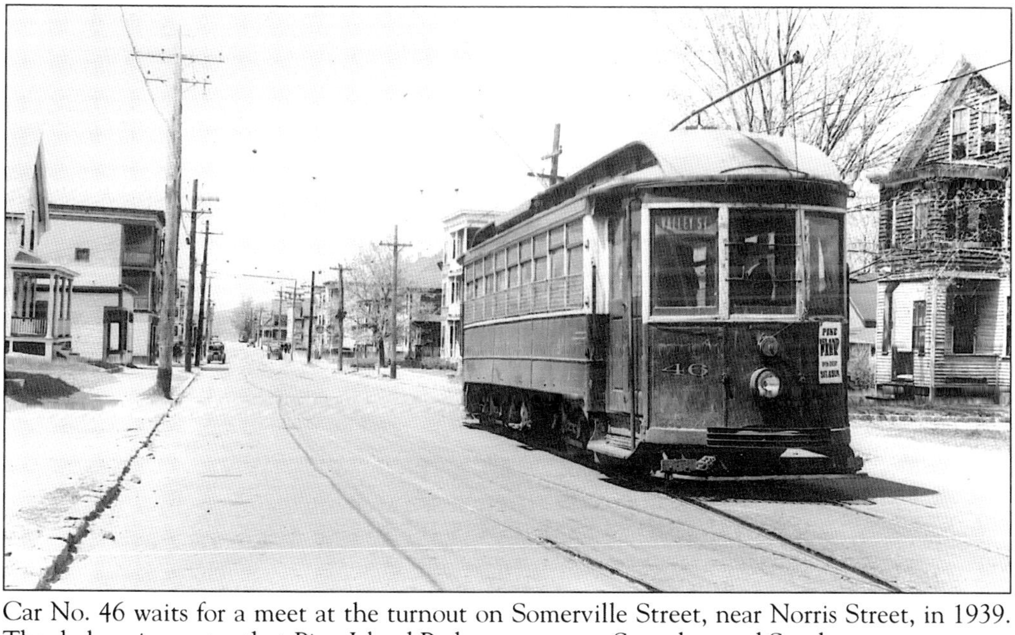

Car No. 46 waits for a meet at the turnout on Somerville Street, near Norris Street, in 1939. The dasher sign notes that Pine Island Park was open on Saturdays and Sundays.

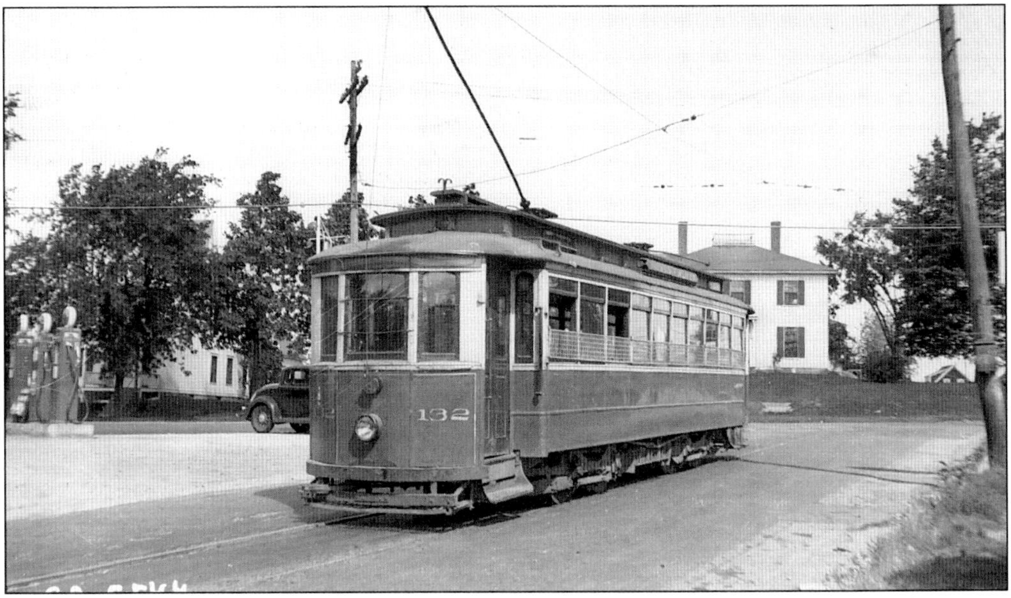

The intersection of Hayward Street and Mammoth Road was the terminus of the Valley Street line for many years, and No. 132 has just arrived there in September 1939.

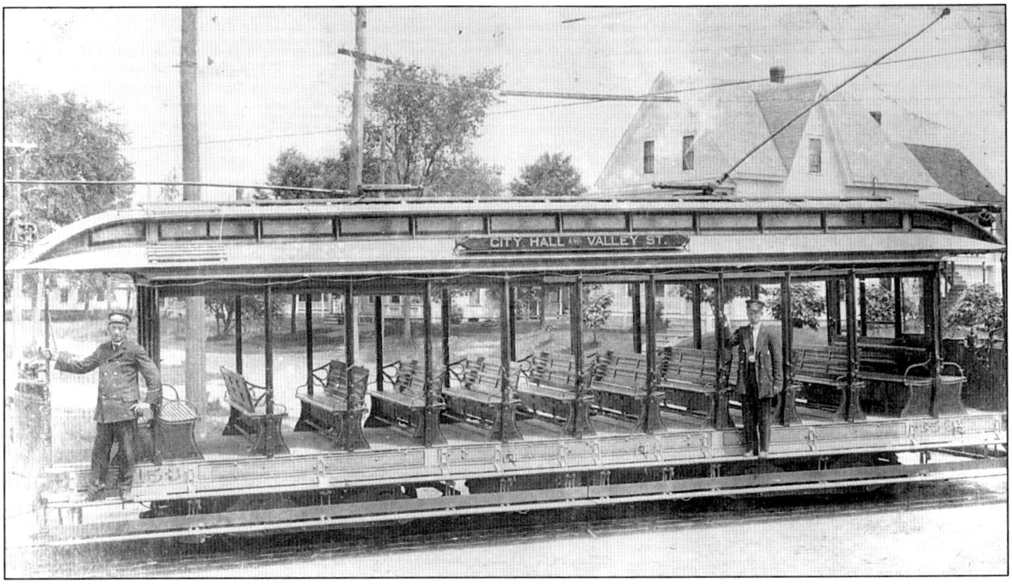

The last 13-bench opens purchased by the Manchester Street Railway were (odd) Nos. 151–159, built by the Laconia Car Company in 1905. Car No. 153 is at the end of the Valley Street line in an unidentified year.

Five

TRACTION, CANAL, AND GRANITE STREETS

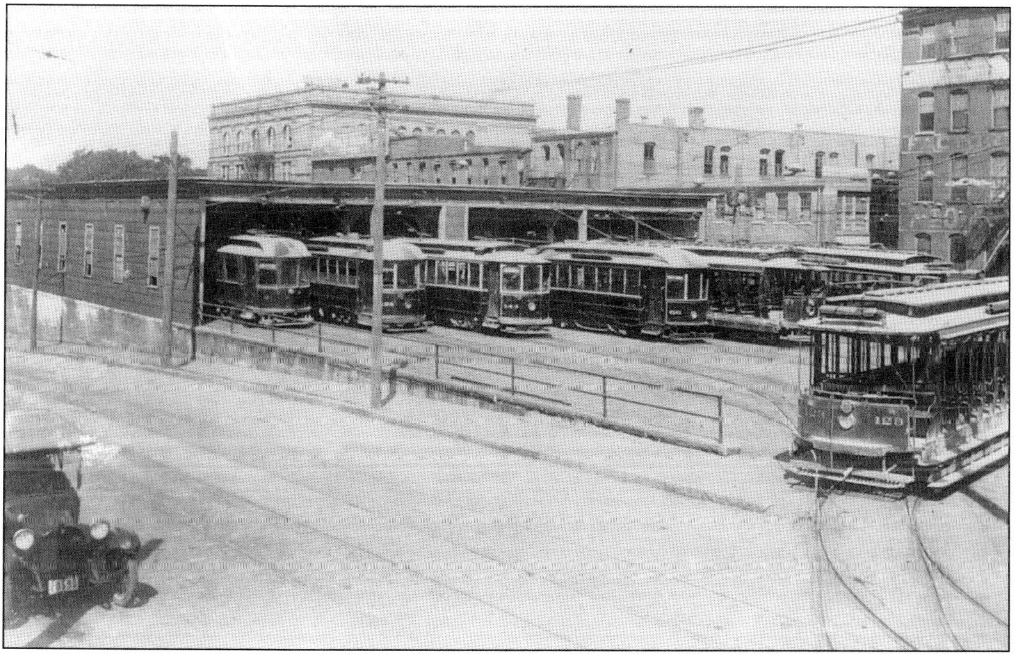

Traction Street, which extended from Elm Street to Canal Street, was so named because it was the site of three carbarns of the Manchester Street Railway for three decades. This view shows the so-called New North Barn erected in 1909, a Rapid and three other types of closed passenger cars, and three open cars. After streetcar service ended in 1940, this carbarn remained standing until it was razed during the construction of the Center of New Hampshire project in the early 1980s. Traction Street was effectively obliterated at that time.

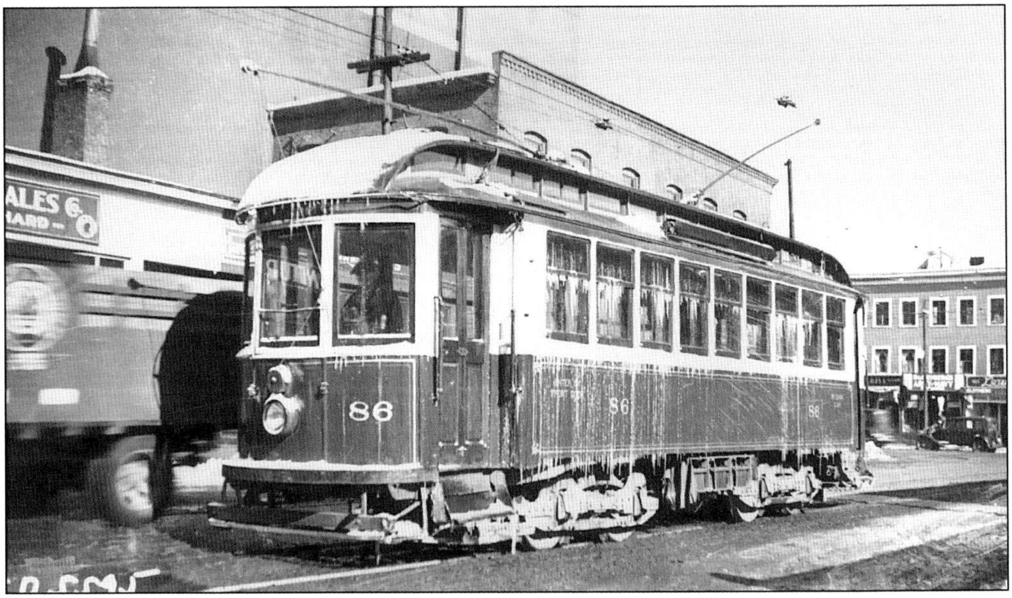

Apparently left outdoors overnight during a winter storm, No. 86 is festooned with icicles as it moves westward on Traction Street near Elm Street on April 12, 1936.

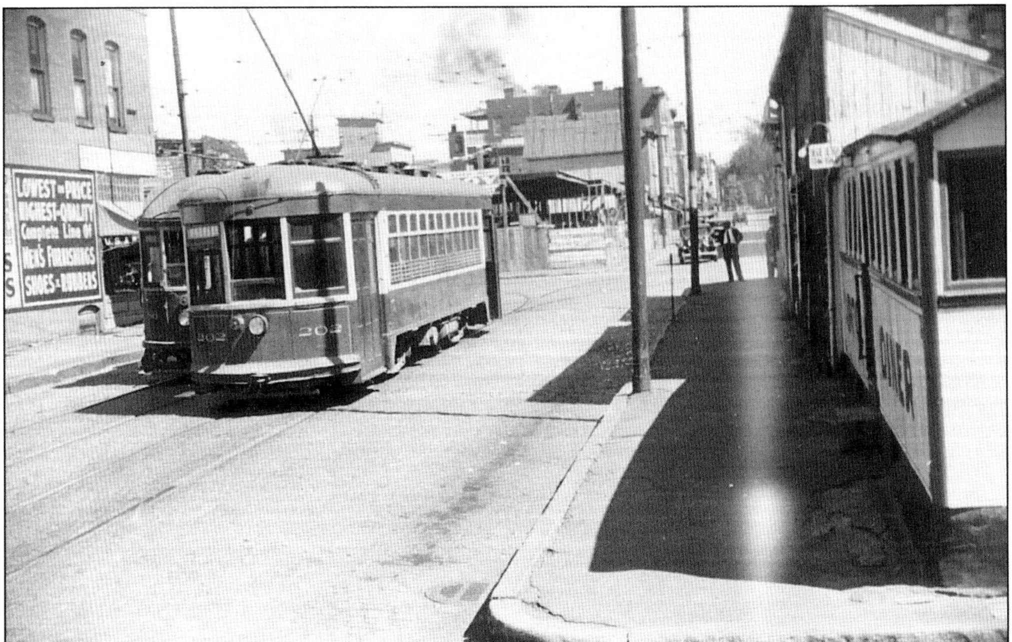

The Capitol Diner is at the right, as No. 202 heads eastward on Traction Street. The car is heading toward Elm Street on its way to Derryfield Park. The diner was built by the Laconia Car Company.

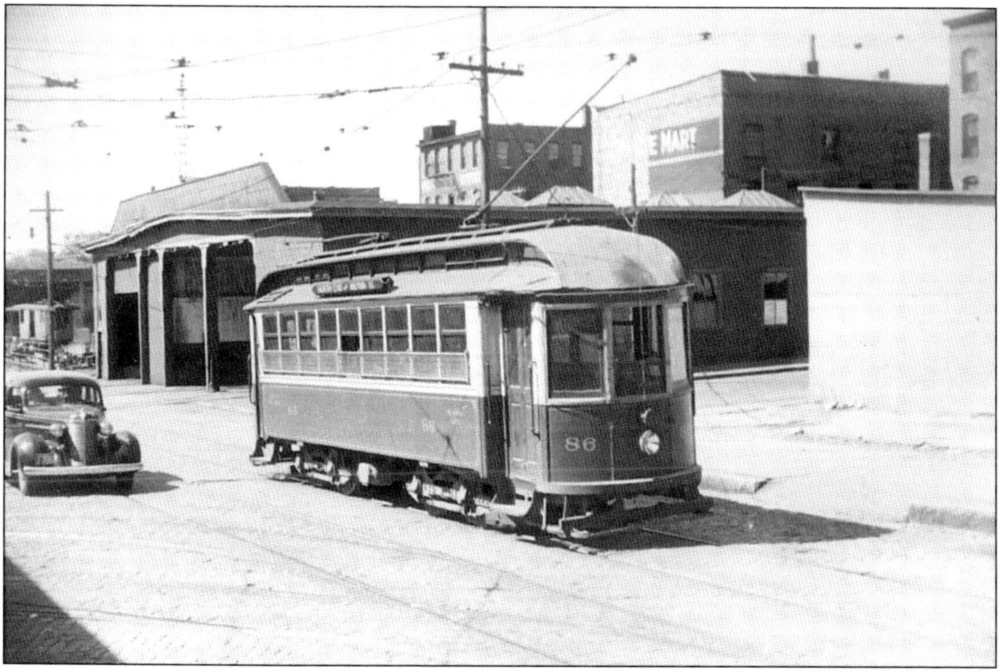

The North Barn of the Manchester Street Railway was situated at the northwest corner of Traction and Franklin Streets. Here, No. 100 passes the North Barn while running as an extra on the Bridge Street–Notre Dame route in the early 1930s.

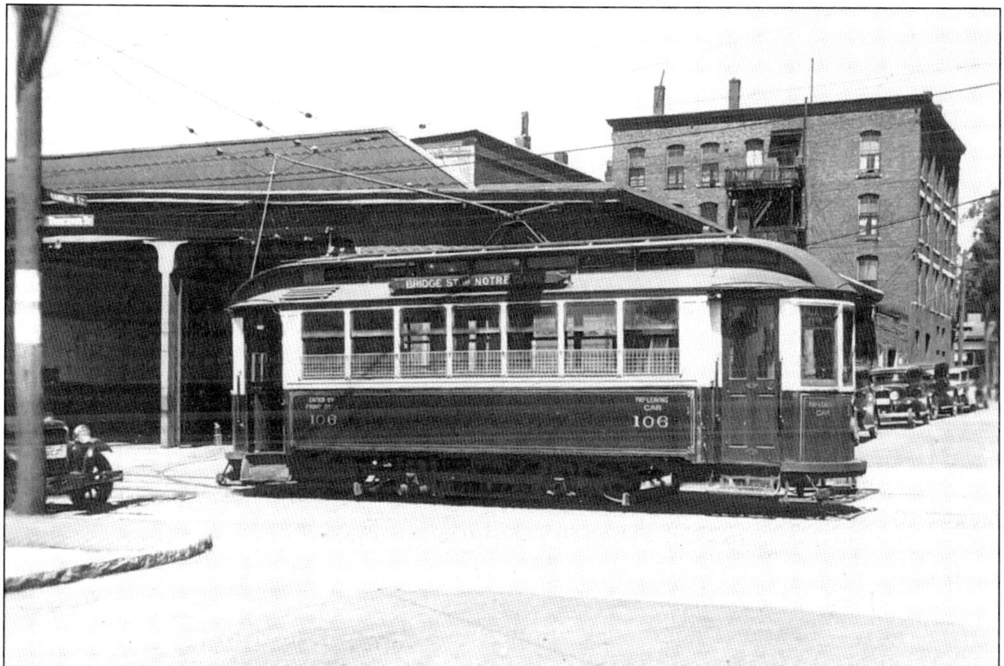

Passing the North Barn on Traction Street is No. 86, bound from St. Joseph Cemetery to the North End. There were seven tracks in the building, which housed the superintendent's office, a crew's lobby, and a paint shop.

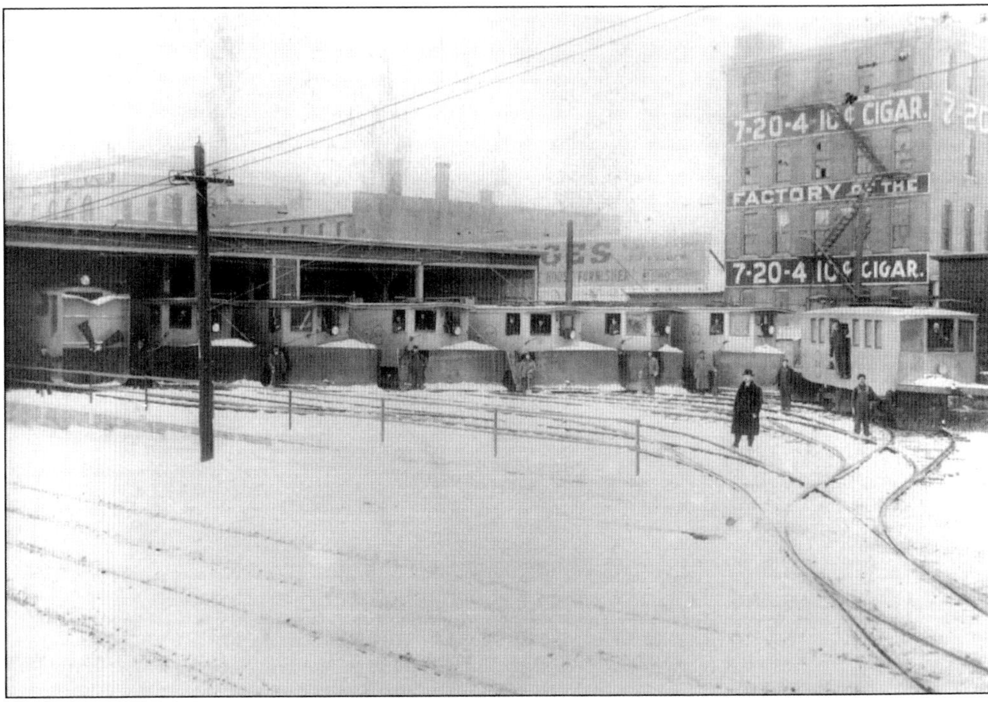

The entire snow-fighting fleet of the Manchester Street Railway was photographed outside the New North Barn in the early 1920s. At the extreme left is rotary plow X-1, acquired in 1901 and retired in 1939.

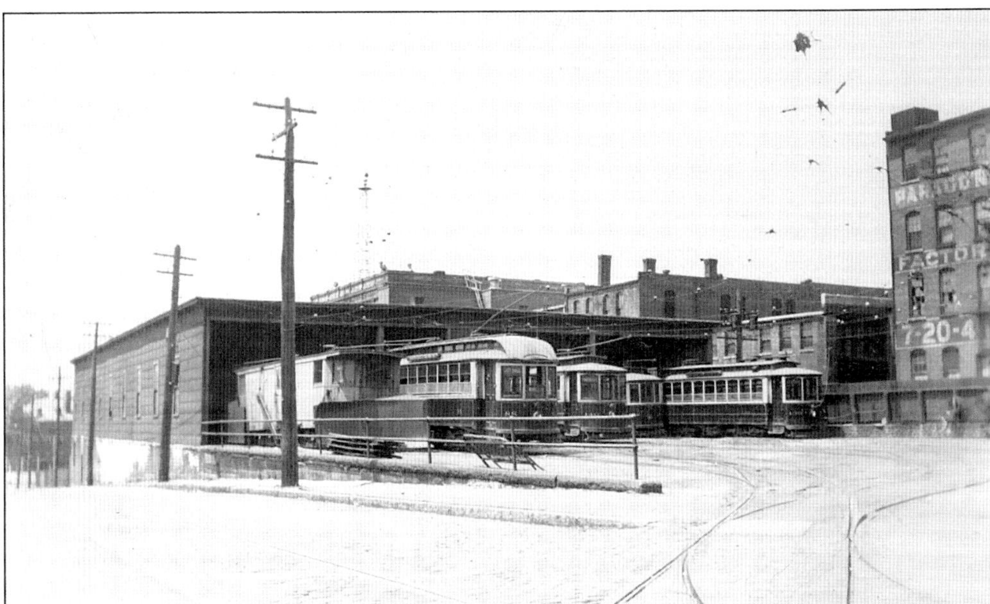

Jerry Cunningham took this view of the New North Barn on May 30, 1936. Shown are, from left to right, snowplow X-9 and passenger cars No. 88, No. 140, No. 132, and No. 138.

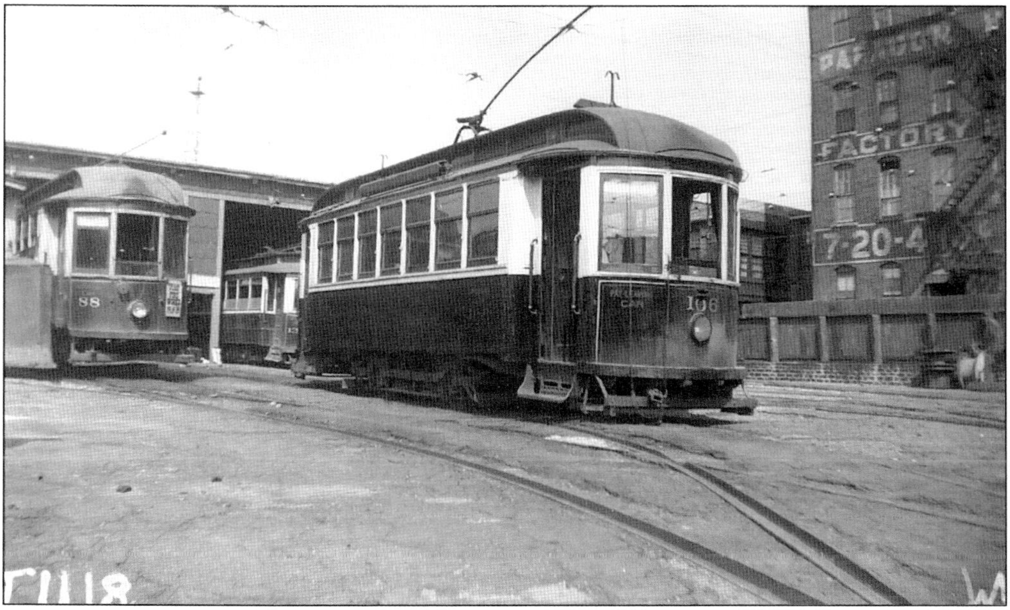

Nearing the end of its days is Laconia-built closed car No. 106, photographed in the yard at the New North Barn in 1938. All cars of this type were retired before the end of that year. Some of their bodies were sold to private parties.

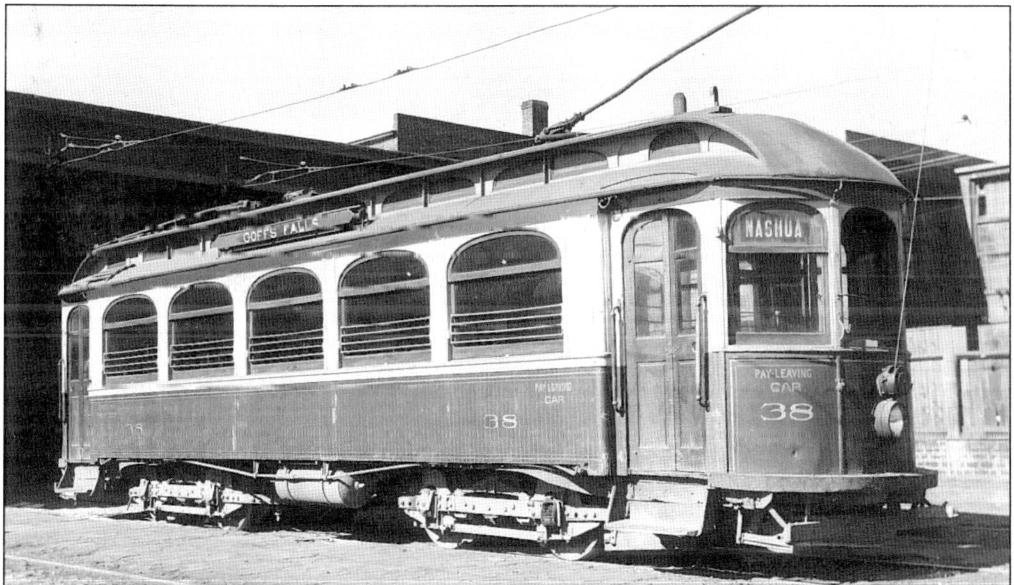

Now preserved at the Seashore Trolley Museum in Kennebunkport, Maine, is No. 38 (formerly Nos. 4 and 32), which was one of the Rapids purchased by the Manchester & Nashua Street Railway in 1906. It is shown in the yard at the New North Barn, *c.* 1939.

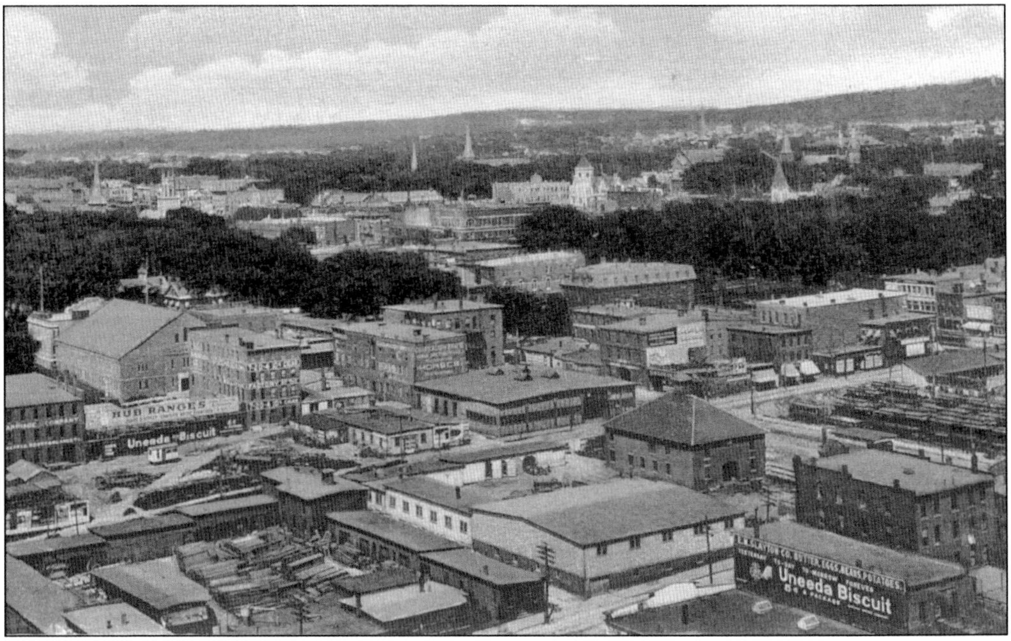

The North Barn of the Manchester Street Railway appears in the approximate center of this 1905 vintage postcard. At the extreme right are cars stored outdoors on the tracks of a carbarn that had been destroyed in March of that year.

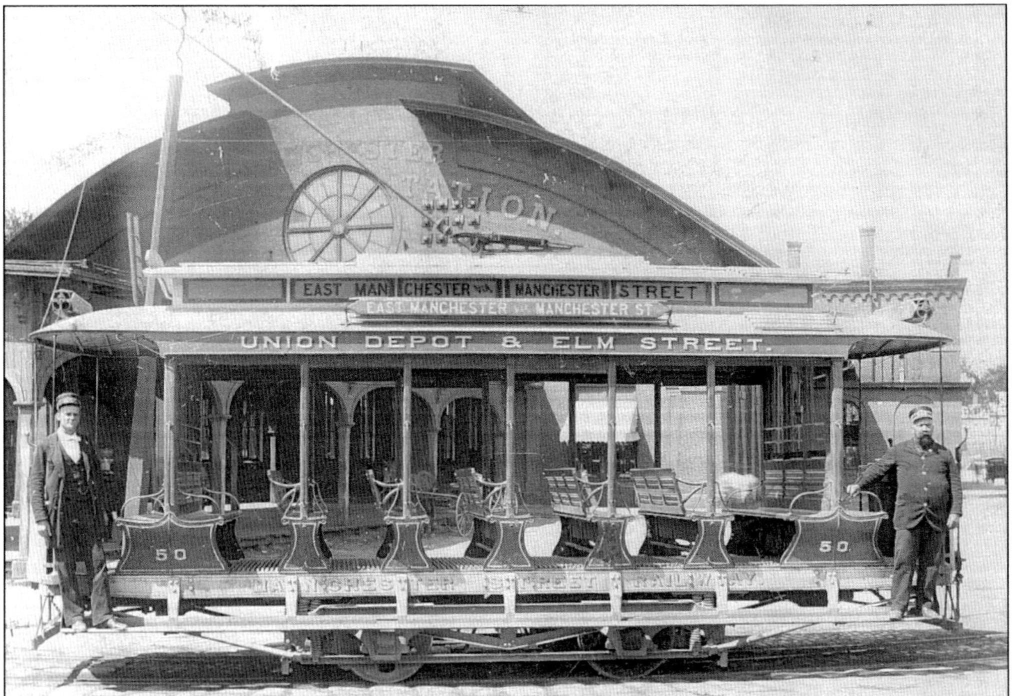

The old Manchester Union Station, which served all the steam railroads entering Manchester, is in the background, as Car 50 pauses on Canal Street *c.* 1895. A new Union Station was opened west of Granite Street in March 1898.

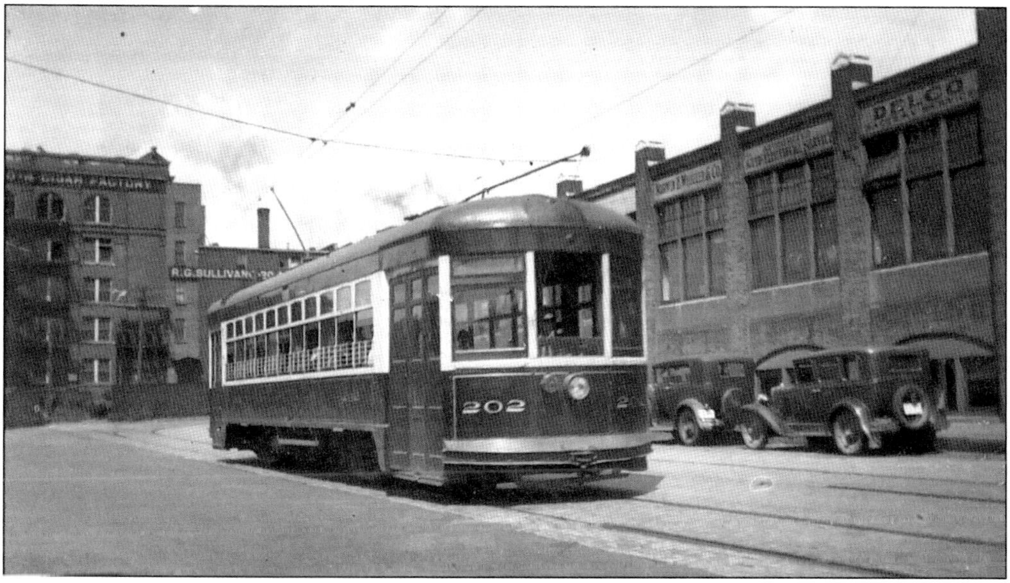

The R.G. Sullivan cigar factory is at the left in this view of No. 202. The car is headed for Notre Dame, on Canal Street between Traction and Granite Streets, on August 8, 1935.

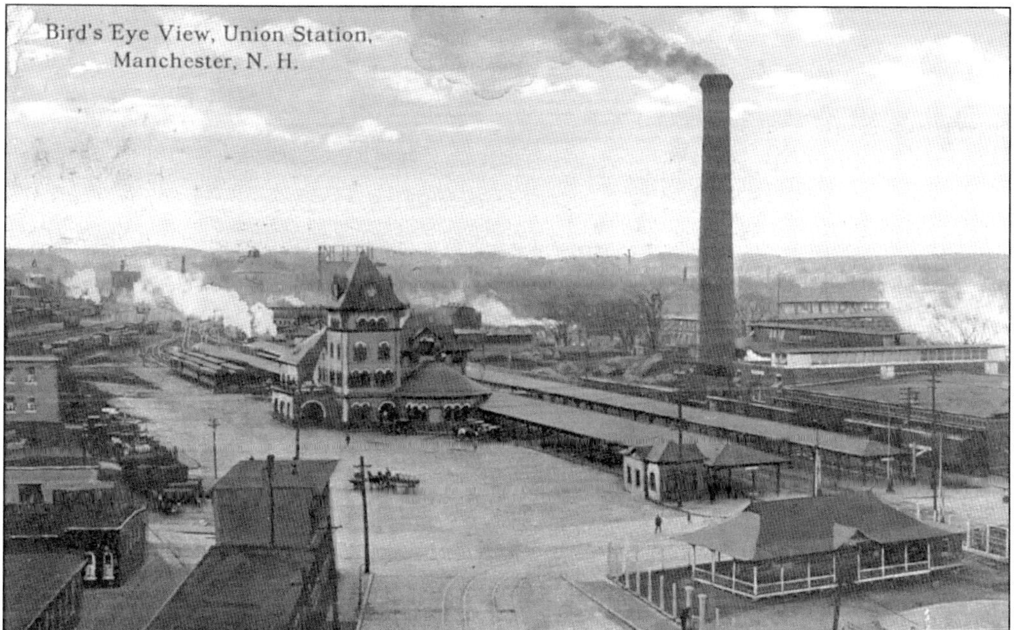

Here is the new Union Station of the Boston & Maine Railroad c. 1910. The small building at the end of one of the station platform canopies is a waiting station of the Manchester Street Railway.

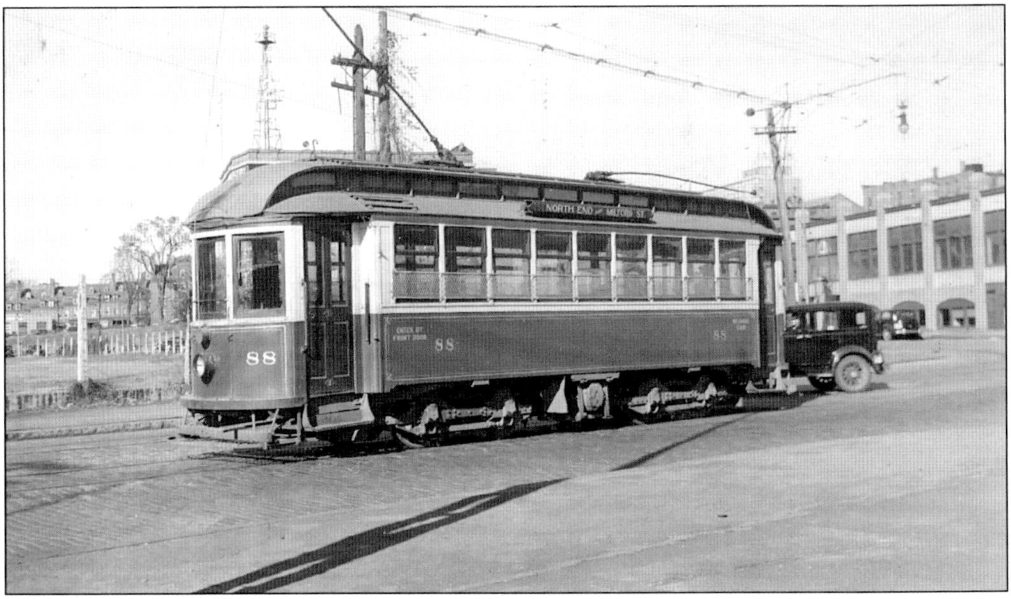

Car No. 88 stops for an errant motorist as it heads for the Elm Street business district and the North End. The car has just crossed the Boston & Maine main line tracks on Granite Street.

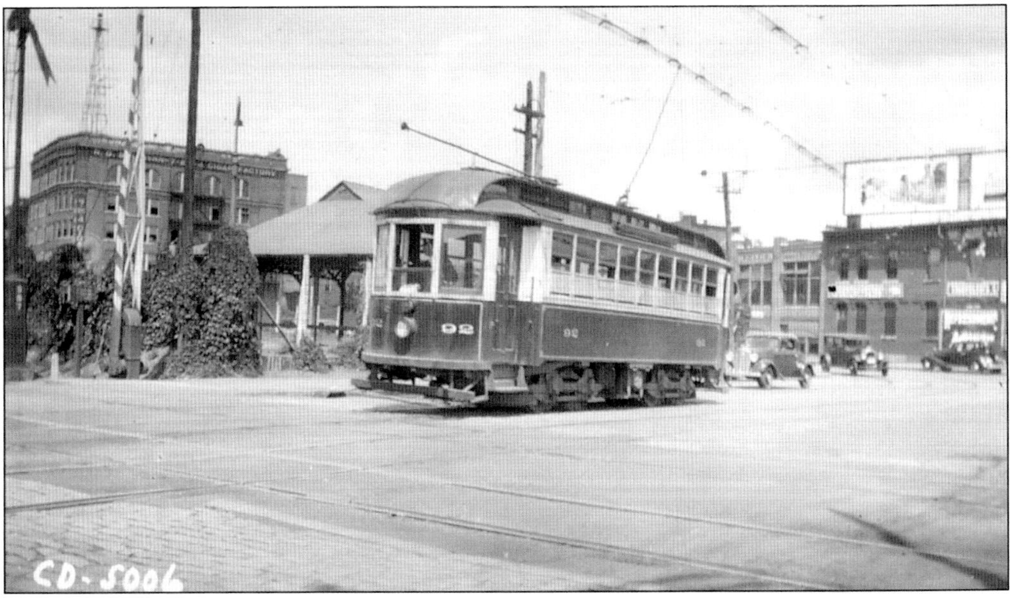

Although the multiple track crossing of the Boston & Maine on Granite Street was protected by gates, streetcar operators were required to stop and look both ways before proceeding. Car No. 92 is en route to the West Side.

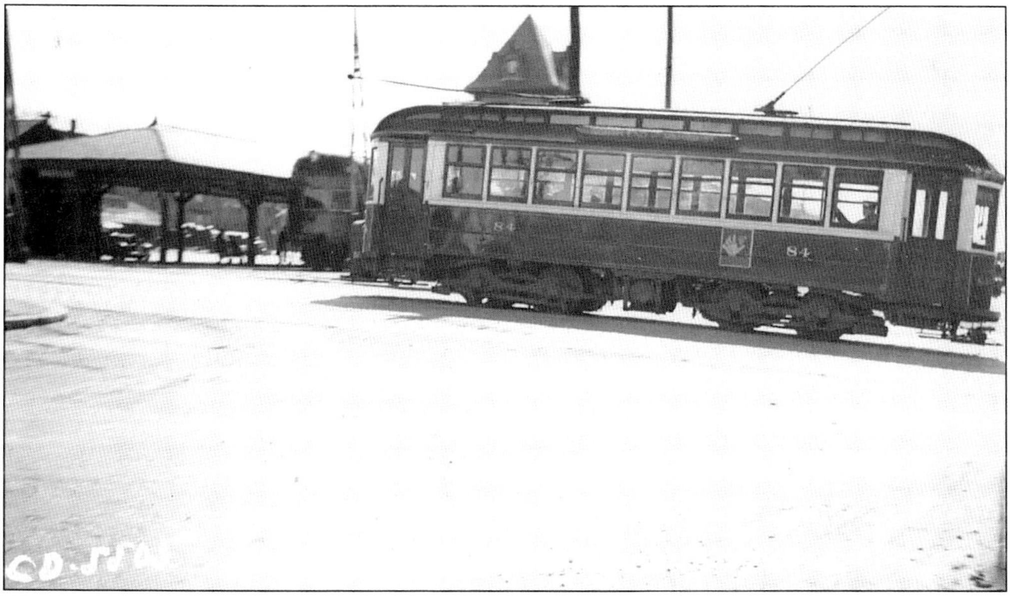

Boston & Maine diesel railcar No. 1140 is at the Manchester depot, as No. 84 approaches on March 29, 1937. The railcar, which normally towed one or more coaches, was commonly known as the "Sacred Cow."

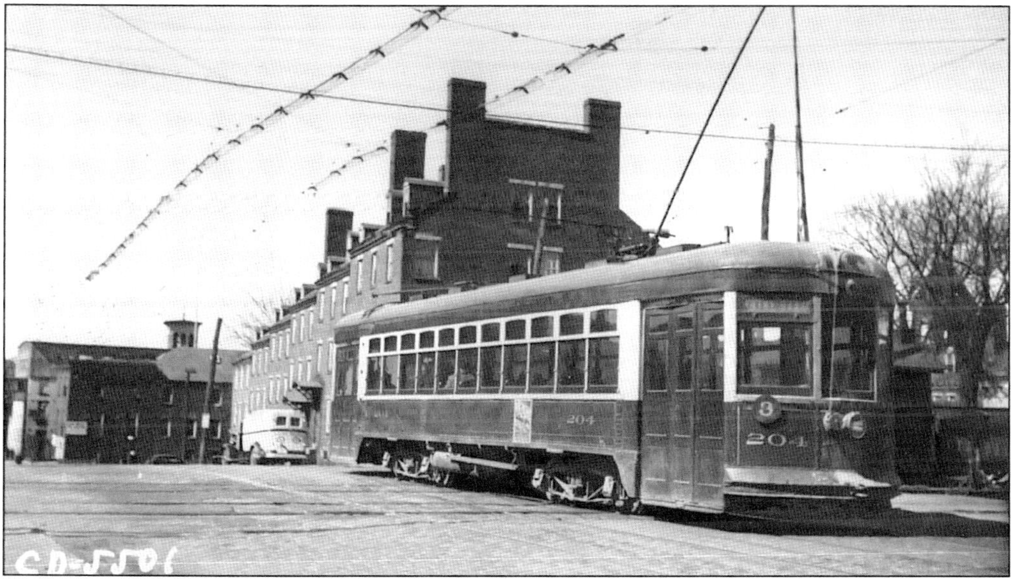

Rumbling over the Boston & Maine tracks, No. 204 moves westward on Granite Street. The car is heading toward the Merrimack River bridge and Granite Square, West Manchester, on March 29, 1937.

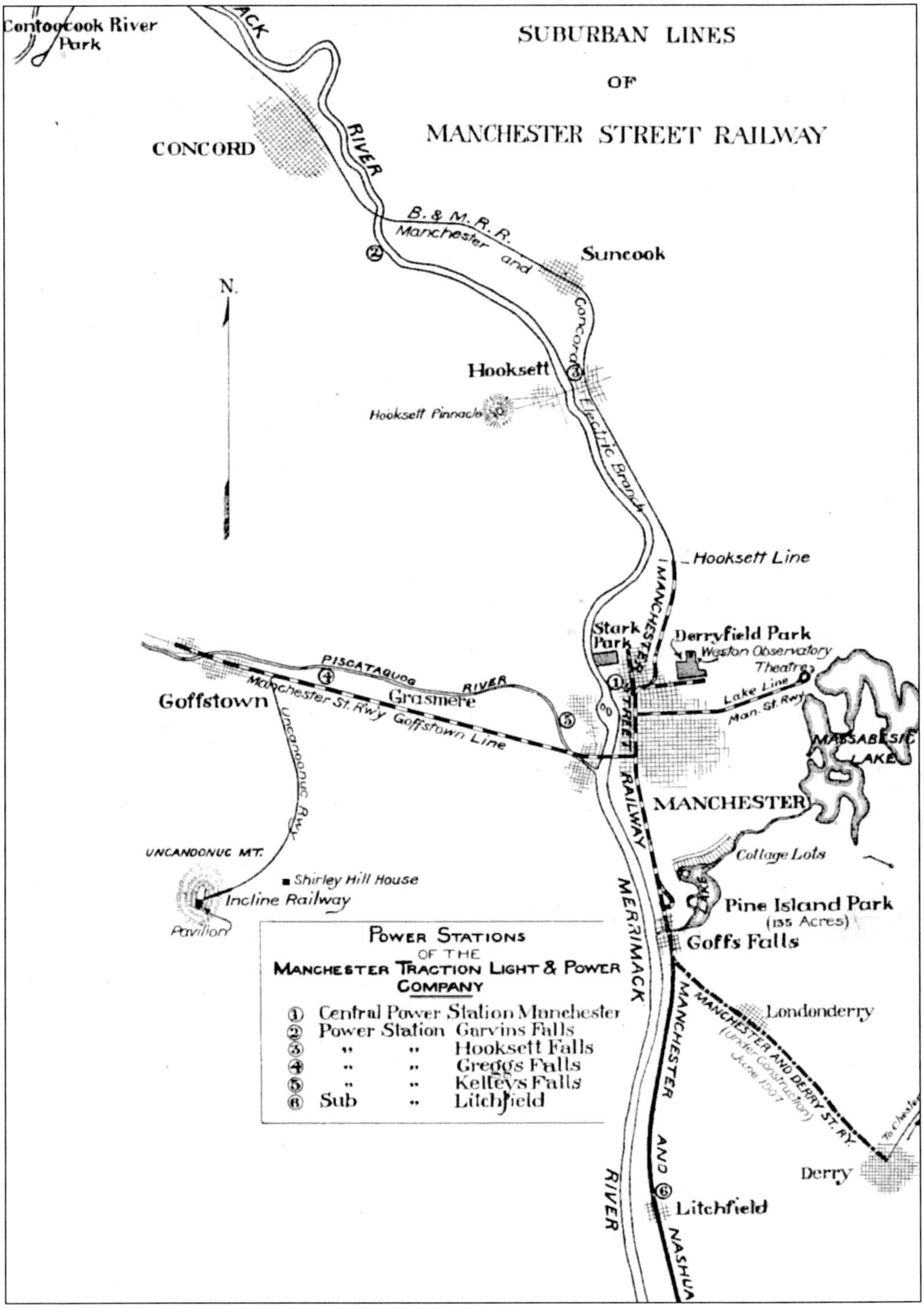

The suburban lines of the Manchester trolley system and connections are shown on this map from the 1907 trolley guide of the Manchester Traction, Light, & Power Company. The Manchester & Derry Street Railway is identified as being under construction; it was completed prior to the end of that year.

Six

West Manchester and Goffstown

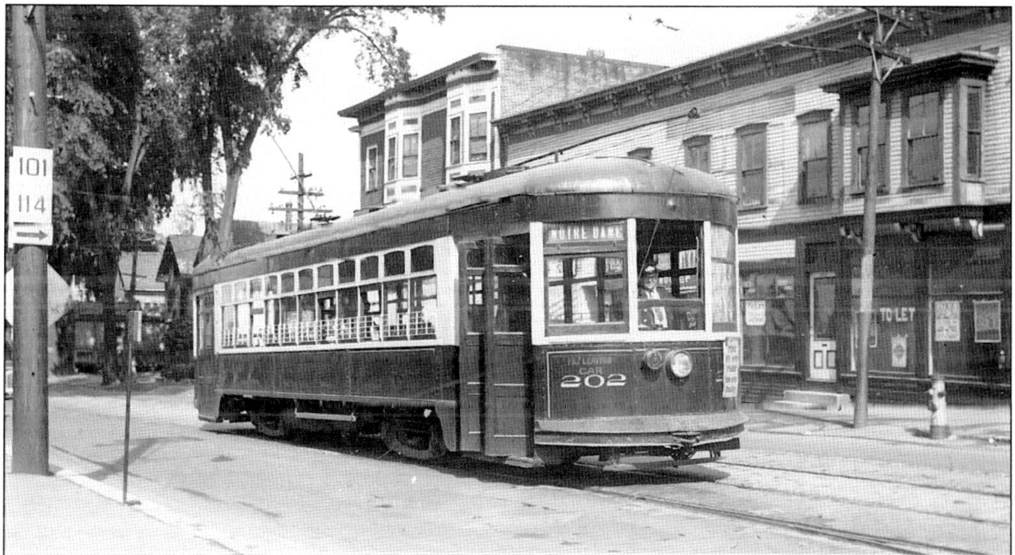

Granite Square was the hub of West Manchester's trolley lines after 1896. Here, car No. 202 takes the switch from Granite Street onto North Main Street on its way to Notre Dame on June 12, 1938.

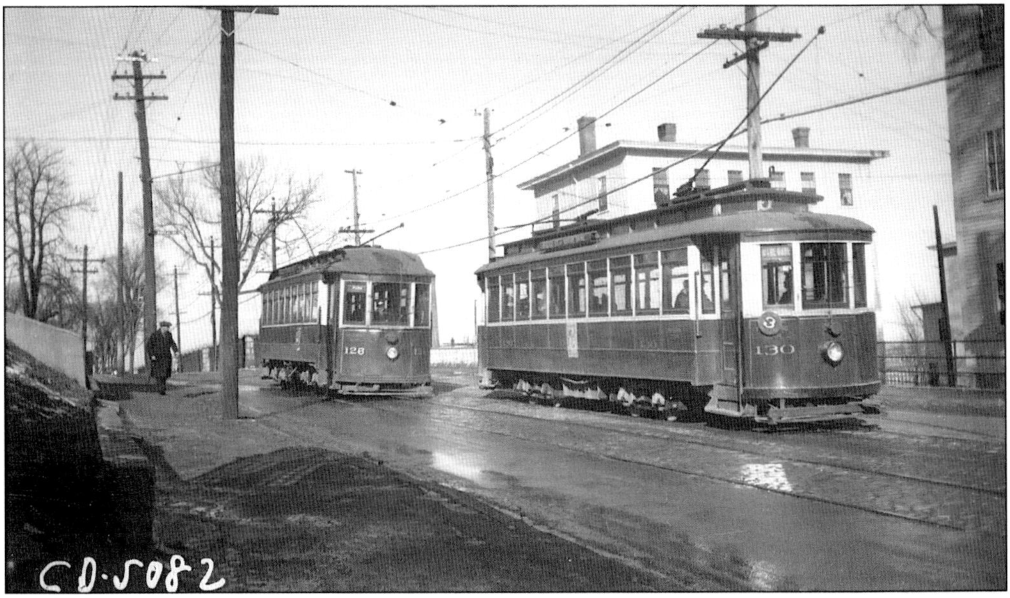

Cars No. 126 and No. 130 meet at the Putnam Street turnout on North Main Street on January 13, 1937. They are running on the Bridge Street–Notre Dame route.

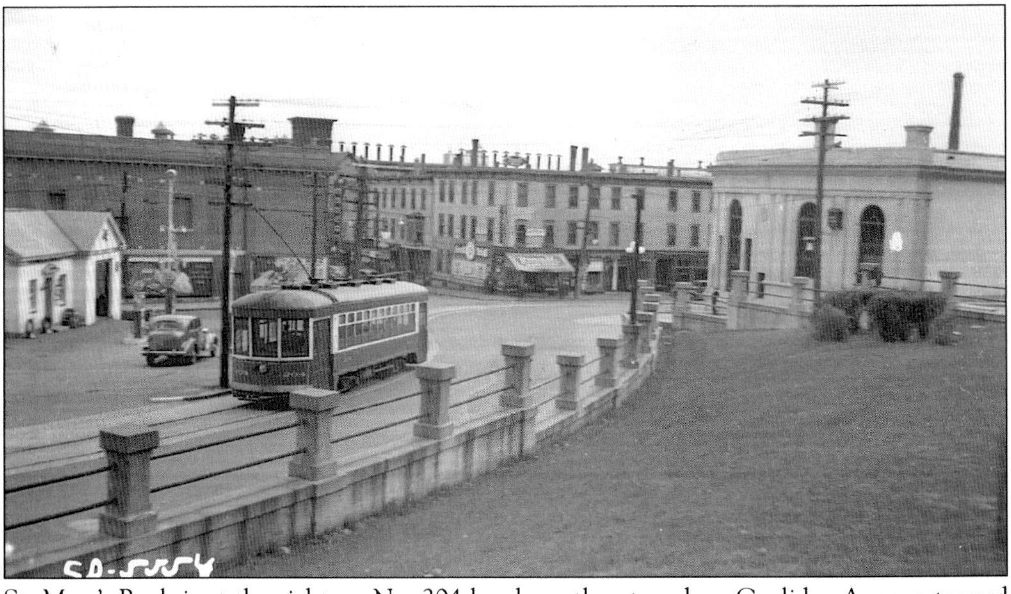

St. Mary's Bank is at the right, as No. 204 heads southeastward on Coolidge Avenue toward North Main Street in September 1939. The buildings in the center of the photograph are long gone.

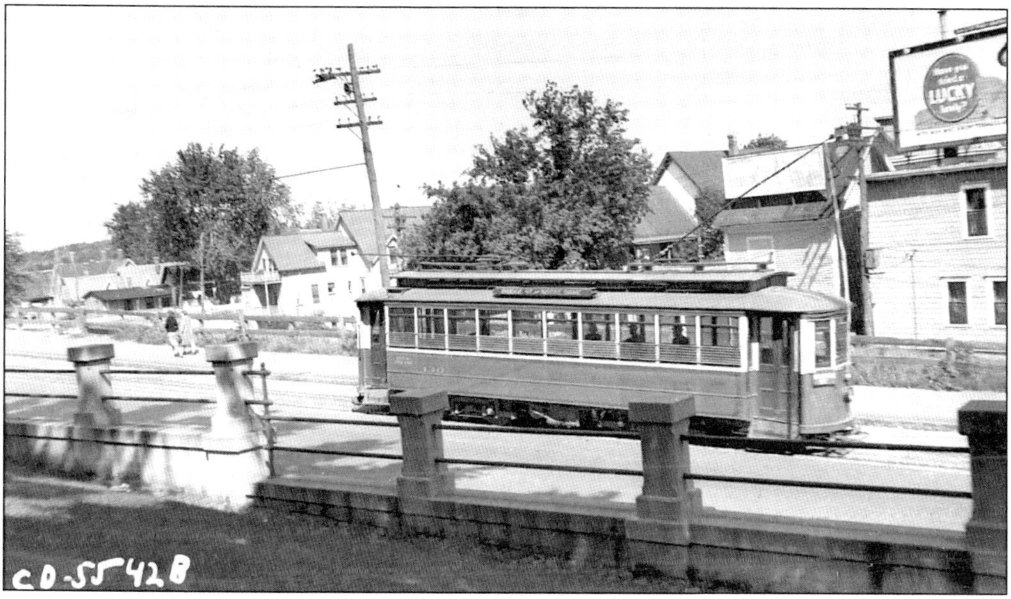

This September 1939 view shows No. 130 just after it crossed Amory Street. The car is on Coolidge Avenue en route to the end of the Notre Dame line on Kelley Street at Morgan Street.

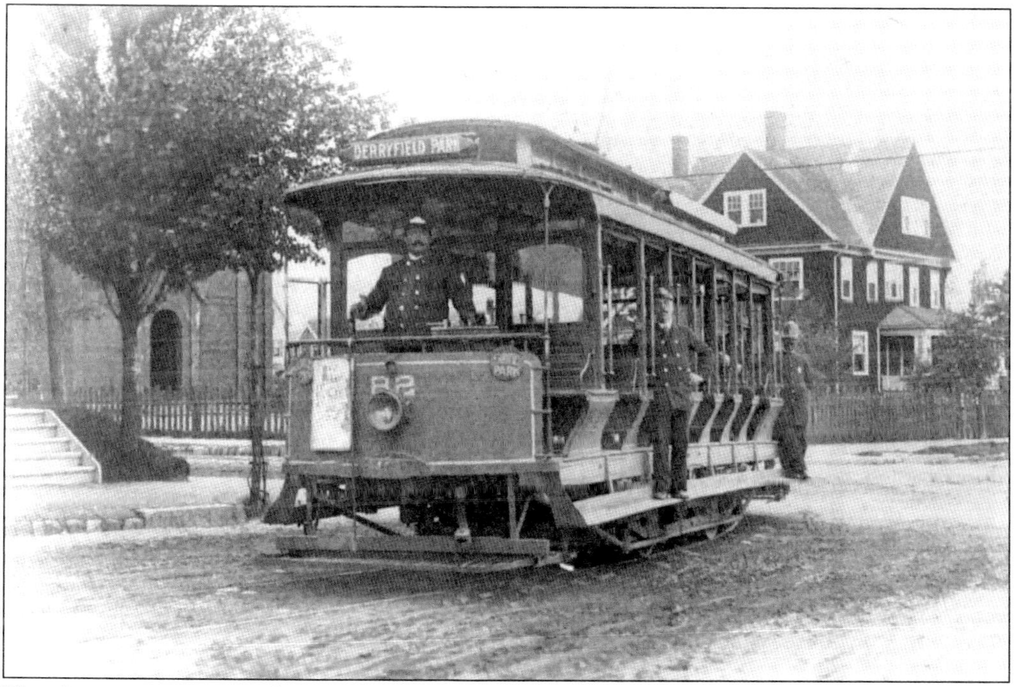

The destination sign reads Derryfield Park as ten-bench open No. 83 turns from Kelley Street onto Coolidge Avenue, *c.* 1904. The St. Patrick parochial school on Kelley Street is at the left.

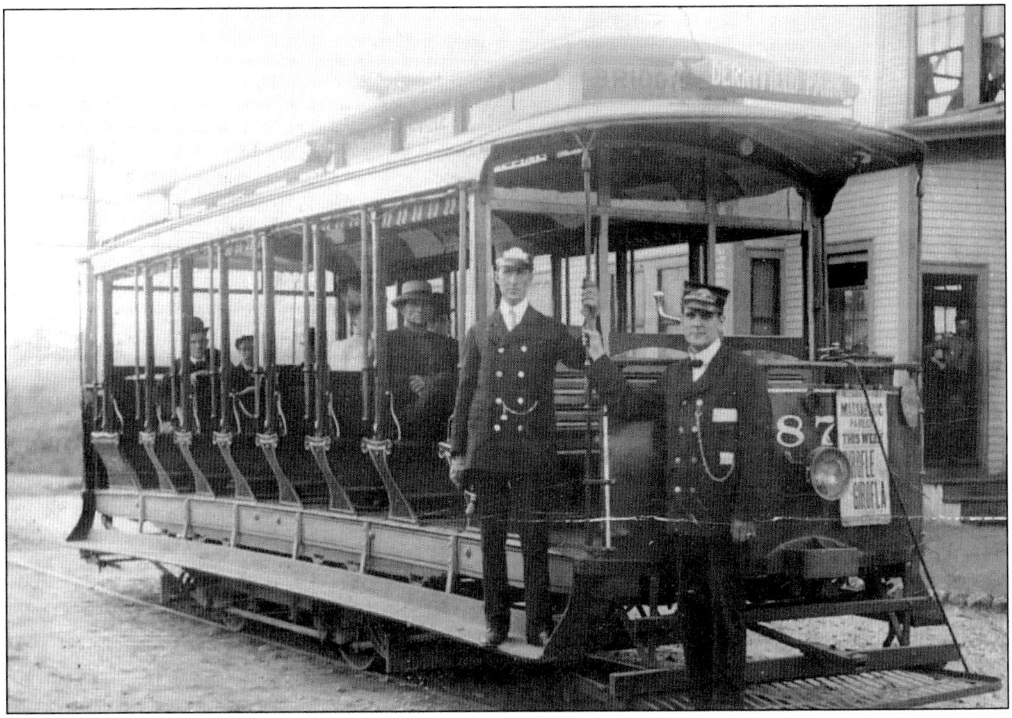

Standing up front, Gene McSweeney, left, is the motorman, and Max Newman, right, is the conductor of ten-bench open No. 87. The car is shown on Kelley Street at Joliette Street in 1909. The track on Kelley Street was extended to Morgan Street in 1912.

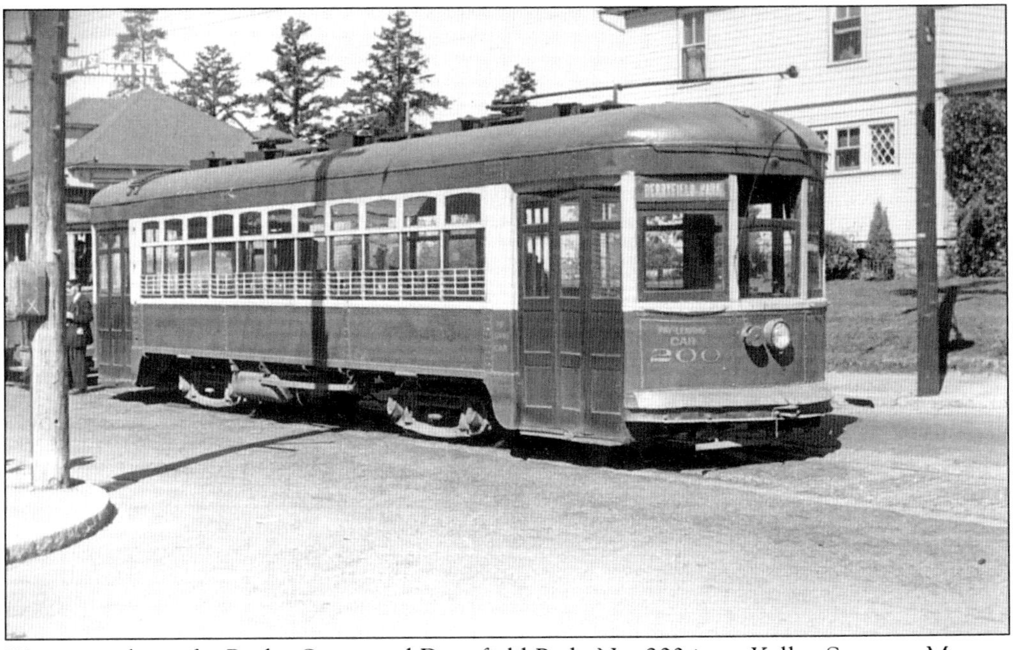

Waiting to leave for Bridge Street and Derryfield Park, No. 200 is on Kelley Street at Morgan Street on August 14, 1937. At the rear is No. 130, running as a trolley enthusiasts' special.

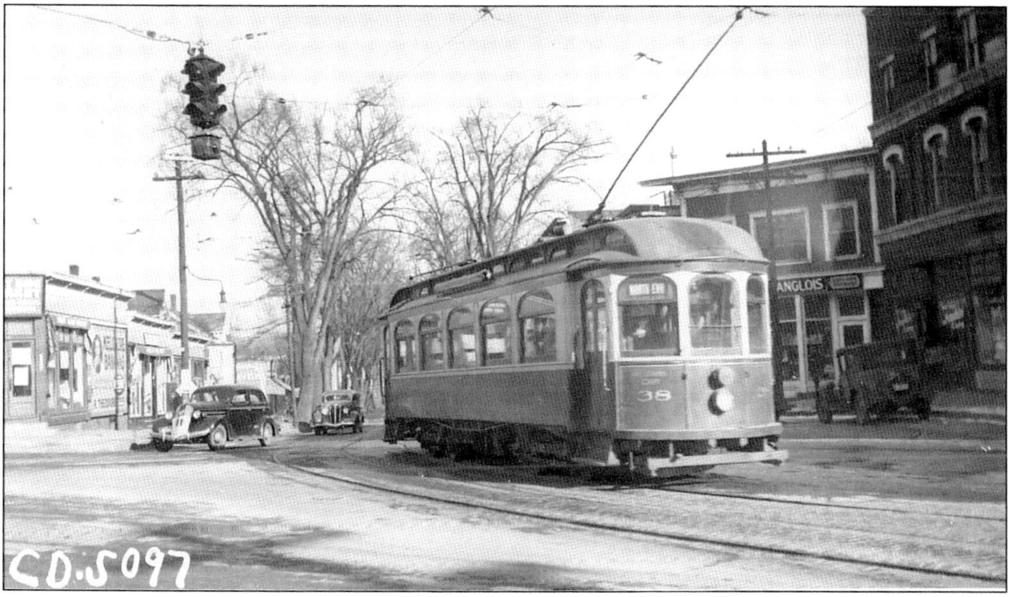

Returning from Goffstown, No. 38 turns from South Main Street onto Granite Street at Granite Square on January 13, 1937. Rapids frequently were assigned to the Goffstown line during the last years of that route.

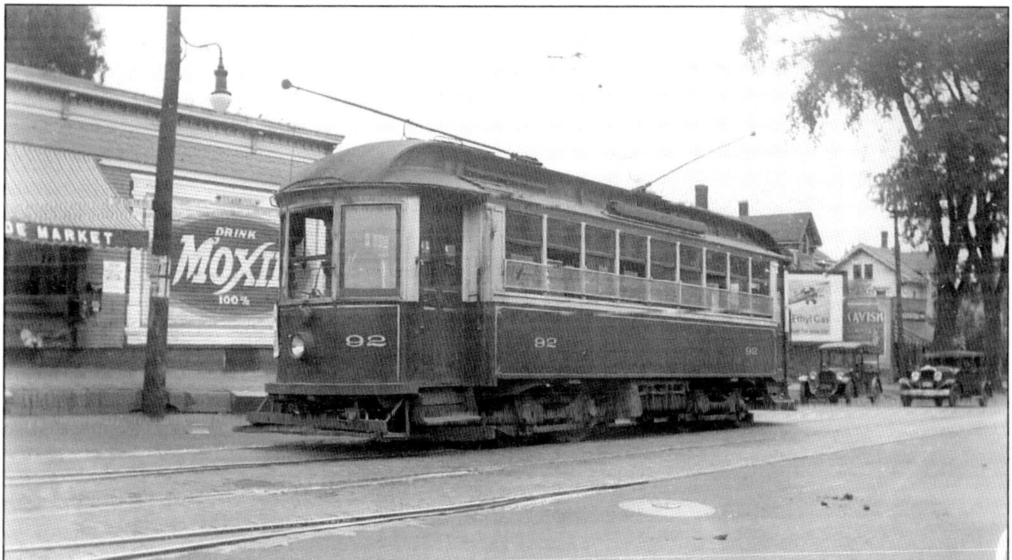

Another Granite Square view shows No. 92 returning from St. Joseph Cemetery and headed for the North End on May 30, 1936. The car was still active when trolley service ended in May 1940.

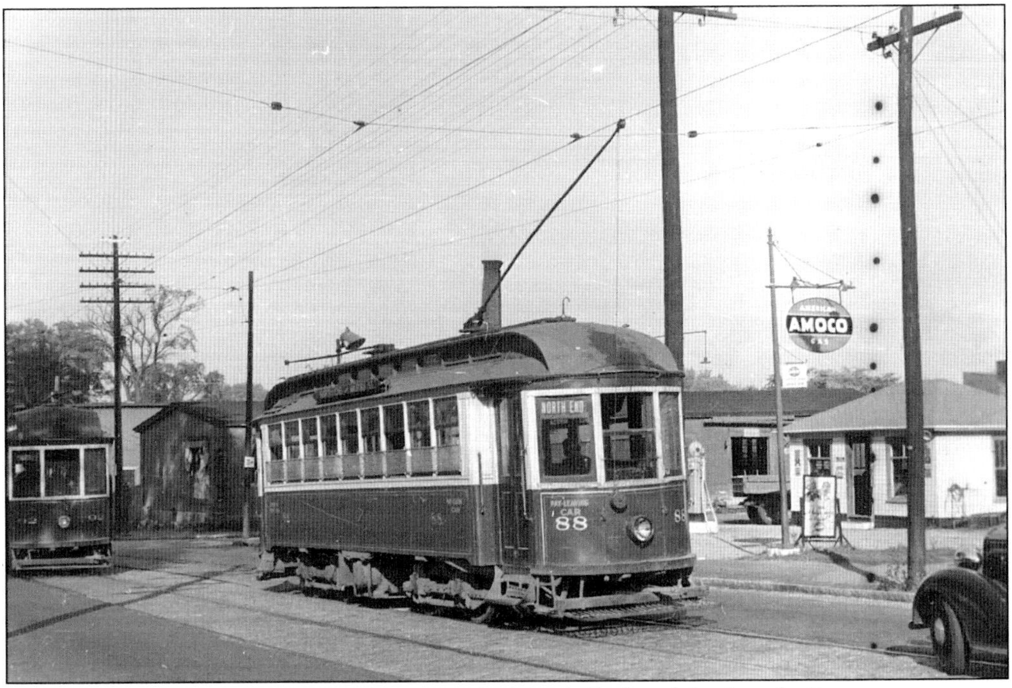

Cars No. 92 and No. 88, running between the North End and St. Joseph Cemetery, meet on the South Main Street double track near Varney Street. This scene was photographed in West Manchester, *c.* 1939.

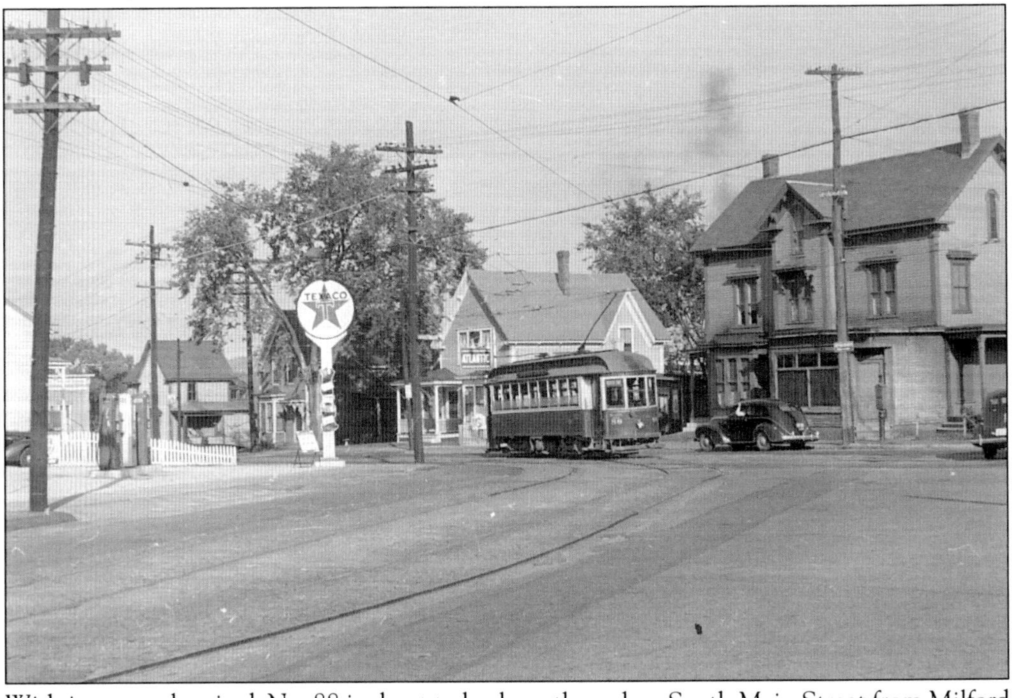

With its rear pole raised, No. 88 is about to back southward on South Main Street from Milford Street to A Street to pick up passengers. The intersection of South Main and Milford Streets was then known as Milford Square.

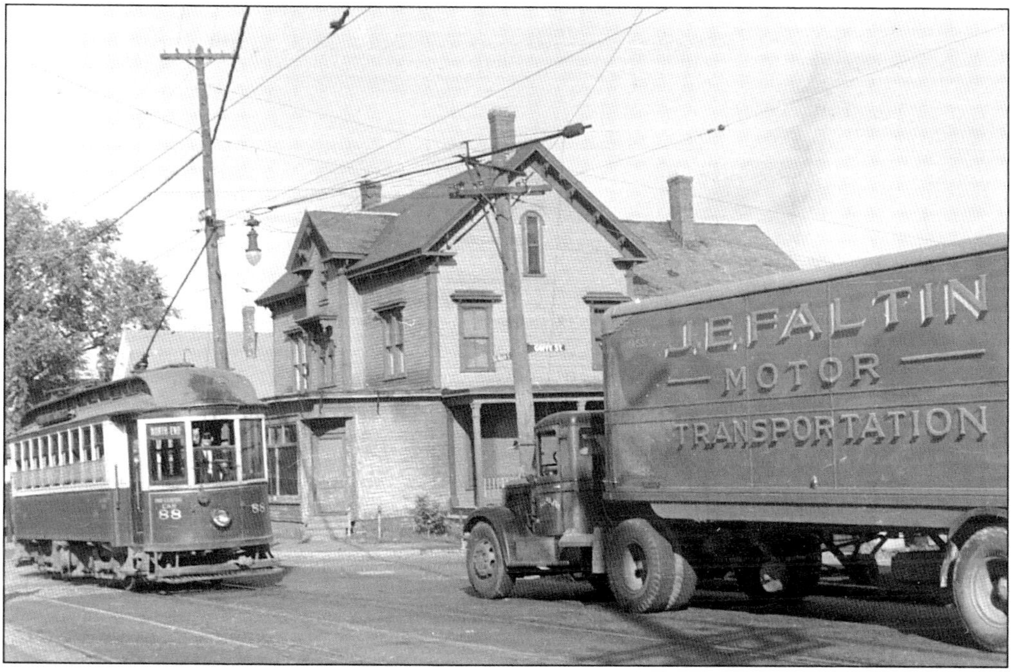

Back poling down South Main Street, No. 88 meets a J.E. Faltin Motor Transportation semitrailer. Once a leading New Hampshire trucking company, Faltin is no longer in business.

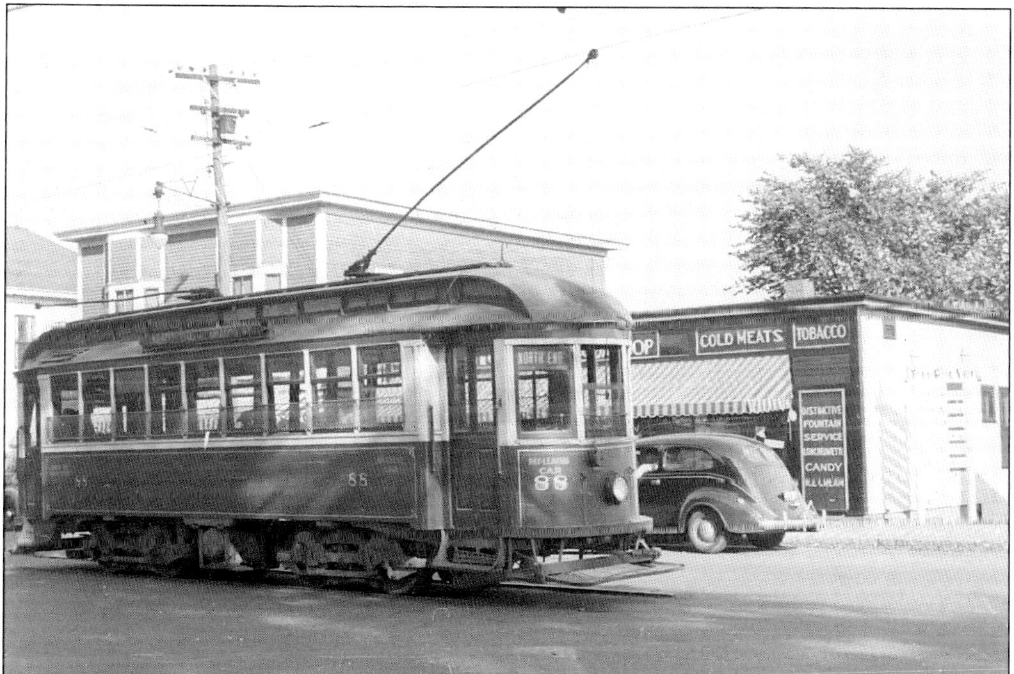

Having arrived at South Main and A Streets, No. 88 is ready to leave for downtown Manchester and the North End. Behind the trolley, at the left, is Sully's Market, which continues to thrive today.

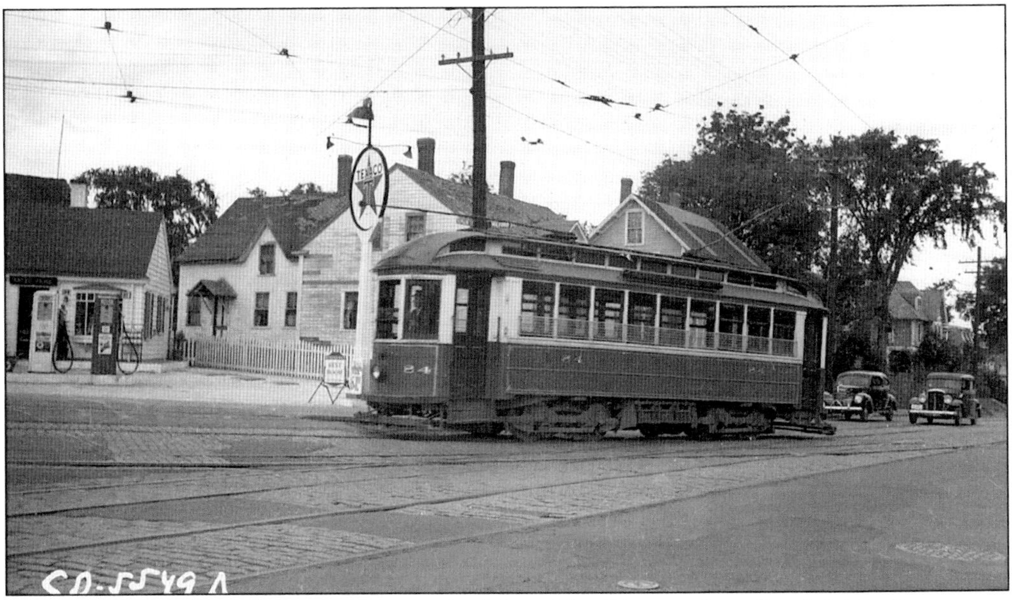

The Smith Brothers Texaco station is at the left, as No. 84 turns from South Main Street onto Milford Street in September 1939. The trolley was heavily damaged by fire in October of that year and was not repaired.

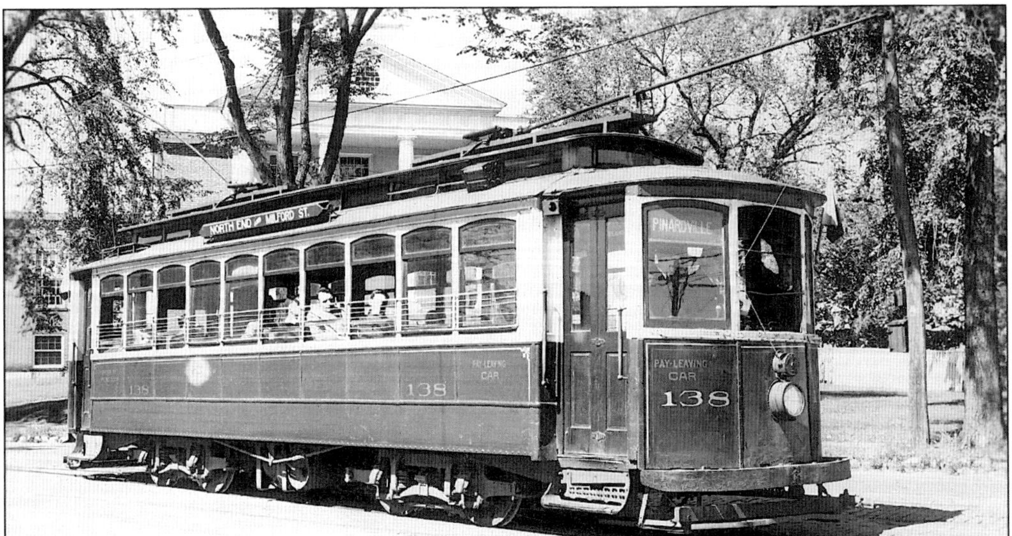

The South Main Street Congregational Church is behind No. 138 on Milford Street near Milford Square *c.* 1939. The church is one of the few Protestant houses of worship on the West Side.

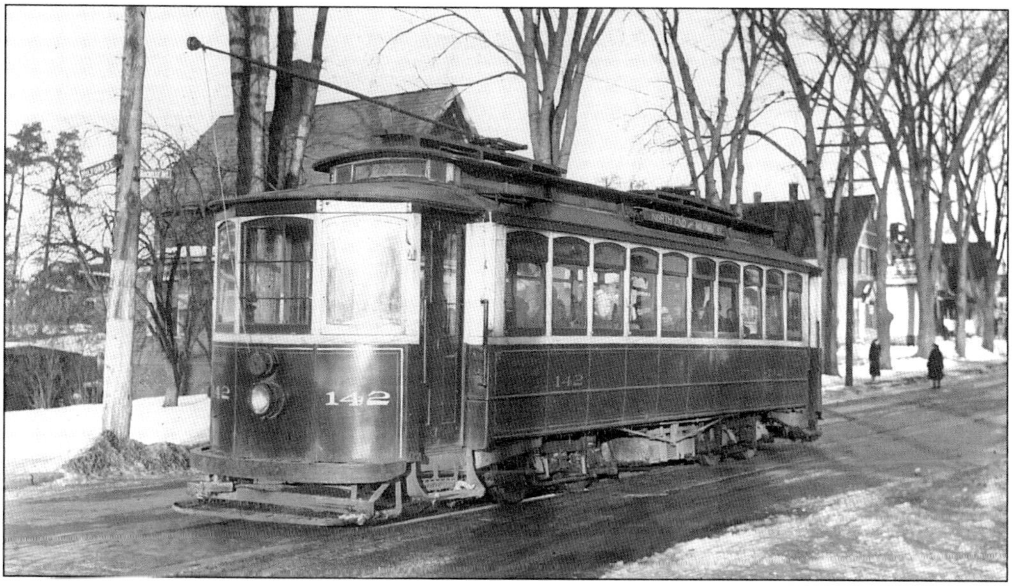

Assigned to the Goffstown line, No. 142 is on Milford Street near Rochelle Avenue on January 8, 1938. This was the last day of trolley service to Monument Square in the Manchester suburb.

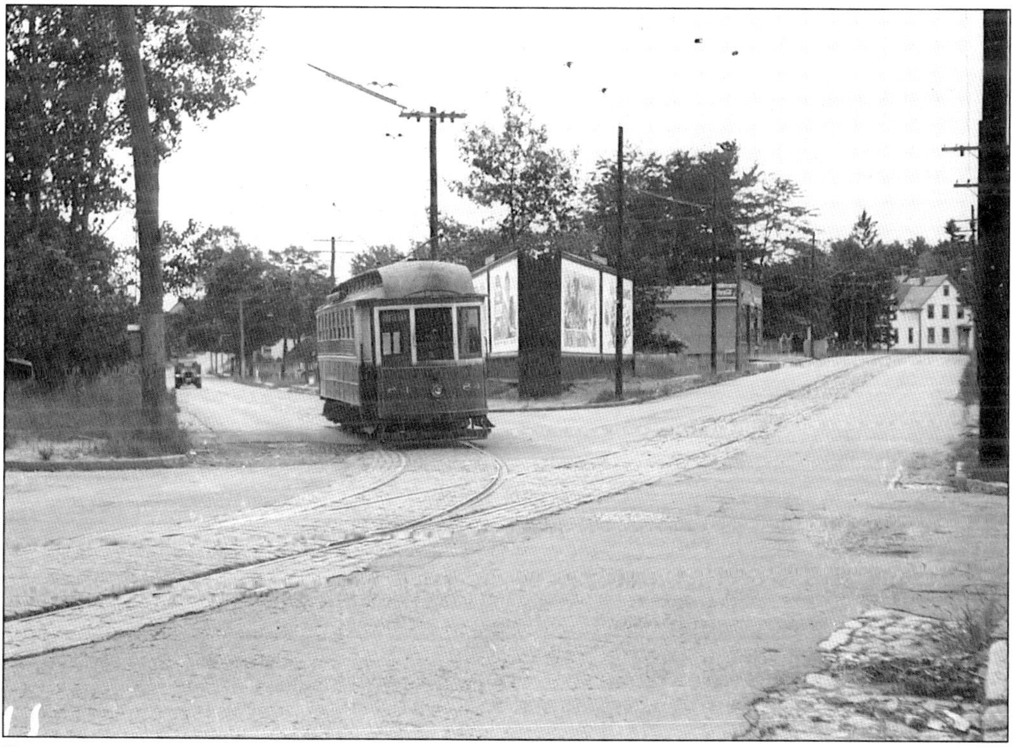

Entering Milford Street from Donald Street, No. 84 is on a run between the North End and St. Joseph Cemetery in September 1939. Trolley service to the cemetery was inaugurated in November 1896.

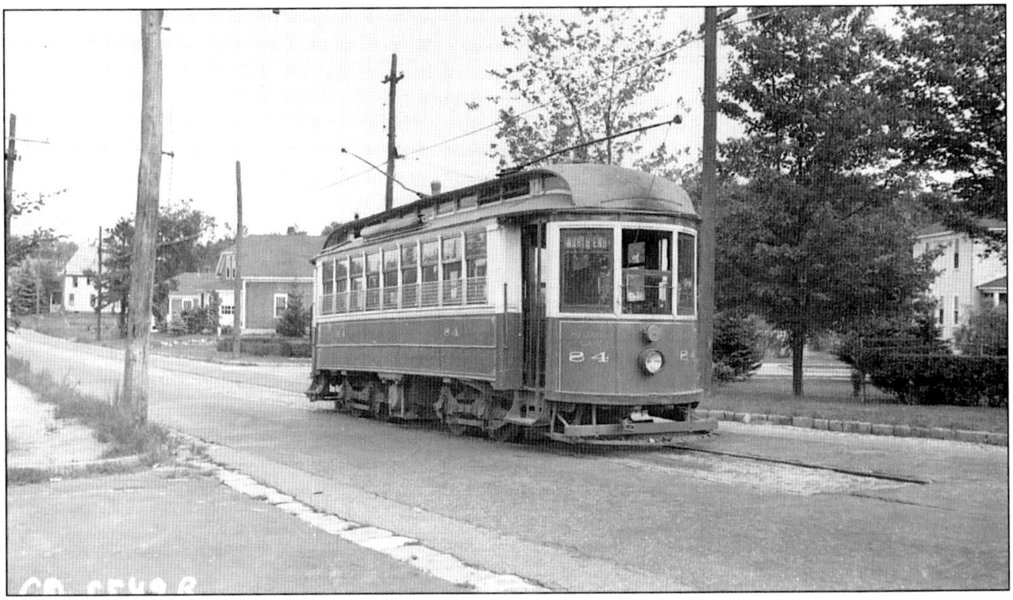

Car No. 84 travels along Donald Street at St. Joseph Cemetery in September 1939. Hourly service was maintained between the North End and the cemetery until trolley service ended.

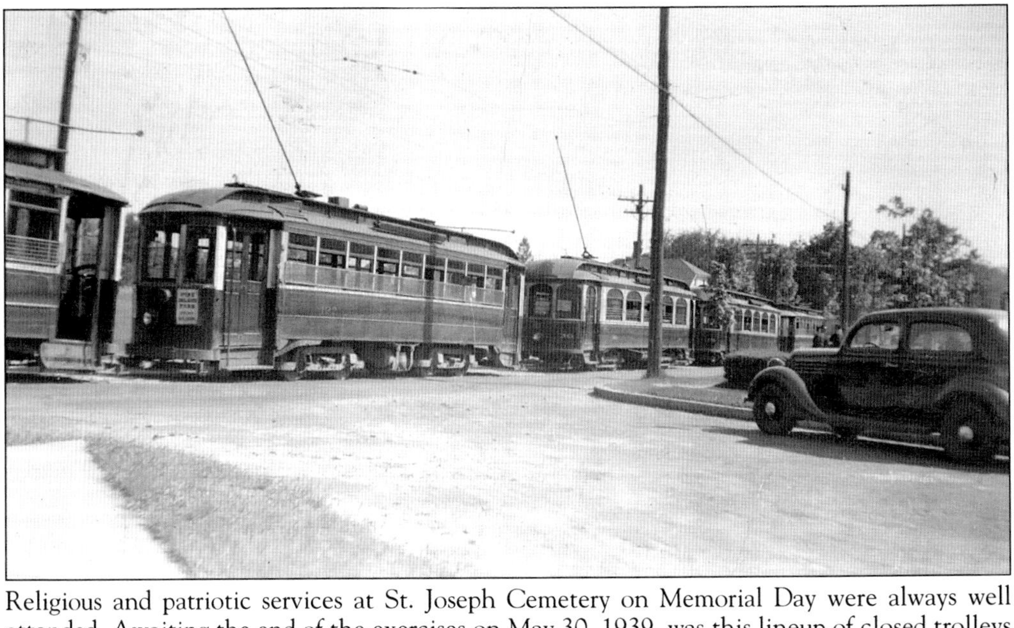

Religious and patriotic services at St. Joseph Cemetery on Memorial Day were always well attended. Awaiting the end of the exercises on May 30, 1939, was this lineup of closed trolleys on Donald Street.

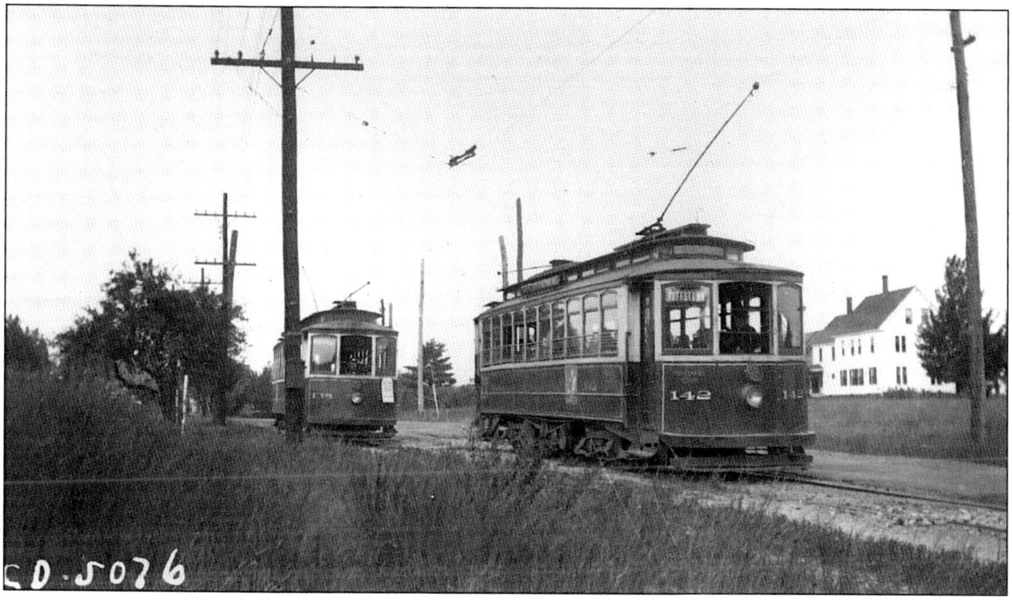

Dickey's turnout on Sylvester Street, West Manchester, was a regular meeting point for Goffstown and Pinardville trolleys. Cars No. 138 and No. 142 were photographed by Charles A. Duncan on September 6, 1936.

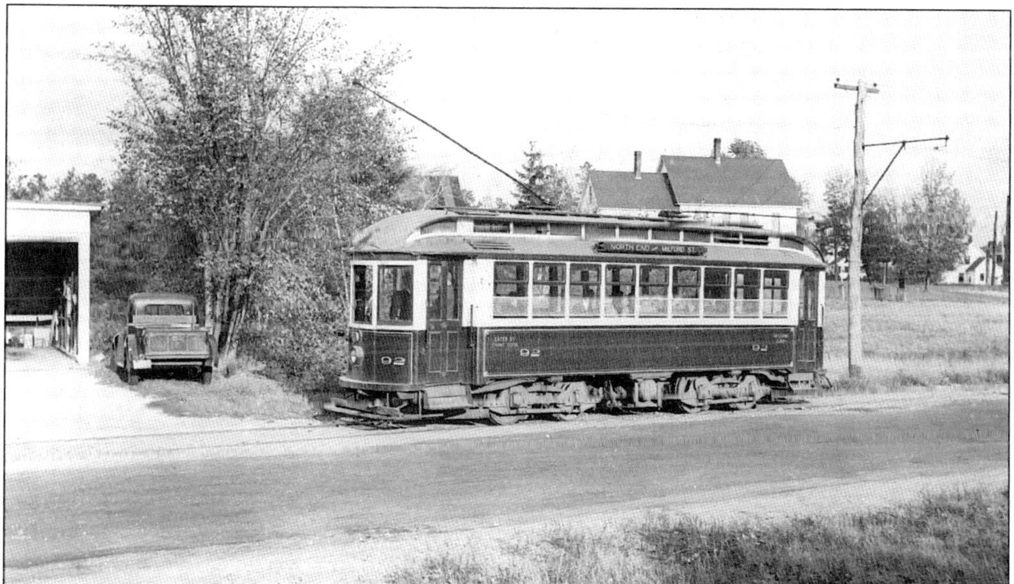

Pinardville-bound No. 92 is on Sylvester Street near Worthley Road in West Manchester on June 22, 1939. At that time half-hourly service was maintained between the North End and Pinardville, a sizable village in the southeastern part of Goffstown.

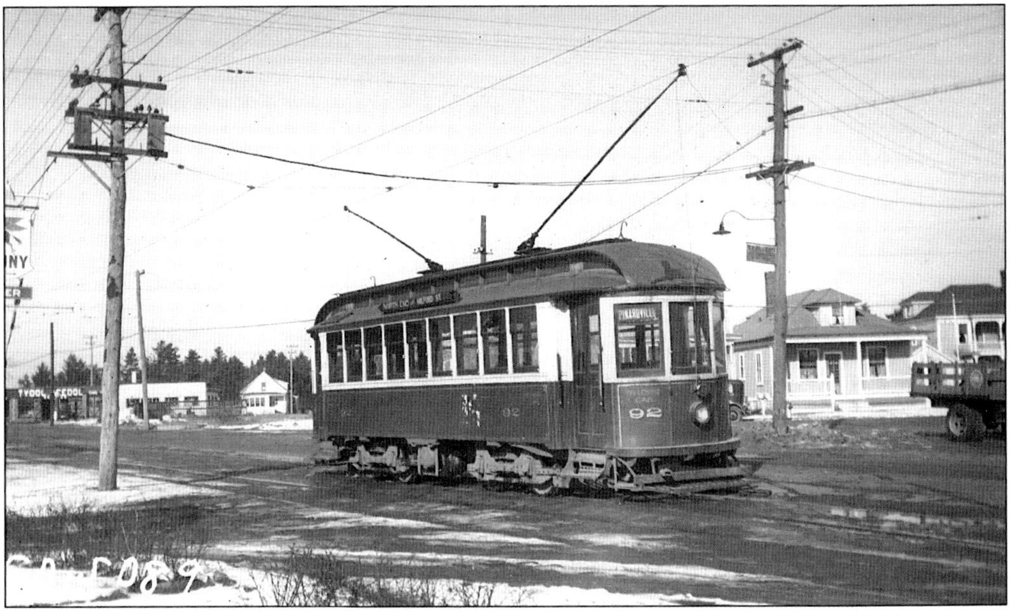

The Pinardville terminus was at the intersection of Mast Road and Pinard Street. The operator of No. 92 is "changing ends" at that point on January 13, 1937.

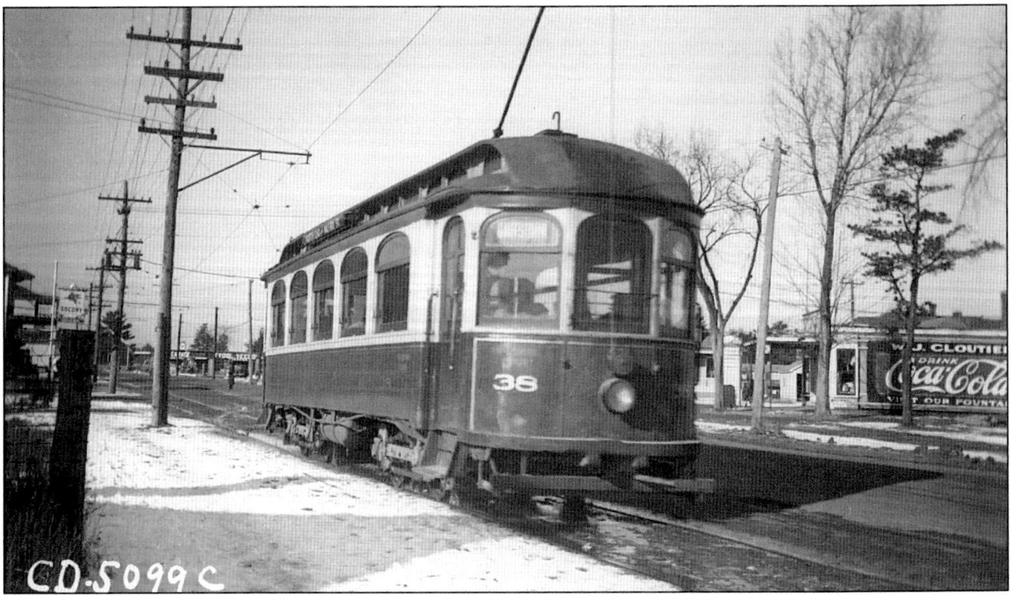

Rapid No. 38 pauses at Pinardville on its way to Monument Square, Goffstown, in January 1937. Nearly six years earlier, the car was acquired as No. 32 from the Manchester and Nashua Street Railway.

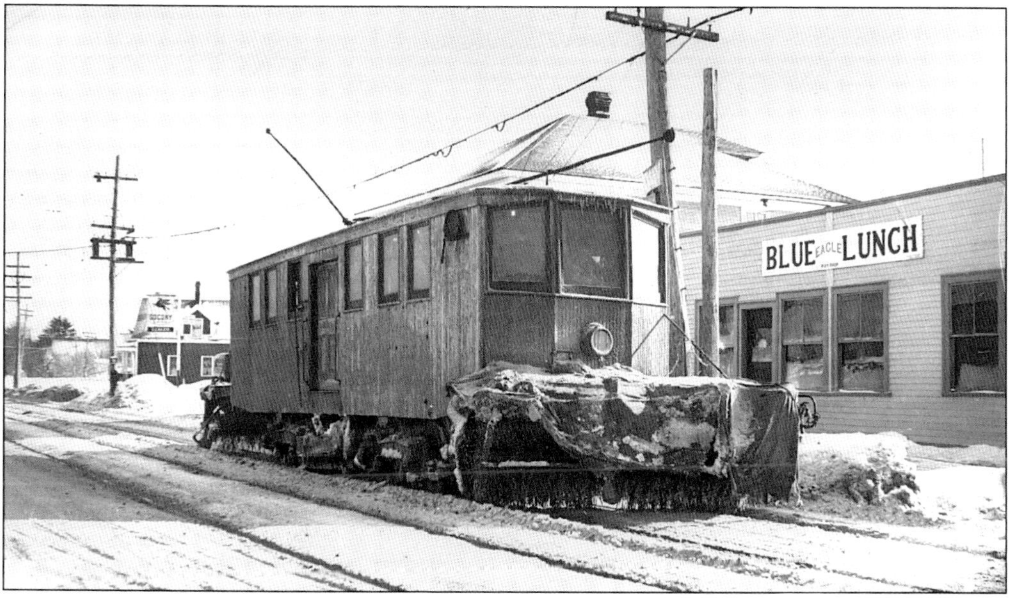

Maybe the crew has adjourned to the Eagle Blue Lunch for coffee, as sweeper X-2 waits at the turnout in Pinardville on February 19, 1936. Sweepers were the most effective in clearing the trolley tracks when snowfall was light to moderate.

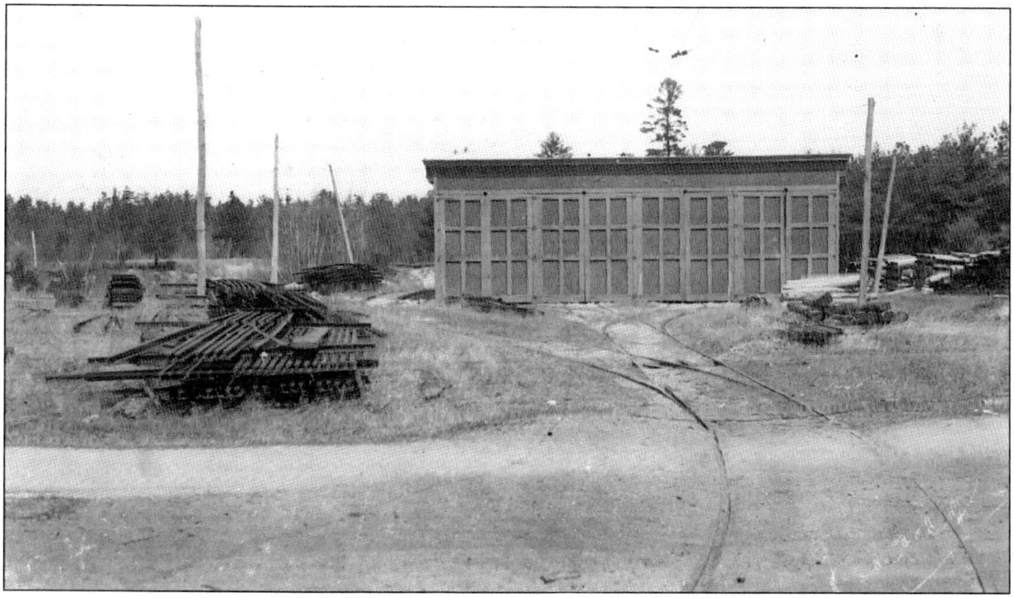

This storage carbarn was on the east side of Mast Road almost opposite Roy Street in Pinardville. It was opened by the Manchester Street Railway in late 1900. There was a sandpit at the rear of the building, which was vacated in mid-1936. Greatly altered, the structure still stands today.

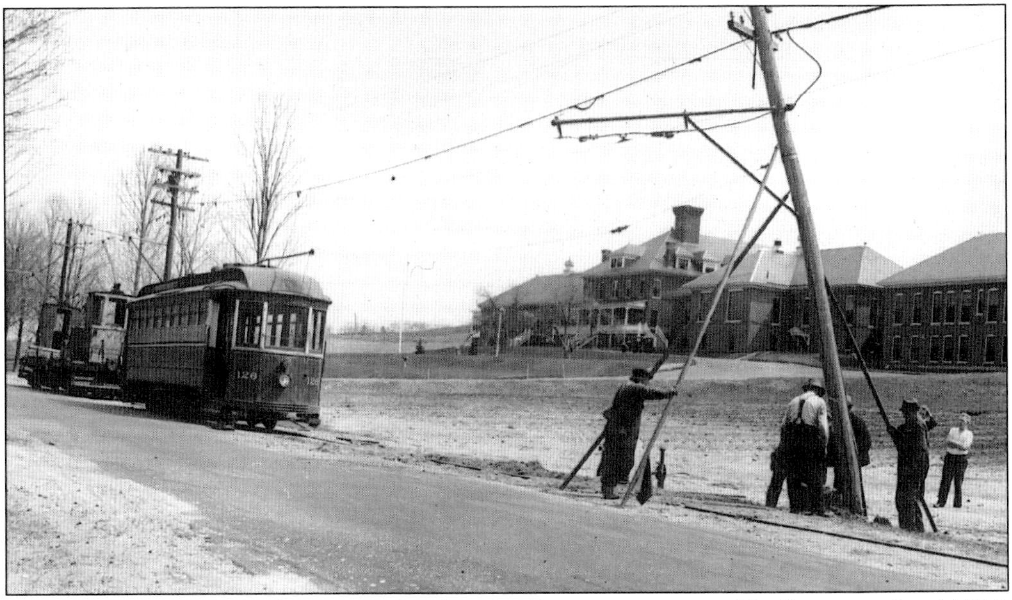

A crew raises a toppled pole on Mast Road in the Grasmere section of Goffstown in April 1936. The old Hillsborough County House of Correction is on the right, and No. 126 is on the left.

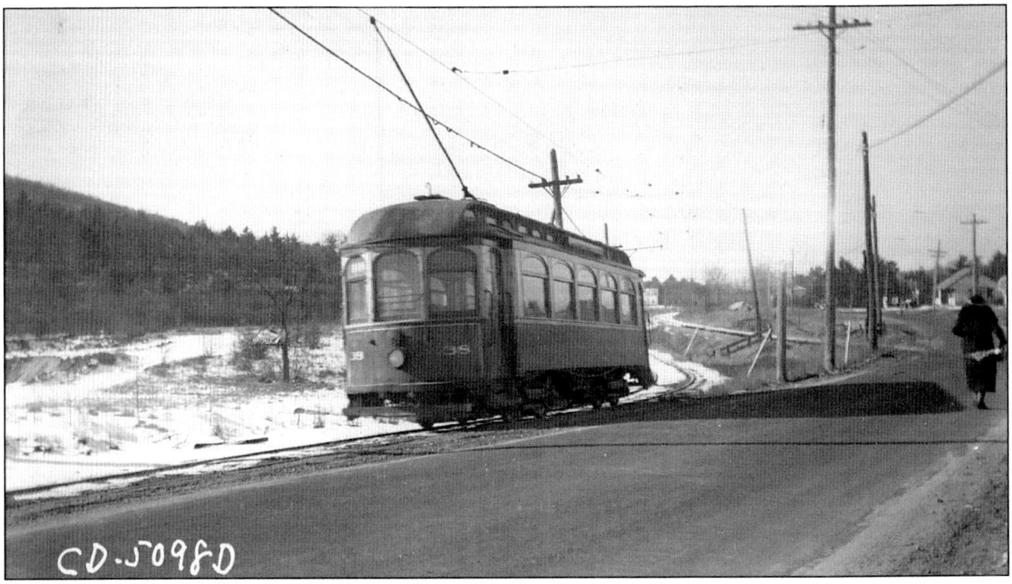

A feature of the Goffstown line was the private right-of-way that extended from the vicinity of Henry Bridge Road in Grasmere to near the intersection of Mast and Normand Roads in Goffstown village. Car No. 38 is at the southern entrance to the private way.

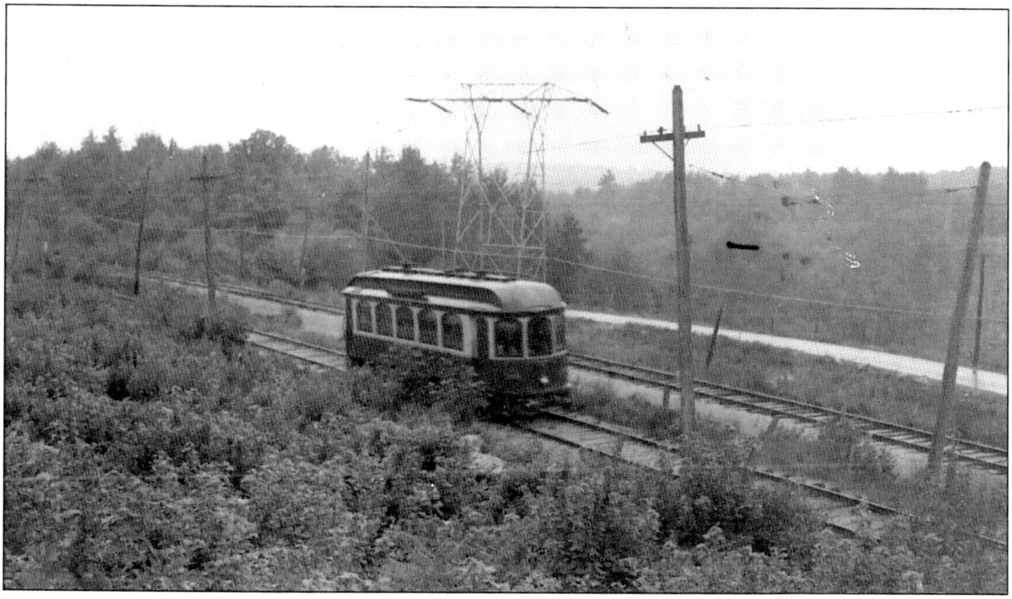

The private right-of-way on the Goffstown line paralleled the Bosston & Maine Railroad much of the way. Here, one of the Rapids passes under a power transmission line of the Public Service Company of New Hampshire.

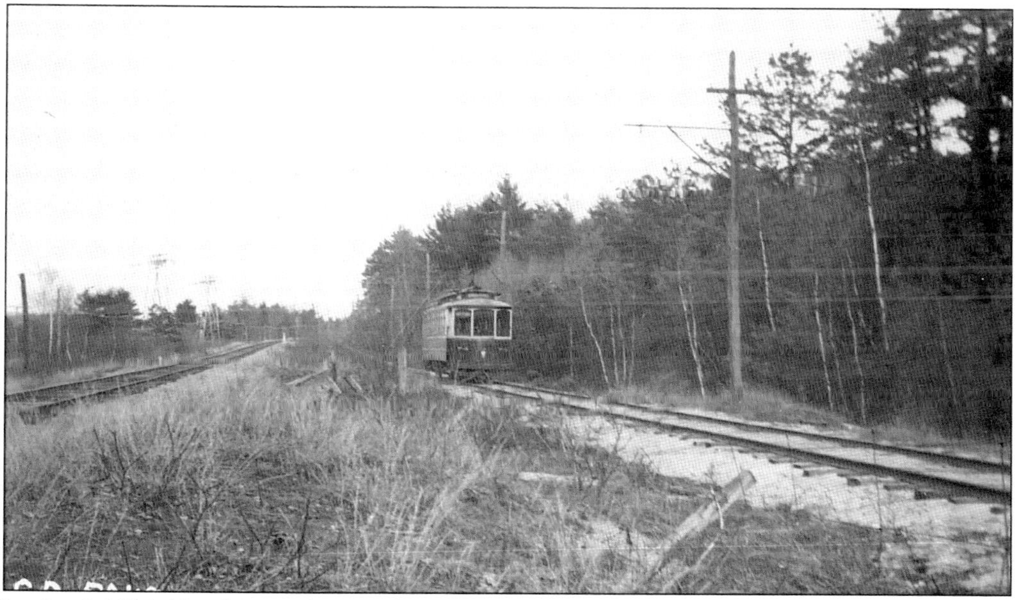

In April 1936, No. 74 speeds over the private right-of-way on its way to Monument Square, Goffstown. The Boston & Maine track at the left was torn up in the 1980s.

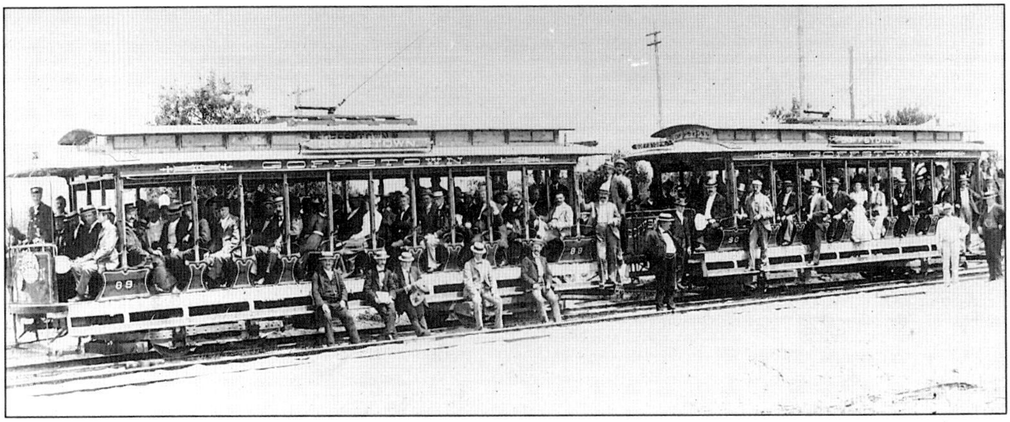

Cars No. 88 and No. 90, both new 12-bench opens, made the very first trip from the Manchester City Hall to the intersection of Main and East Union Streets in Goffstown village. This trip was made on July 24, 1900, and regular service began the next morning.

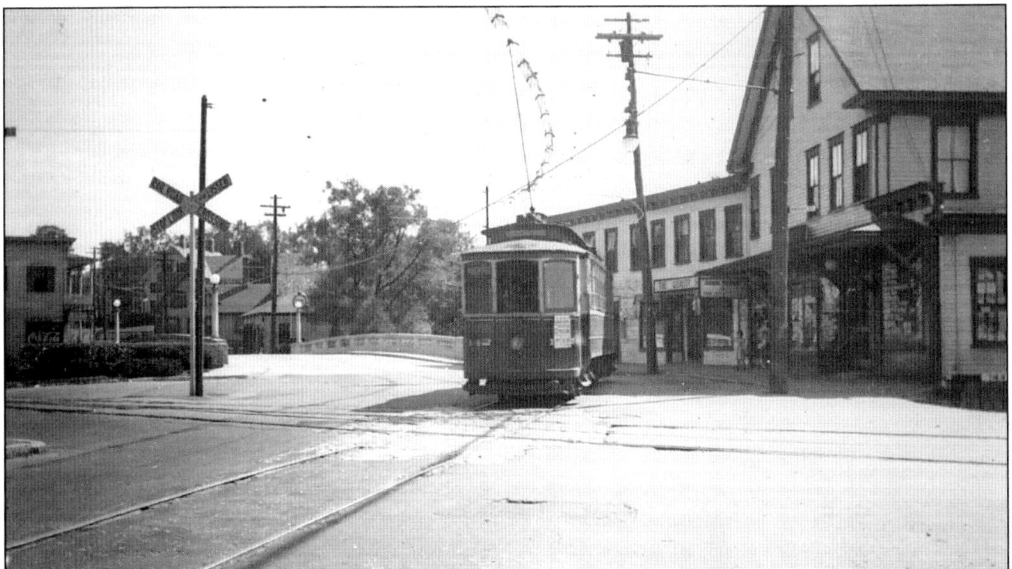

On its way back to Manchester, No. 142 bumps across the Boston & Maine tracks on Main Street and approaches the Piscataquog River bridge on Main Street, Goffstown, on September 6, 1936. The Goffstown–Manchester running time was 40 minutes.

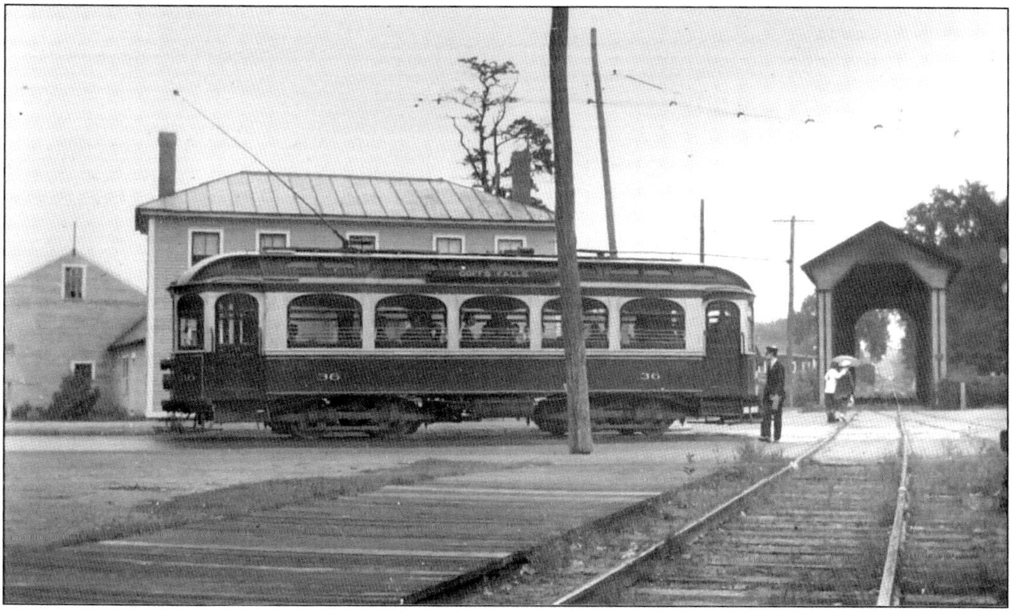

Rapid 36 stops just short of the railroad tracks on September 19, 1937. The covered bridge that carried the Boston & Maine tracks across the Piscataquog River on Main Street, Goffstown, is at the right.

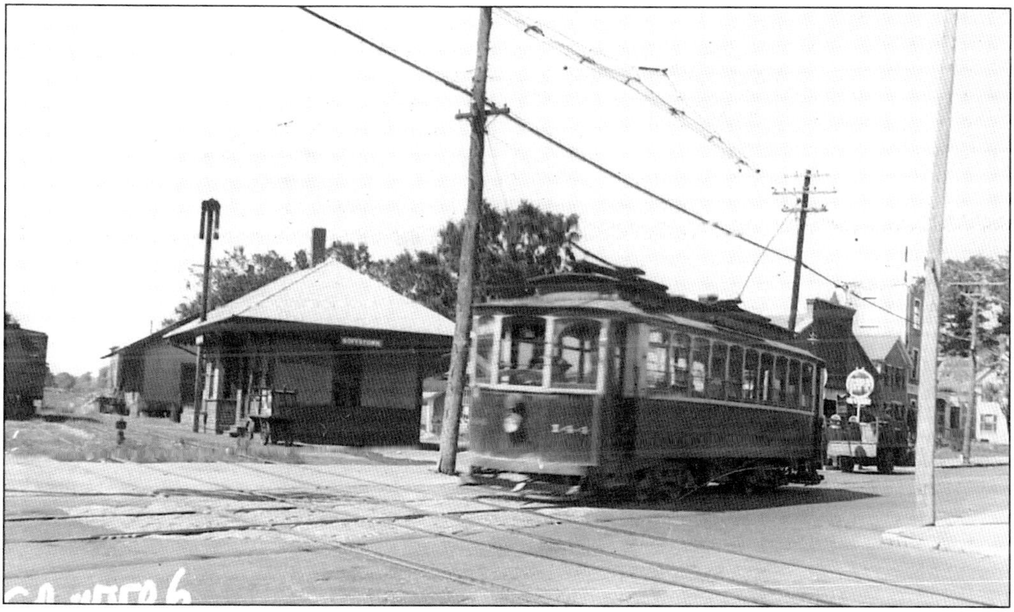

What appears to be a loaded baggage cart stands on the station platform, as No. 144 passes the Goffstown depot of the Boston & Maine Railroad on its way to Manchester c. 1935. Railroad passenger service between Manchester and Goffstown ended in 1936.

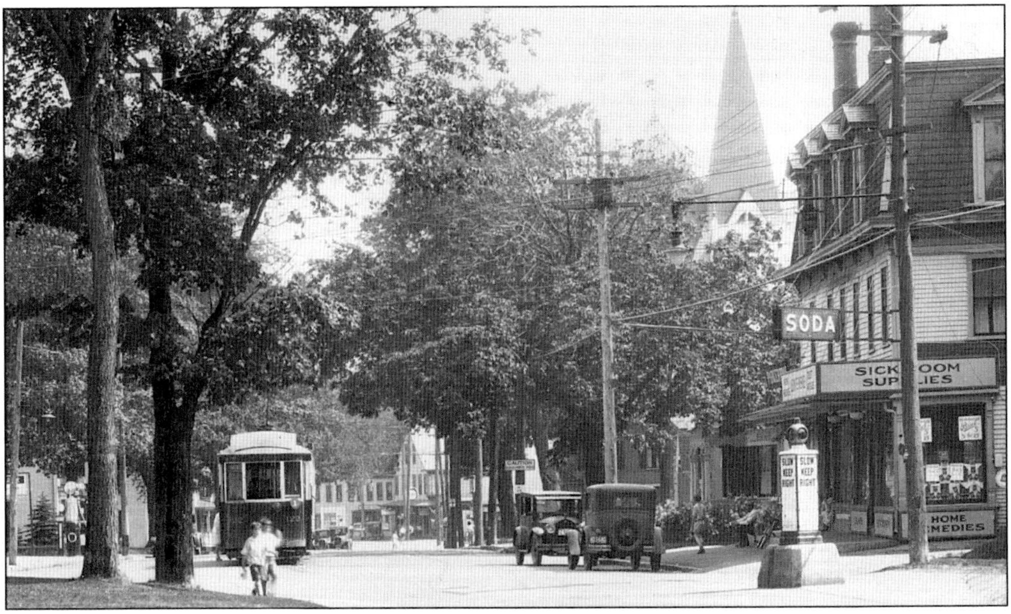

Because of the need to build a new bridge across the Piscataquog River, trolleys from Manchester did not start running through service to Monument Square, Goffstown, until April 1901. Car No. 122 is in front of the Parker Brothers store in the early 1930s.

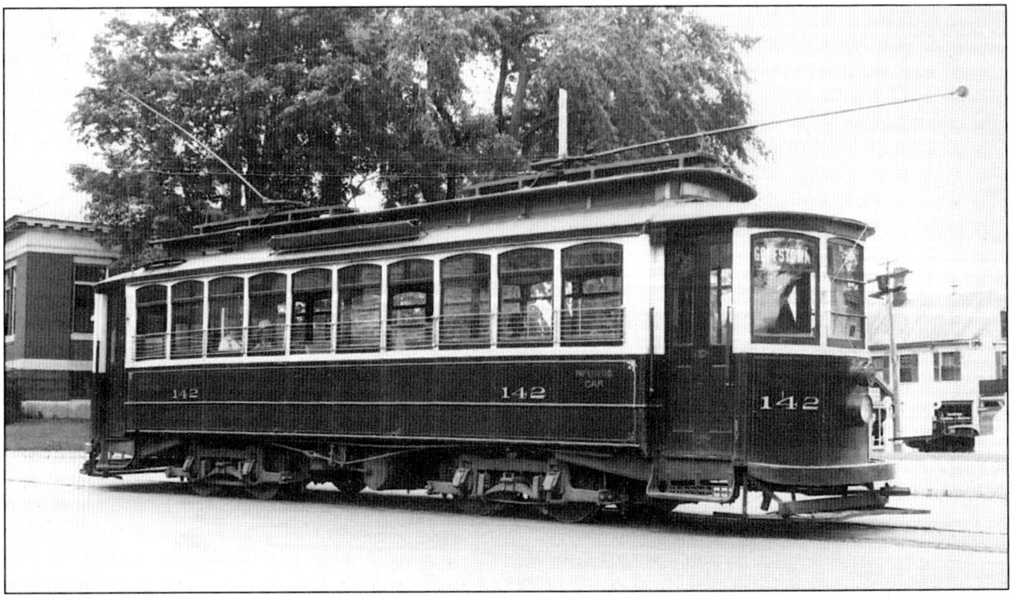

Equipped with cross seats for suburban service, No. 142 is shown at Monument Square, Goffstown, on January 22, 1935. The exterior livery was red with white trim.

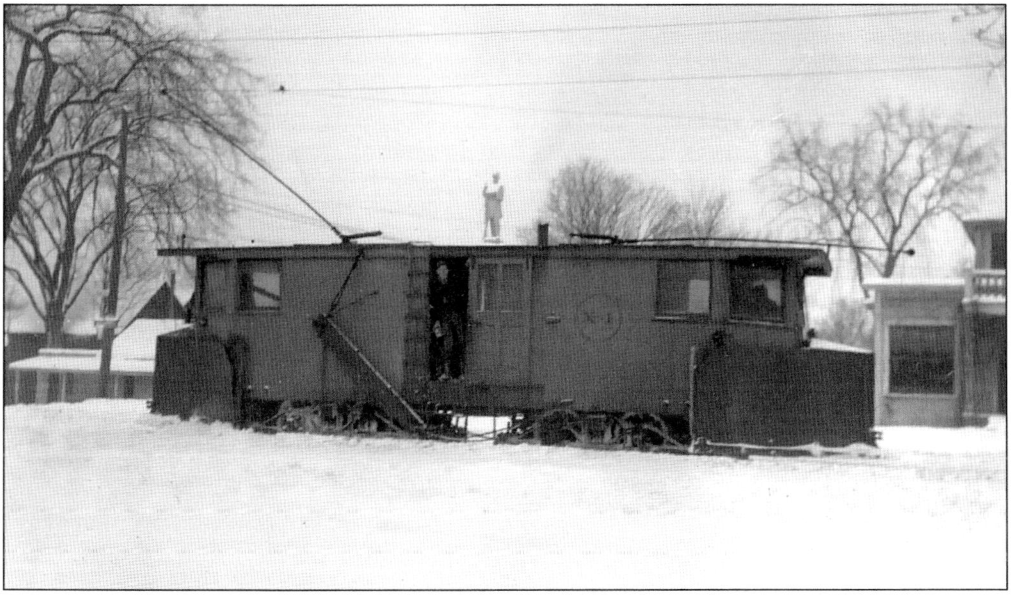

Snowplow X-4 is at the end of the line in Goffstown village on January 1, 1938. This view was taken exactly one week before the end of trolley service between Pinardville and Monument Square.

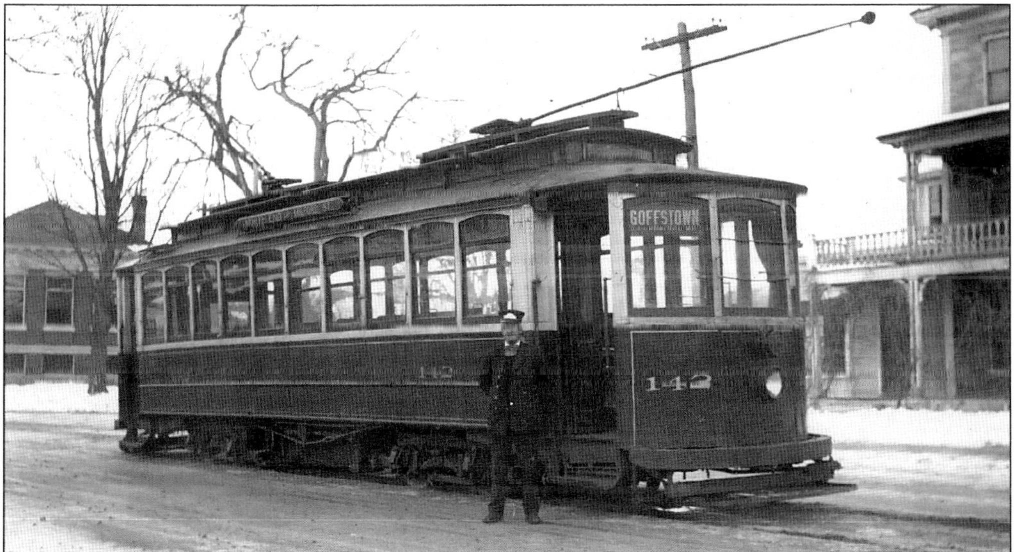

It is January 8, 1938, and No. 142 is in Monument Square on the last day of trolley service between Manchester and Goffstown village. Bus operation commenced the following morning.

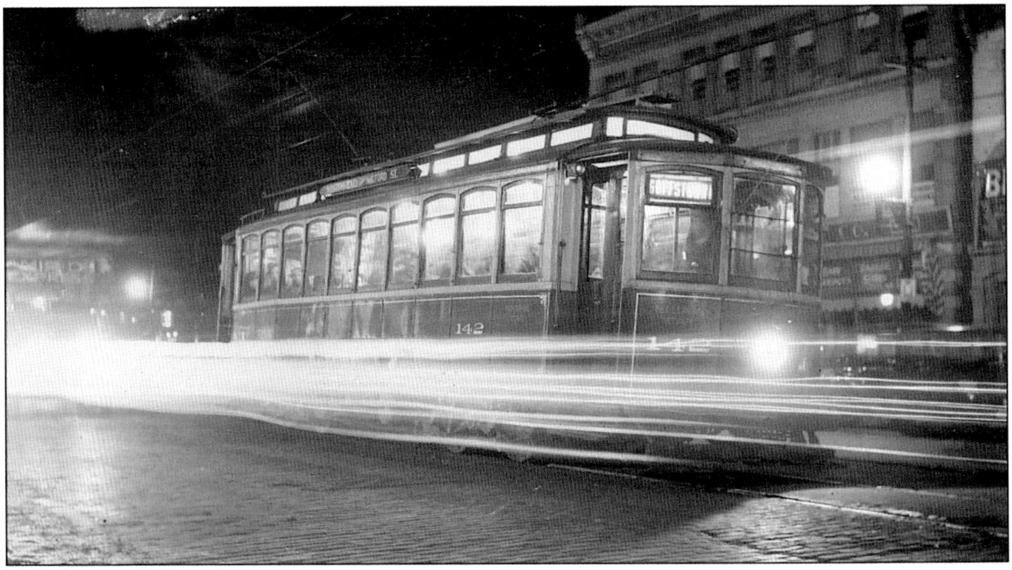

The very last car from Manchester to Goffstown, No. 142, leaves the Transfer Station at 11:15 p.m. on January 8, 1938. Thomas F. Burke is the operator, and among the passengers are many Goffstown residents taking a sentimental final ride.

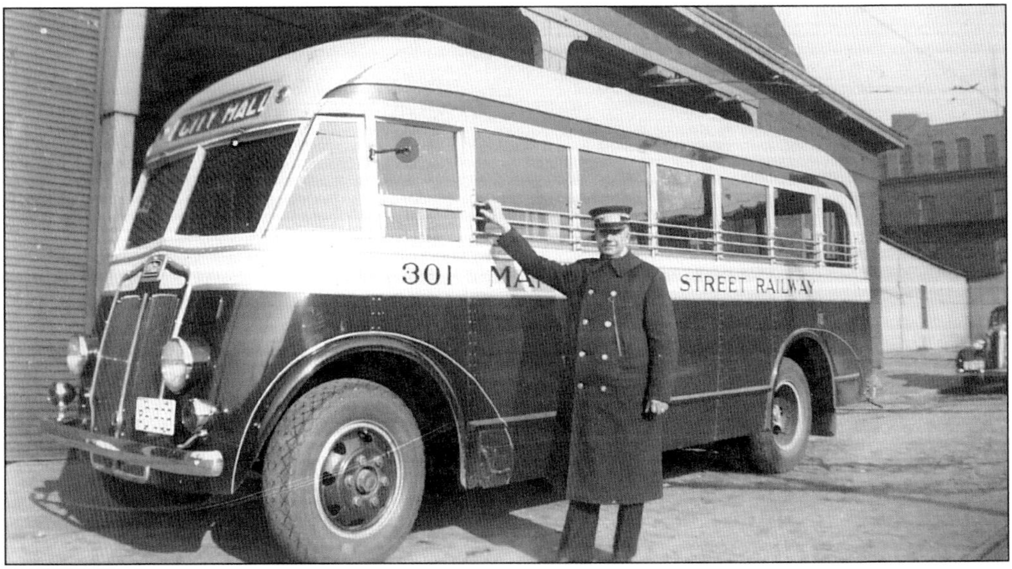

Cars No. 301 and No. 331, both small motor coaches acquired in 1937, were placed in service between Manchester and Goffstown village on January 9, 1938. Car No. 301 is at one of the Traction Street carbarns shortly after delivery.

Seven

UNCANOONUC

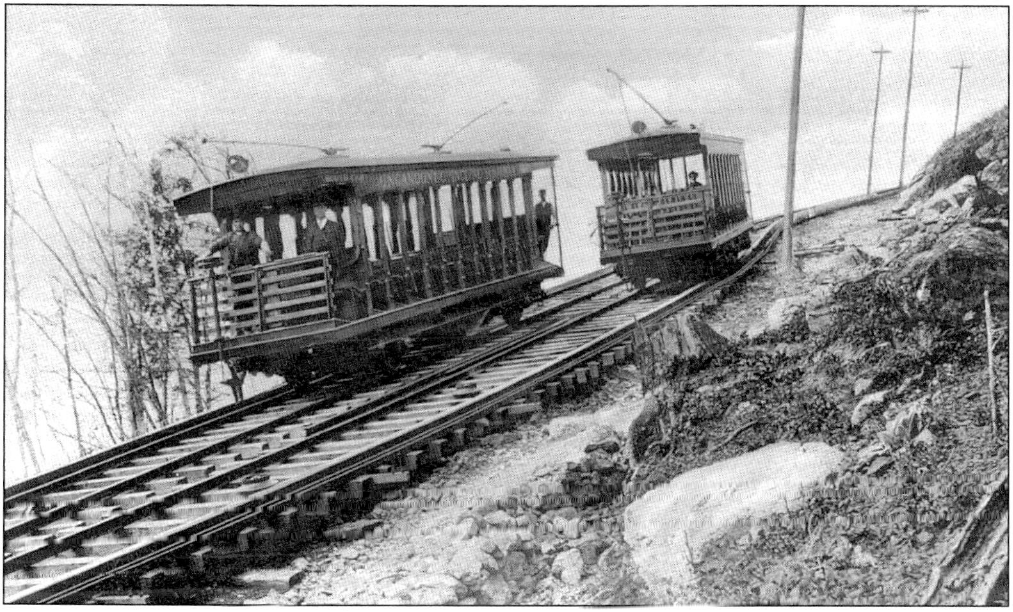

Two open cars meet at the midway turnout on the 2,380-foot Uncanoonuc Incline Railway, which opened on June 8, 1907. Owned by the Uncanoonuc Incline Railway & Development Company, the railway extended from the base to the summit of South Uncanoonuc Mountain in Goffstown. In 1905, the company constructed a conventional 2.5-mile trolley line from a connection with the Manchester Street Railway on South Mast Street (at Shirley Junction) to the mountain base. The two incline cars were connected by a steel cable and were operated on the counterbalance principle: when one ascended, the other descended. The ruling grade was 35 percent and the running time was five minutes. The single track from Shirley Junction to the mountain base was abandoned in 1938, but the incline railway remained intact until 1941. That year, a woods fire destroyed about 500 feet of track and ruined the cable. No effort was made to replace the track or cable and soon after the end of World War II, the remaining track was torn up and the incline cars were junked.

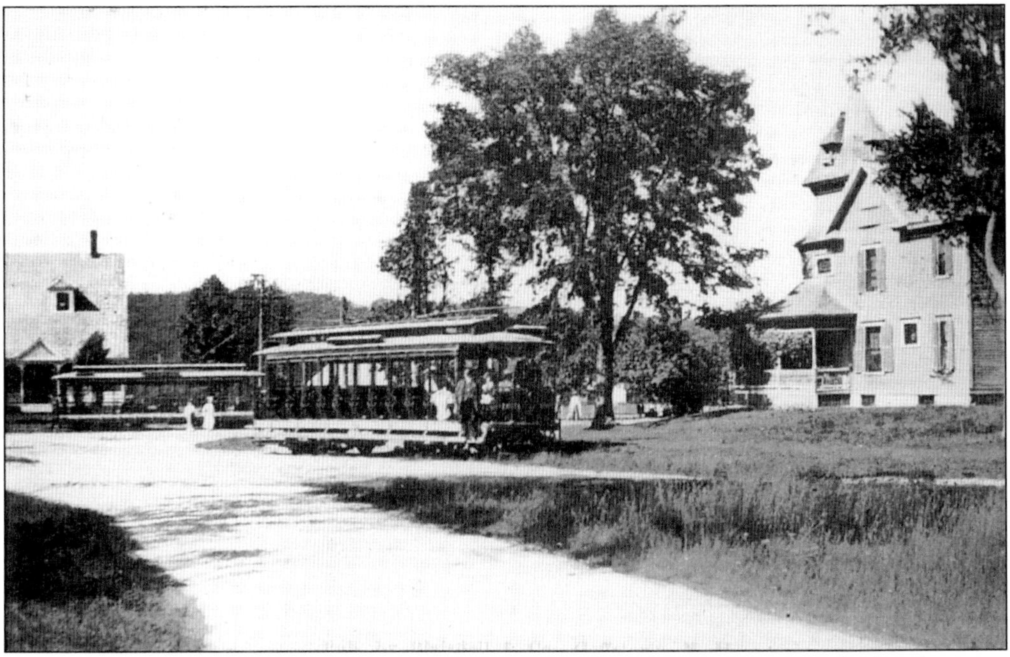

This view shows two Manchester Street Railway 13-bench open cars at Shirley Junction *c.* 1910. The trolley on the left is headed for Monument Square, Goffstown, and the other one is on the Uncanoonuc company's track.

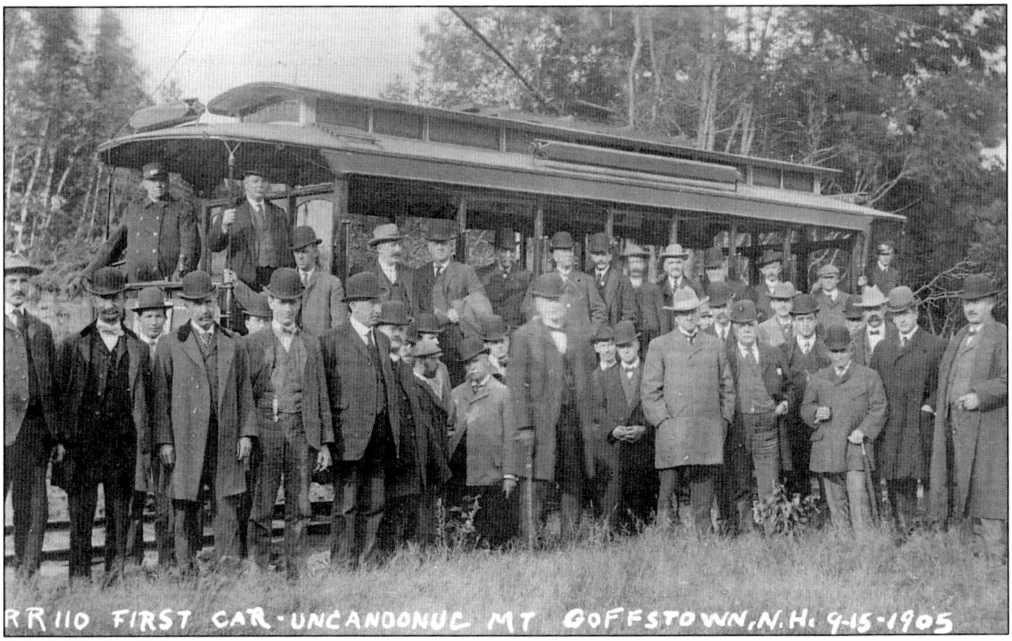

A ten-bench open of the Manchester Street Railway made the first trial trip from Shirley Junction to the base of South Uncanoonuc Mountain on September 15, 1905. Among the passengers were a number of Goffstown town officers and prominent residents.

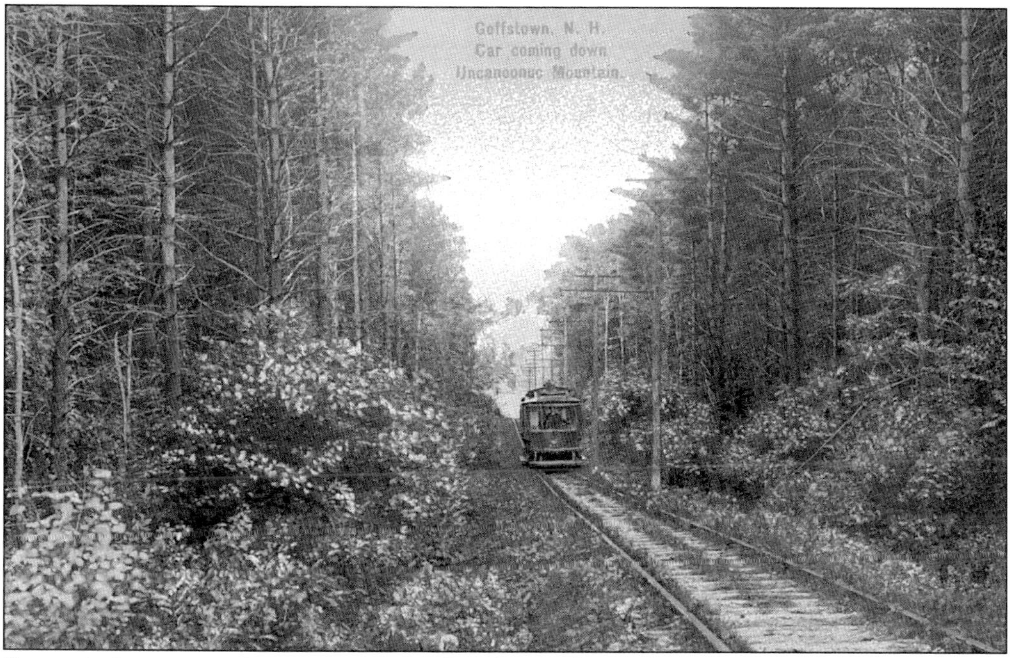

Situated almost entirely on a private right-of-way, the trolley line from Shirley Junction to South Uncanoonuc Mountain had an average grade of 4.5 percent. The running time for "up" cars was 15 minutes, and that for "down" cars was 6 minutes.

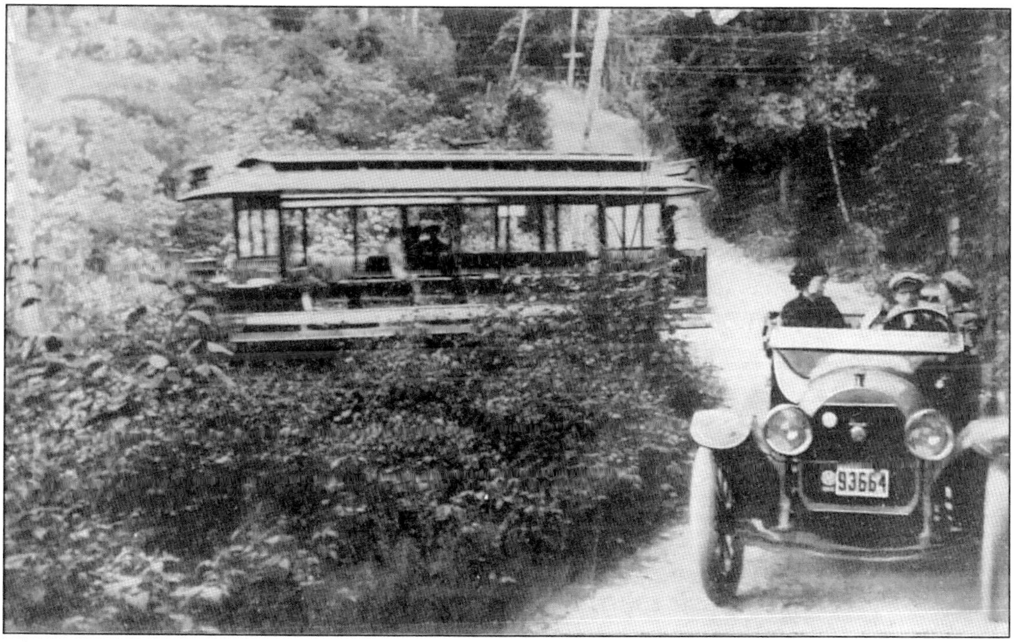

The mountain laurel is in full bloom in June, as an open trolley travels between Shirley Junction and the South Uncanoonuc Mountain base. The automobile on the right appears to be an Oldsmobile.

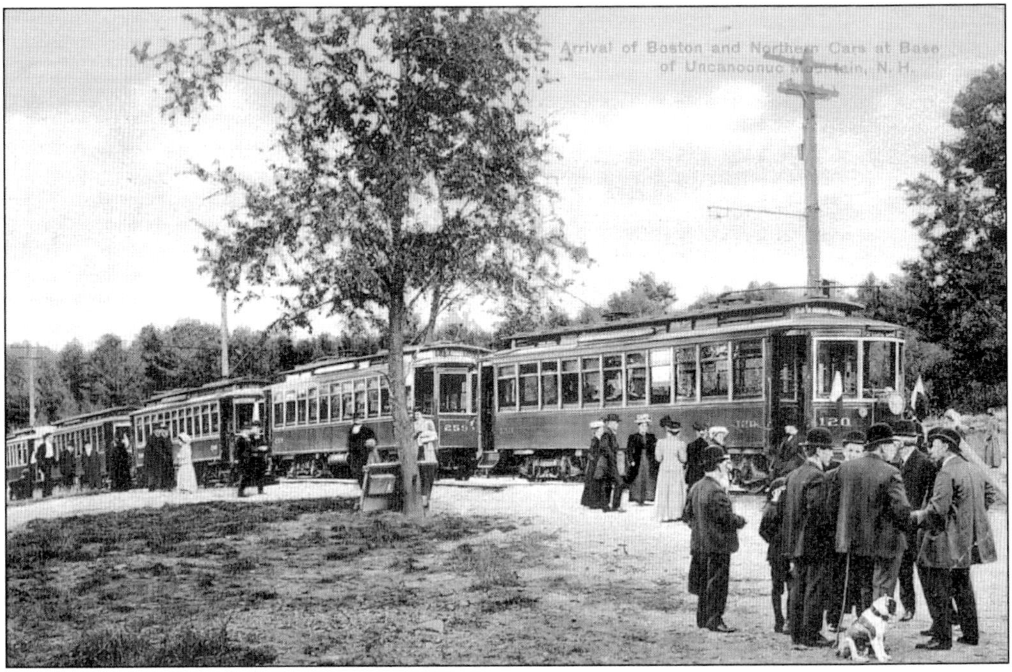

Only six were expected, but 16 trolleys of the Boston & Northern Street Railway brought some 600 excursionists from Eastern Massachusetts to the Uncanoonuc Incline Railway on Sunday, October 6, 1907.

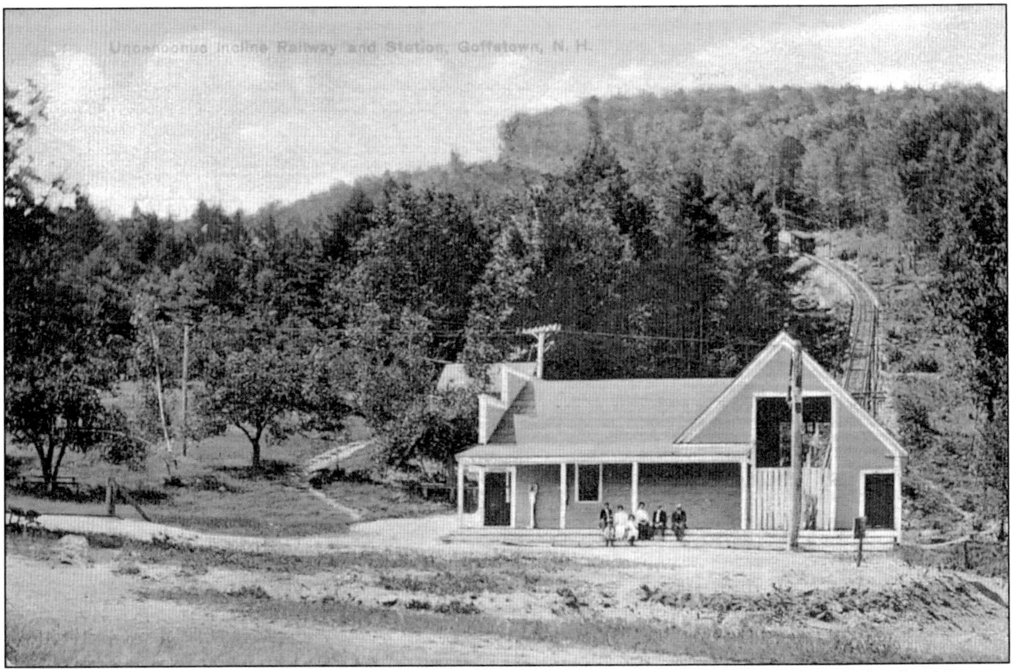

Shown is the base station of the Uncanoonuc Incline Railway in 1907. Behind the building is the incline railway track, on which a car is either ascending or descending.

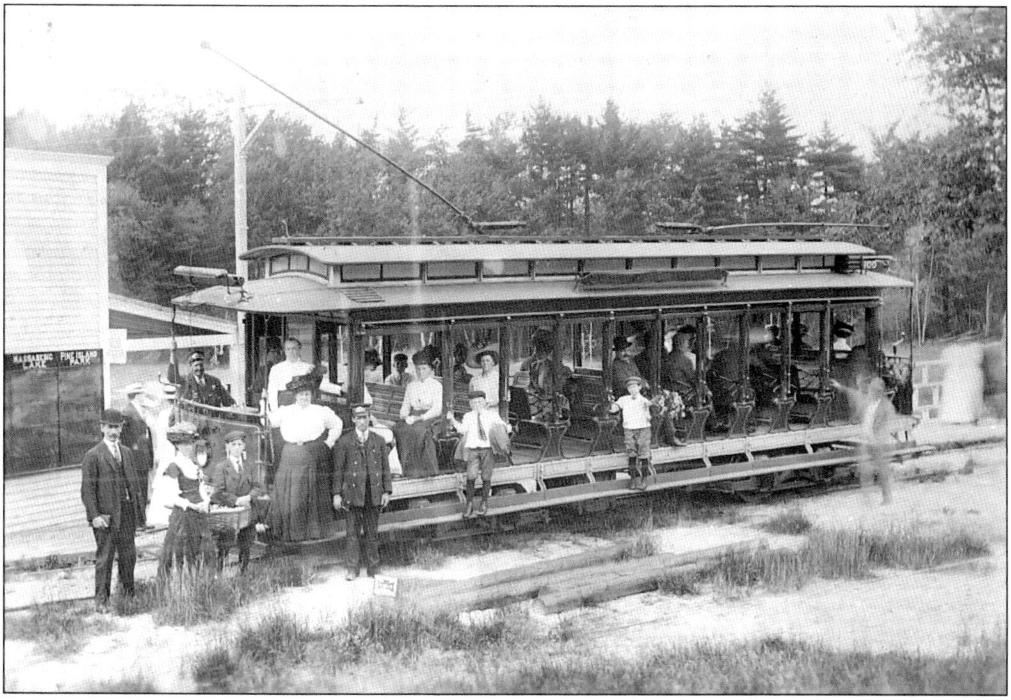

No through cars were ever run regularly between downtown Manchester and the Uncanoonuc base station. However, charter parties were carried from time to time, especially when the mountain laurel was at its peak. Shown is one of the 13-bench opens of the Manchester Street Railway.

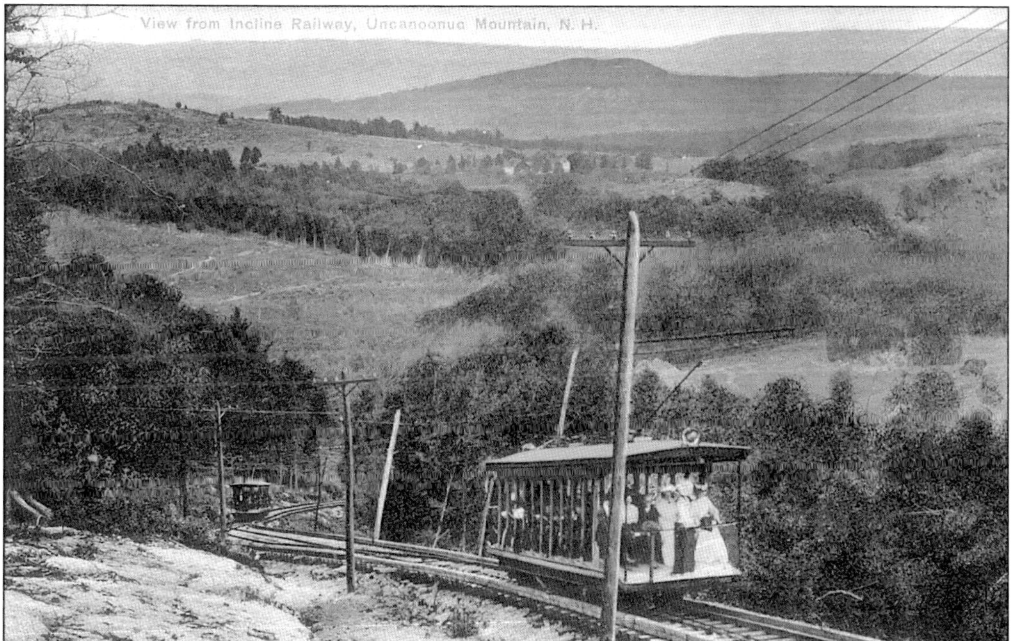

Two incline railway cars approach the midpoint turnout *c.* 1908. The widespread view from the summit of South Uncanoonuc Mountain is apparent in this scene.

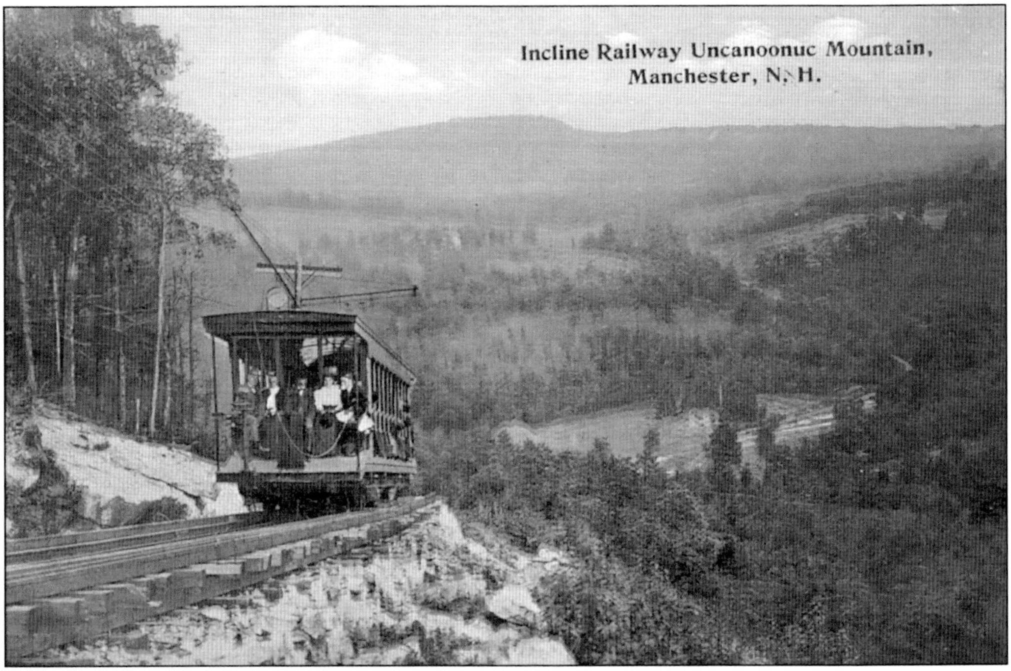

Five passengers occupy the rear bench of one of the incline cars as it descends the railway toward the base station c. 1910. For many years service was maintained only from May 1 to October 15; however, during the 1930s, winter trips were run for skiers.

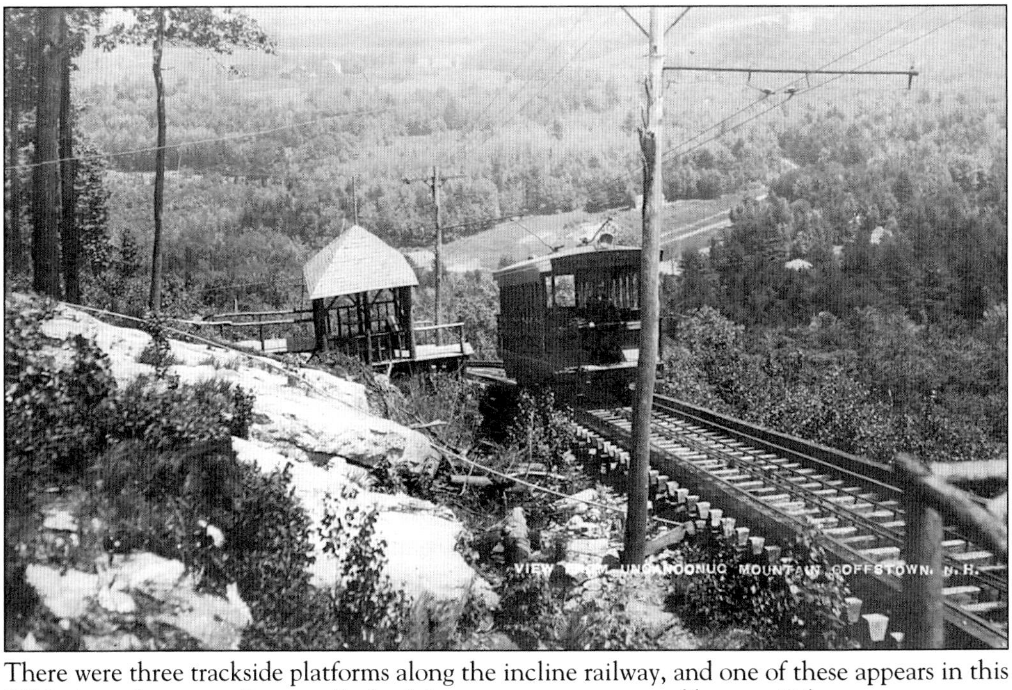

There were three trackside platforms along the incline railway, and one of these appears in this 1910 view of an ascending car. Each of the two cars was powered by two 40-horsepower motors and carried both a motorman and conductor.

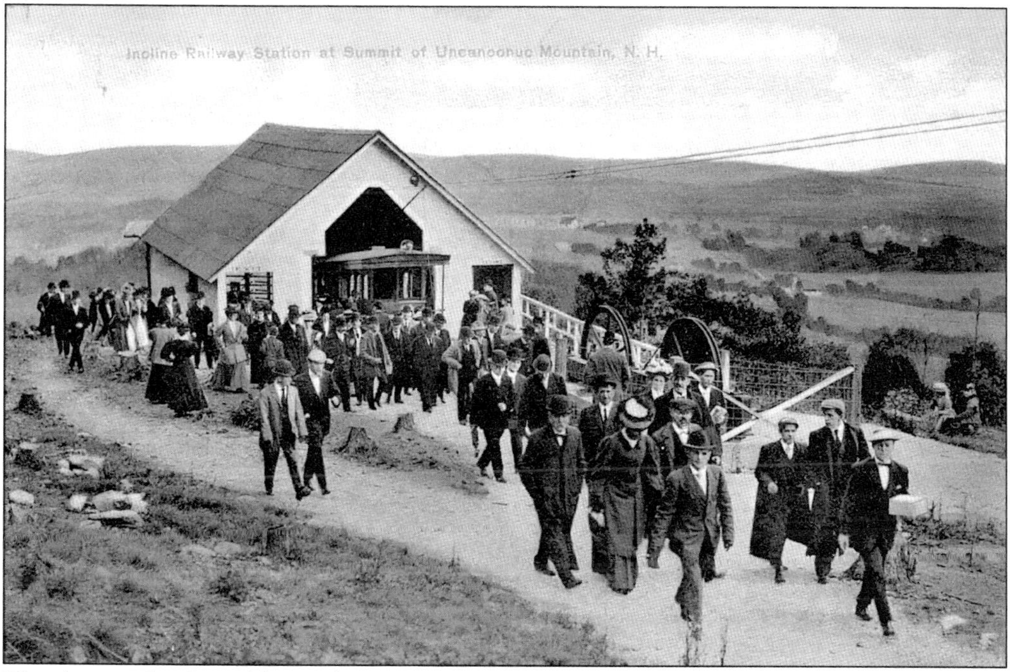

The sheaves for the cable can be seen in this view of the summit station of the Uncanoonuc Incline Railway, taken shortly after its opening. The group leaving the station is walking to the Uncanoonuc Hotel, a short distance away.

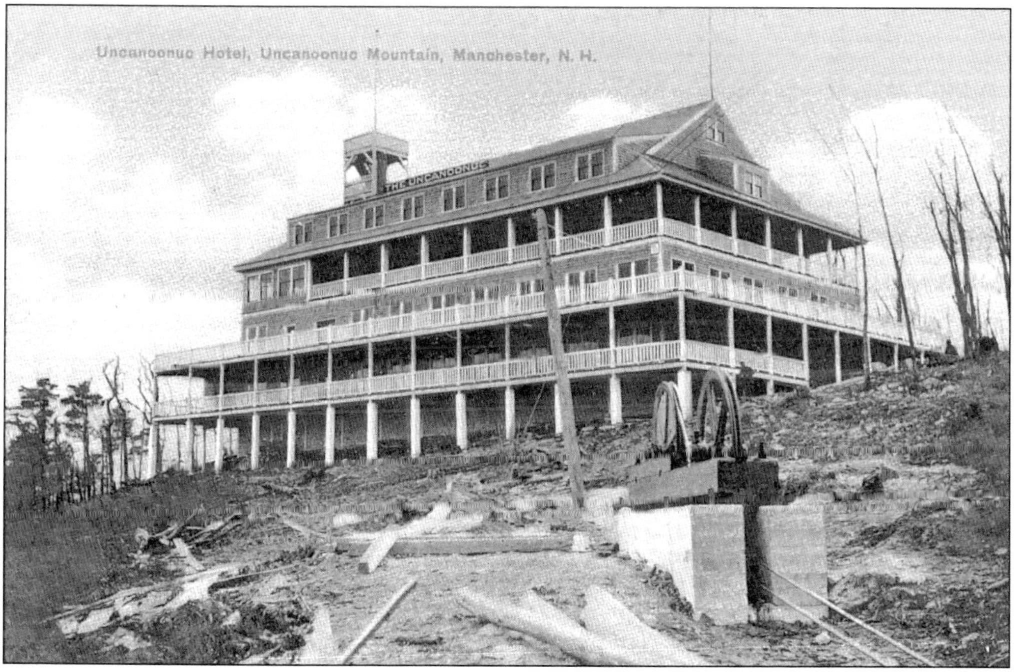

Opened the same day as the incline railway was the five-story Uncanoonuc Hotel, located on the summit of South Mountain. Famous for the quality of its dining room cuisine, the building was destroyed by a fire in February 1923. The replacement pavilion burned in 1930.

STOP! LOOK AND LISTEN

RAPID TRANSIT LINE

SCHEDULE AND CONNECTIONS

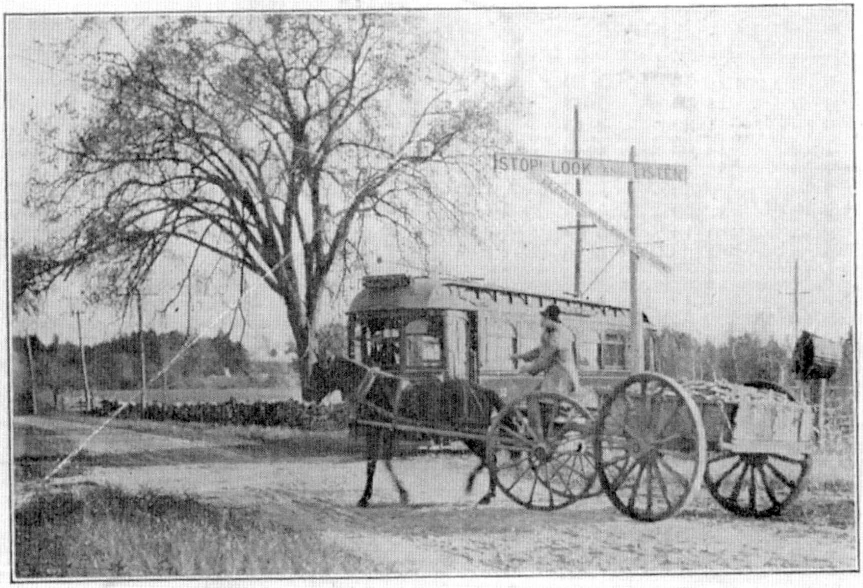

TROLLEY GUIDE No. 5

Manchester, N. H.

In Effect September 14, 1908. Subject to delays, changes, and corrections without notice.

This is the cover of one of the Manchester trolley guides, published by the Manchester Traction, Light, & Power Company between 1907 and 1921. It shows one of the Rapids and a horse-drawn cart at one of the grade crossings on the Manchester & Nashua Street Railway.

Eight

Rapid Transit Lines

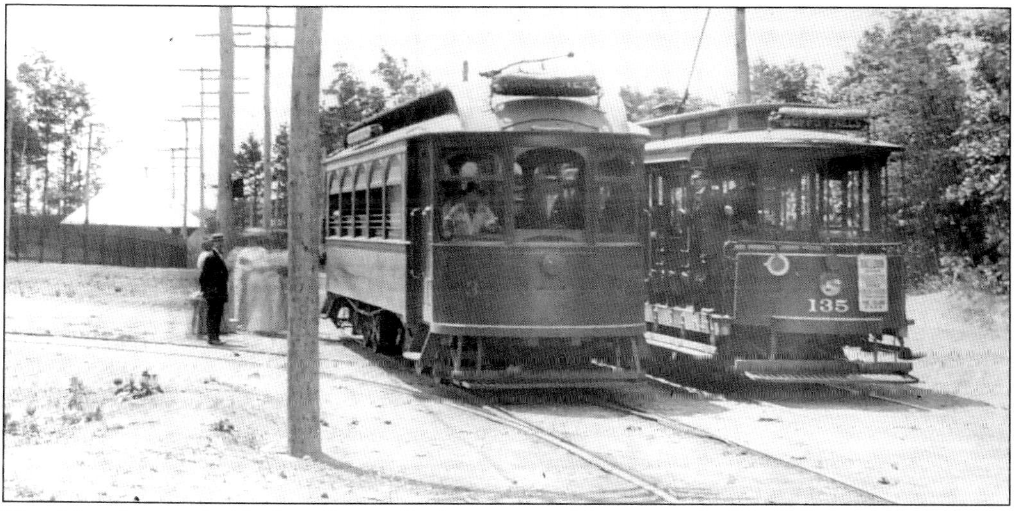

The Manchester & Nashua Street Railway opened between Goffe's Falls and Hudson on January 1, 1907. On December 7 of the same year, the Manchester & Derry Street Railway commenced operation between the Queen City and what was then known as West Derry via North Londonderry and Londonderry. Both companies were identified as the Rapid Transit Lines of the Manchester trolley system. The Manchester & Nashua connected in Hudson with the Nashua Street Railway and held track rights over the latter to Tremont Square in the Gate City. The distance between the Manchester City Hall and Tremont Square was 18.25 miles, the running time was 55 minutes, and the through fare was 25¢ initially. The Manchester & Nashua was reasonably profitable through 1919 but thereafter saw steady losses. The line was abandoned on September 13, 1931. Pictured is Manchester & Nashua Rapid No. 3, inbound to Manchester, meeting Goffe's Falls-bound open No. 135 at Pine Island Park.

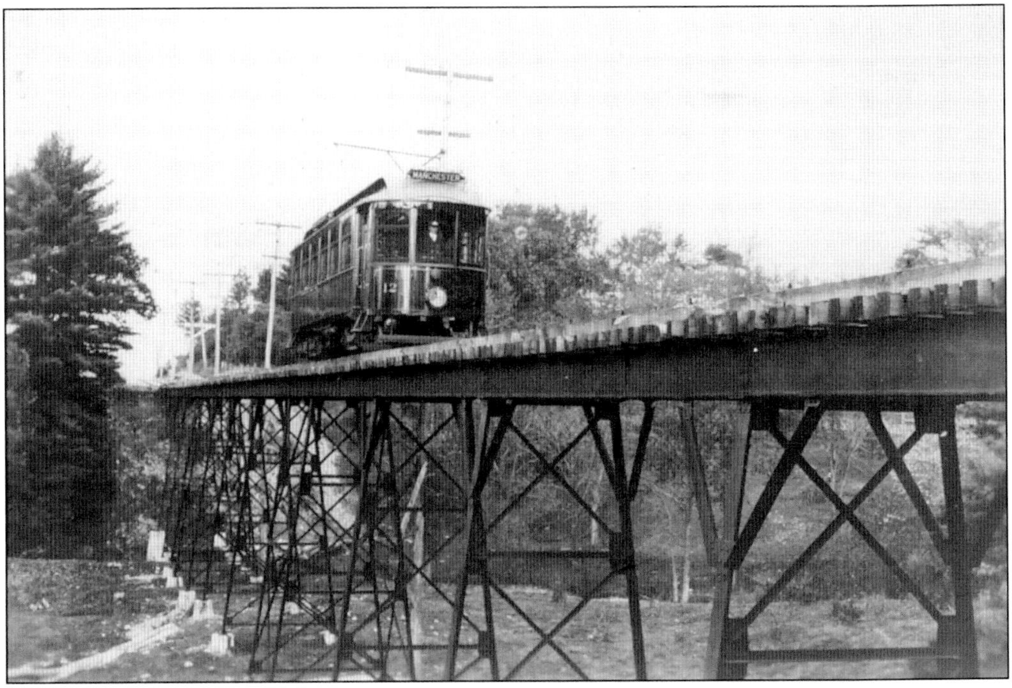

Among the features of the Manchester & Nashua was a 410-foot steel viaduct across Little Cohas Brook on the private right-of-way that is now Hazelton Avenue at Goffe's Falls. Crossing the structure is Rapid No. 12, on its way to the Manchester City Hall.

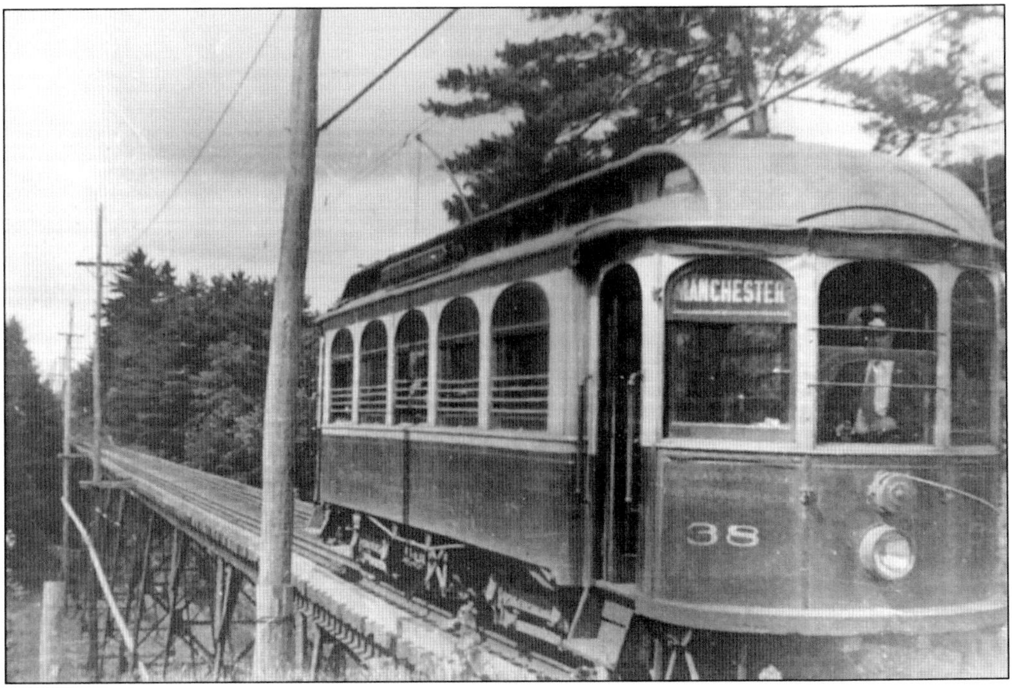

Running as a one-man car, northbound Rapid No. 38 crosses another of the three viaducts on the Manchester & Nashua after 1925. By that time, the Manchester–Nashua through fare had risen to 50¢.

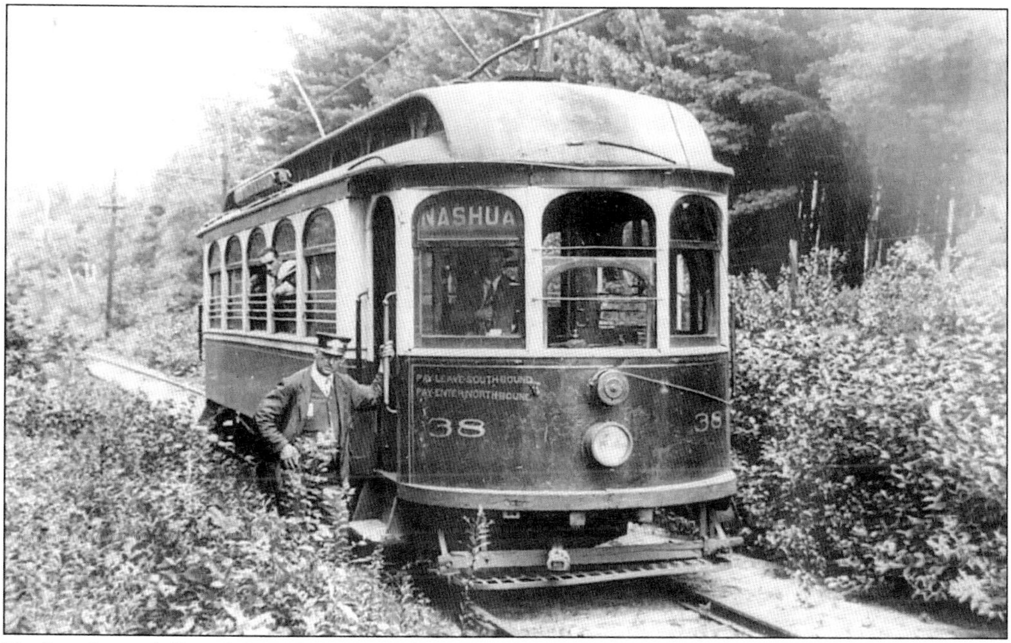

Nashua-bound Rapid No. 38 is on the Manchester & Nashua private way, somewhere in Litchfield. The railway owned 8.14 miles of track in that town.

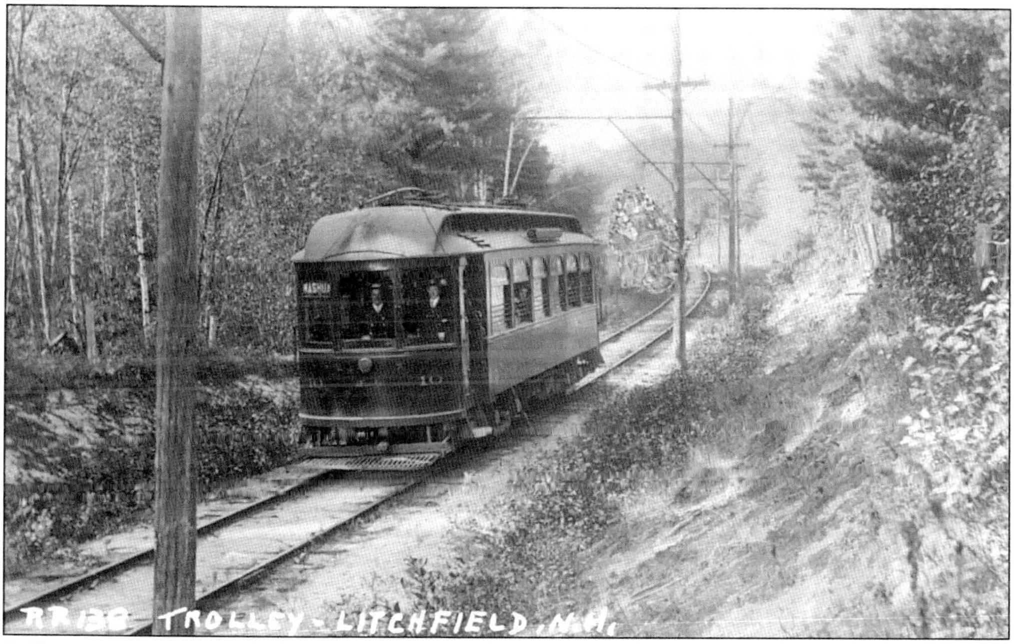

Still in its original dark green paint scheme, Rapid No. 10 passes through Litchfield on its way from Manchester to Nashua. The body of this car became the Maple Diner in Danvers, Massachusetts, *c.* 1932.

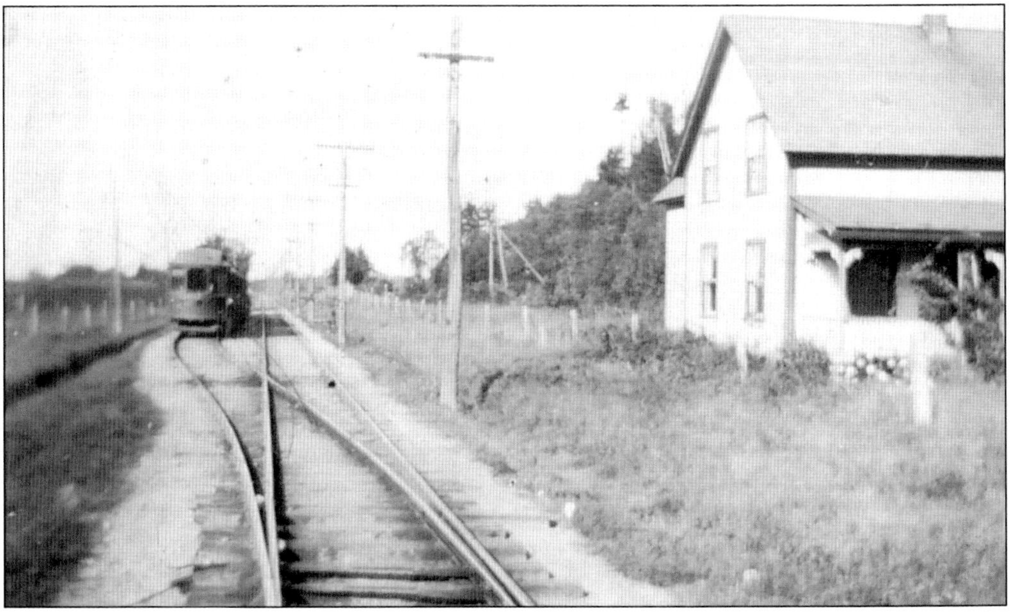

A Rapid waits on Manchester & Nashua's Litchfield turnout for an opposing car to arrive. The private right-of-way between Goffe's Falls and Hudson was fenced on both sides, and a number of cattle passes were provided.

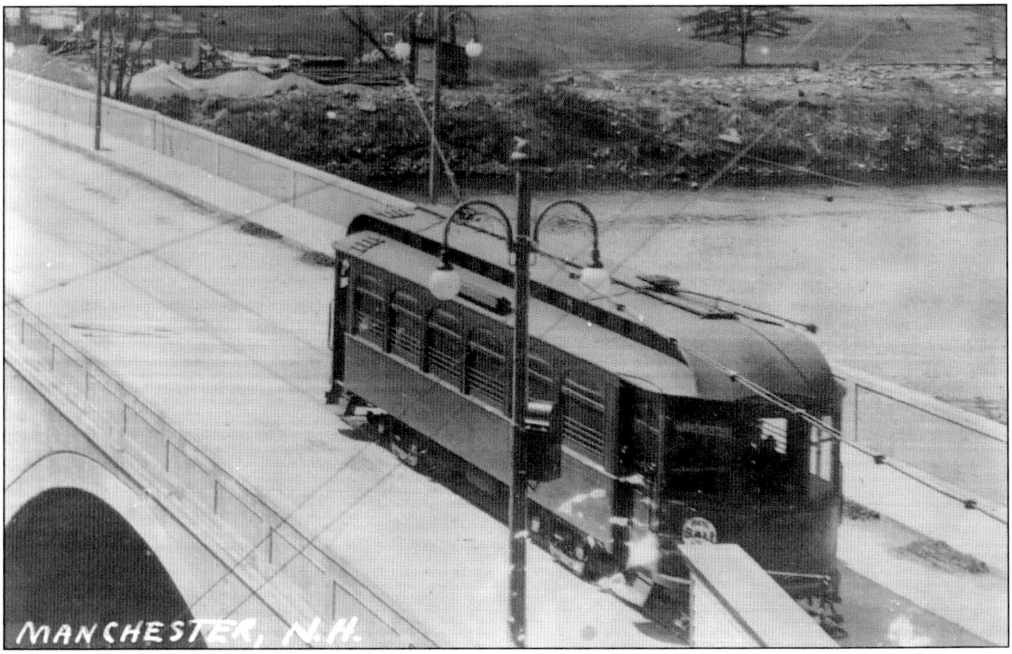

A reinforced concrete bridge replaced an 1881-vintage iron structure across the Merrimack River between Hudson and Nashua in 1910. Crossing the bridge is one of the Rapids en route from the Gate City to Manchester *c.* 1915.

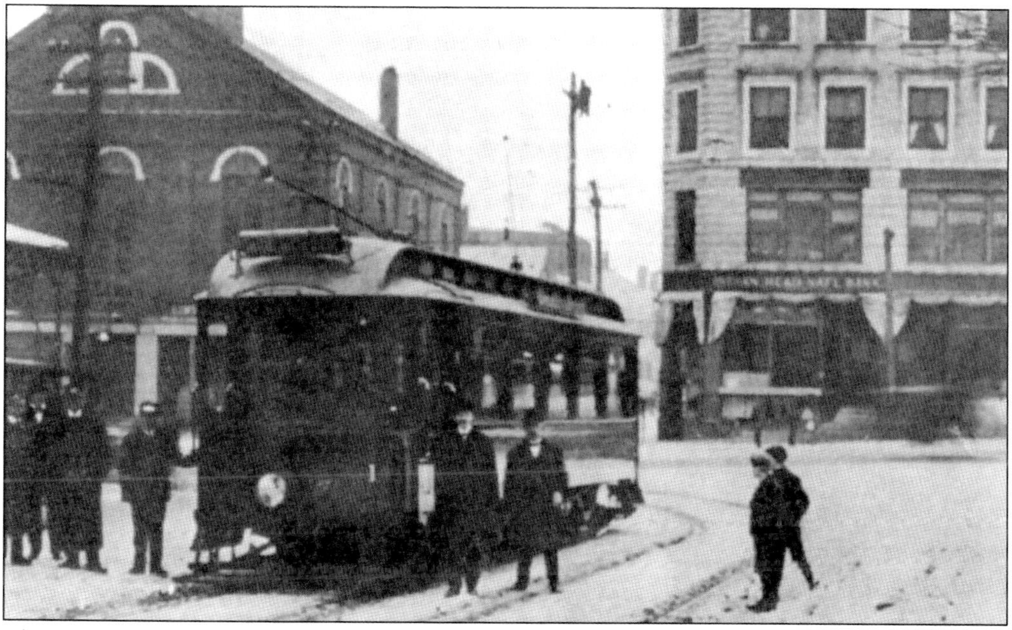

The first trial trip over the Manchester & Nashua Street Railway was made on December 28, 1906 by Rapid No. 1. The car, which left Manchester at 9:50 a.m., is shown shortly after it arrived in Nashua at 10:33 a.m.

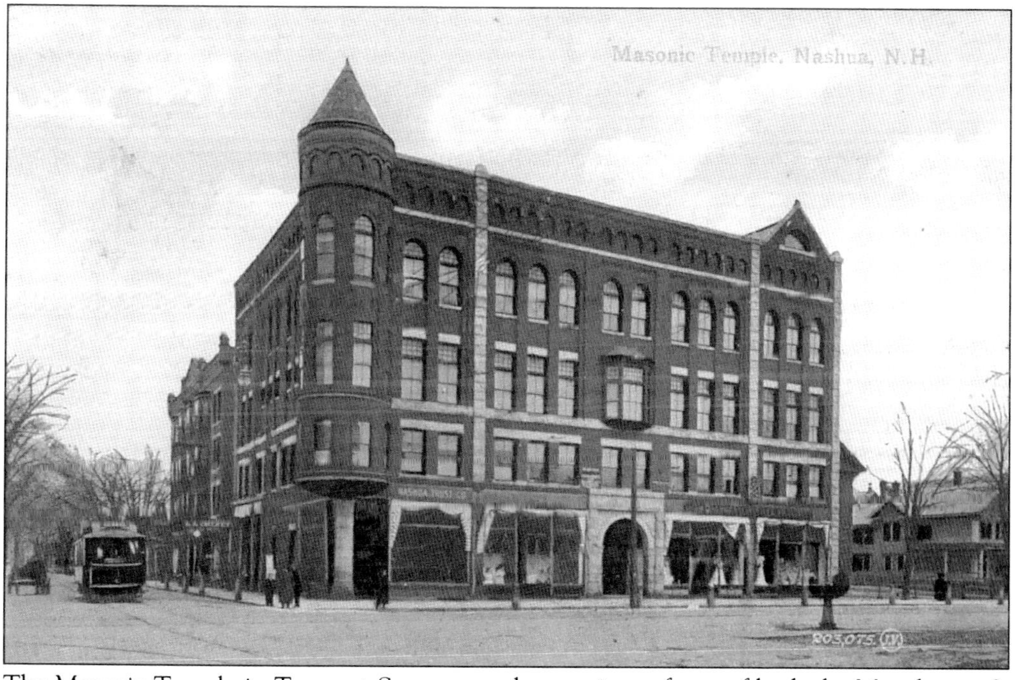

The Masonic Temple in Tremont Square was the terminus of cars of both the Manchester & Nashua and the Hudson, Pelham, & Salem Street Railways after 1907. One of the Hudson, Pelham, & Salem cars is shown on East Pearl Street.

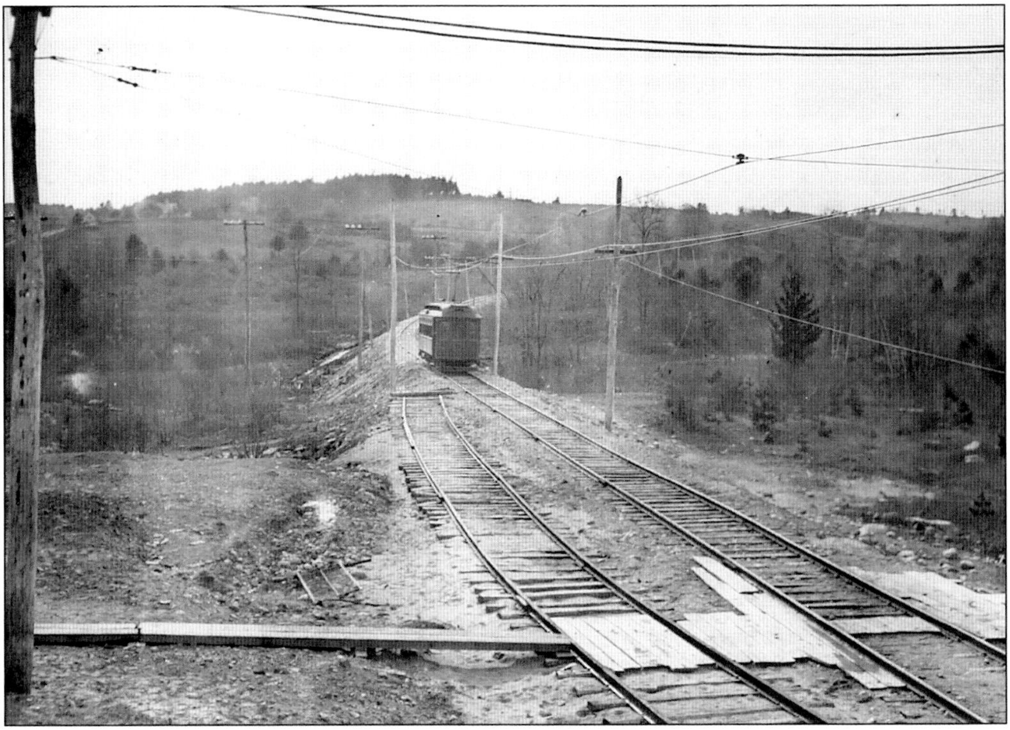

The Manchester & Derry branched from the Manchester & Nashua at Cohas Junction, immediately south of the Little Cohas Brook viaduct. One of the Rapids leaves the junction en route to North Londonderry and West Derry.

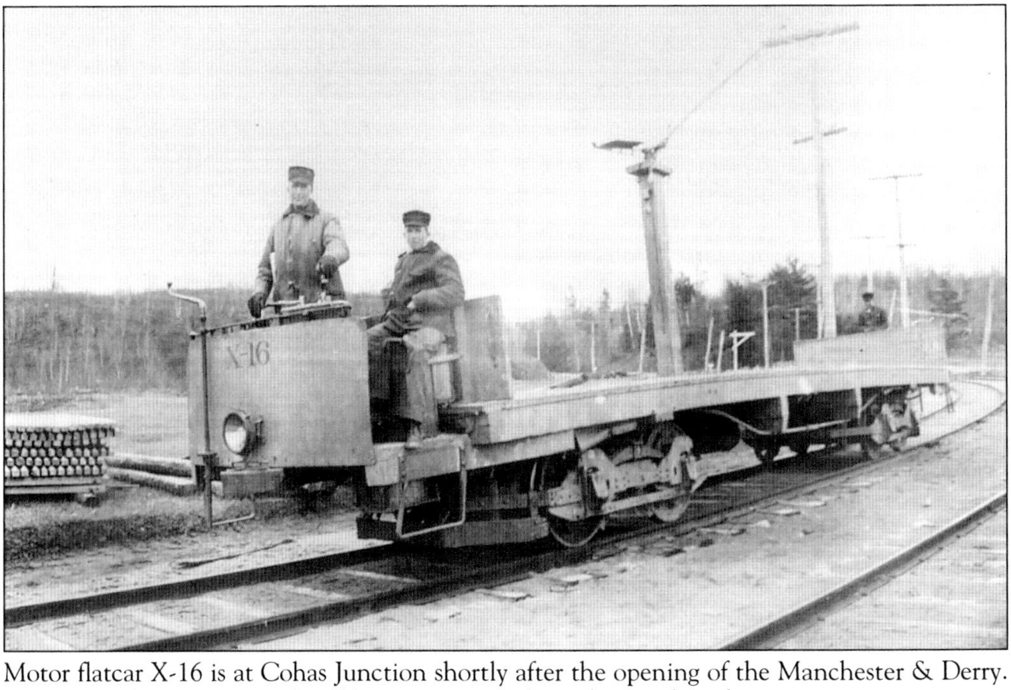

Motor flatcar X-16 is at Cohas Junction shortly after the opening of the Manchester & Derry. A few years later, it was replaced by a new car with a cab at each end.

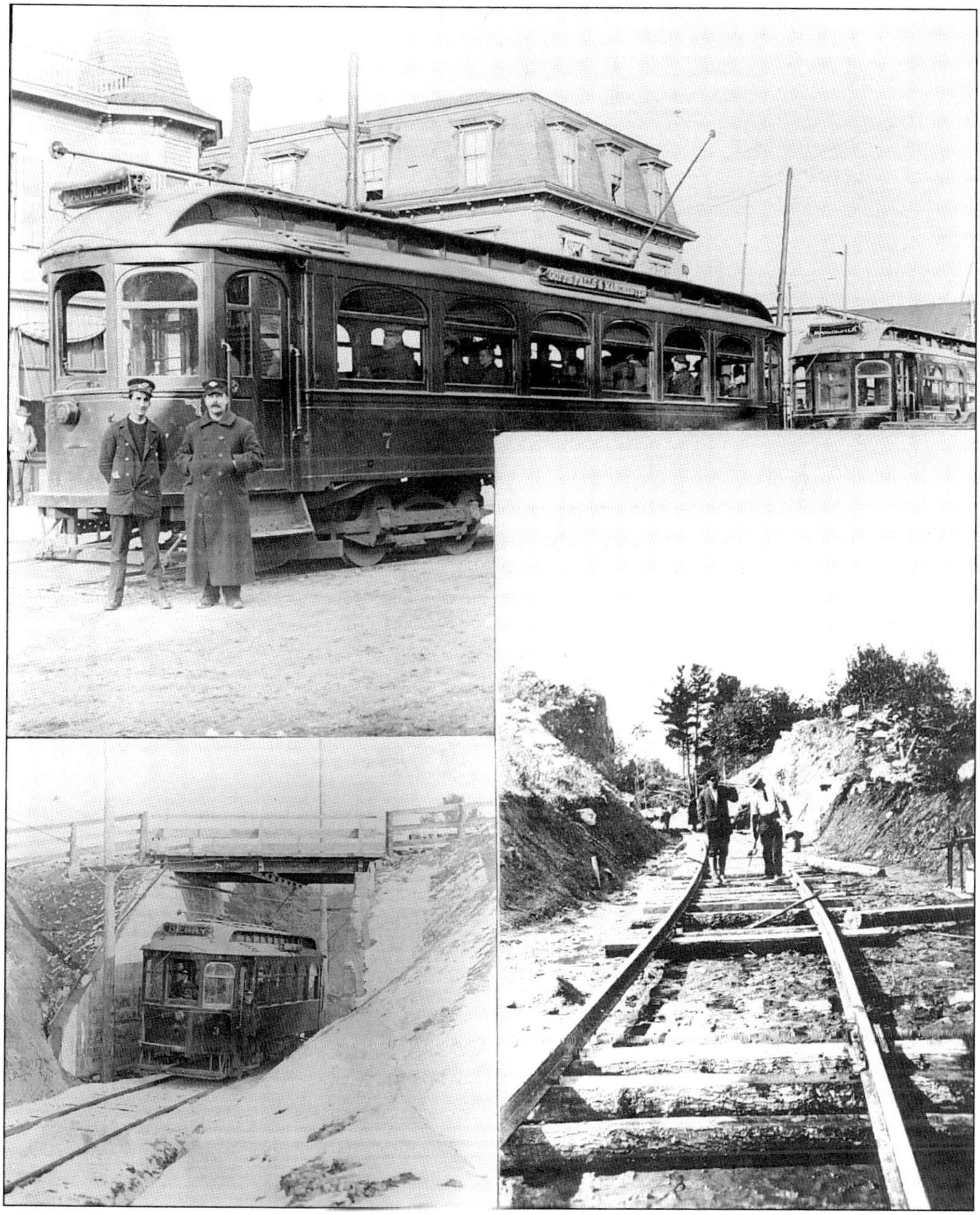

The upper view in this montage shows Manchester & Derry No. 7 and another Rapid in West Derry, possibly on Sunday, December 8, 1907. At that time, riding was so heavy that some scheduled trips had to be run with two cars. At the lower left, Manchester & Nashua No. 3 passes under a highway bridge. At the right, track is being laid through a rock cut between Cohas Junction and North Londonderry.

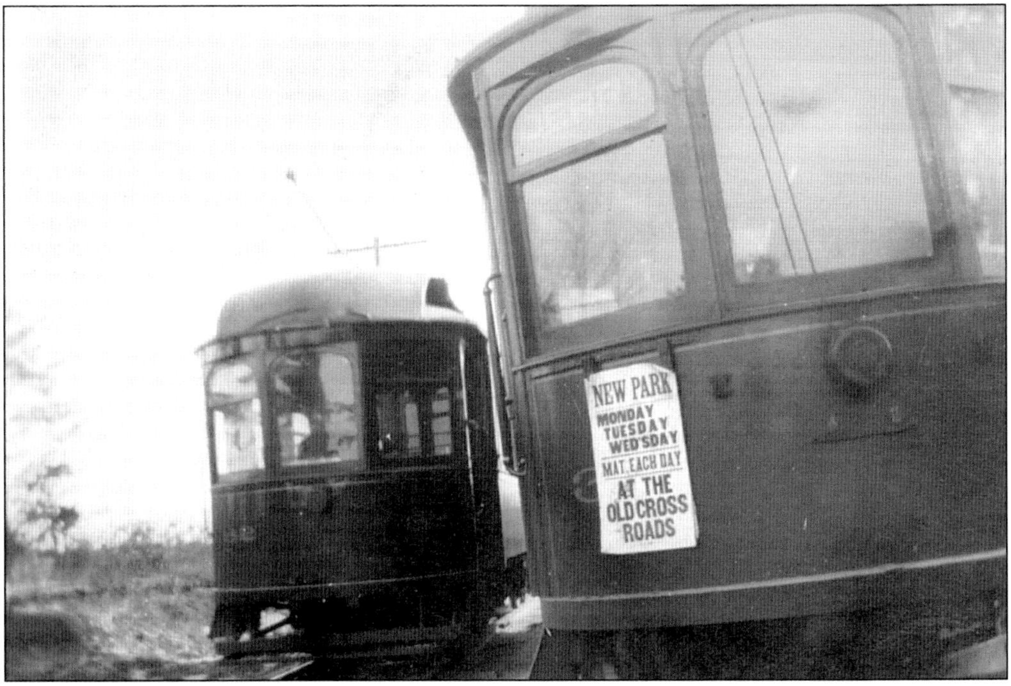

This meet of two Manchester & Derry cars is believed to have taken place at Hartford's turnout on Mammoth Road, North Londonderry. Car No. 12 is at the left; the other car is one of the 30-class Rapids.

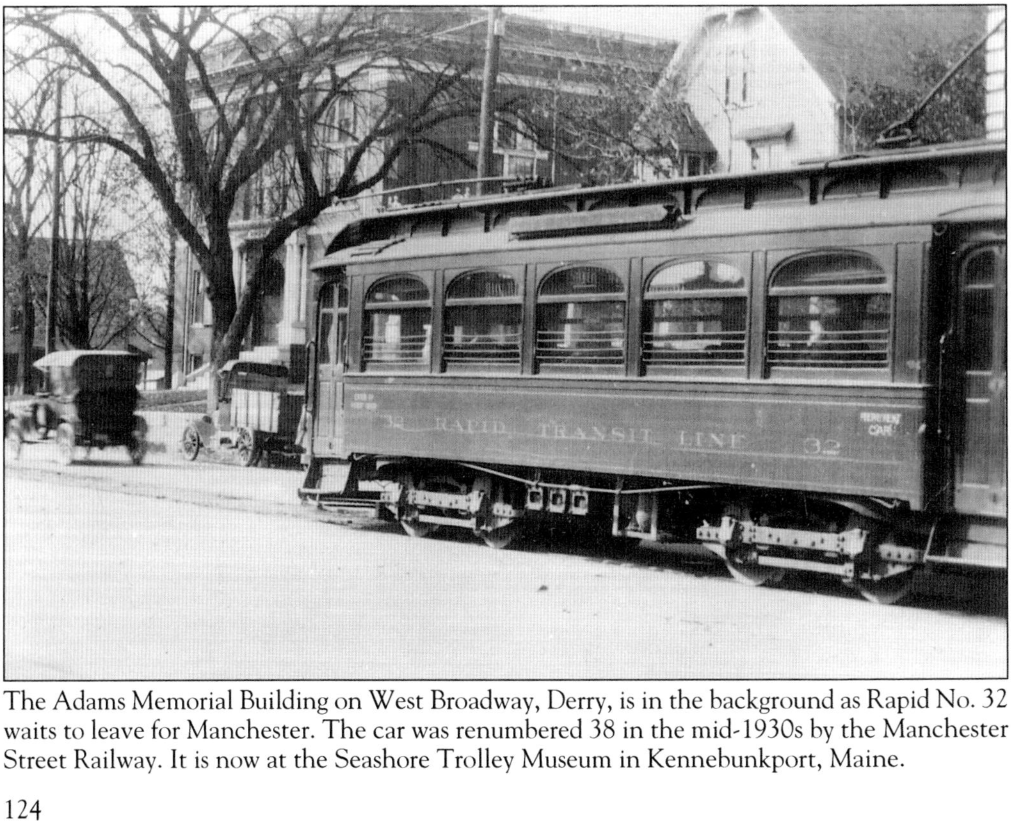

The Adams Memorial Building on West Broadway, Derry, is in the background as Rapid No. 32 waits to leave for Manchester. The car was renumbered 38 in the mid-1930s by the Manchester Street Railway. It is now at the Seashore Trolley Museum in Kennebunkport, Maine.

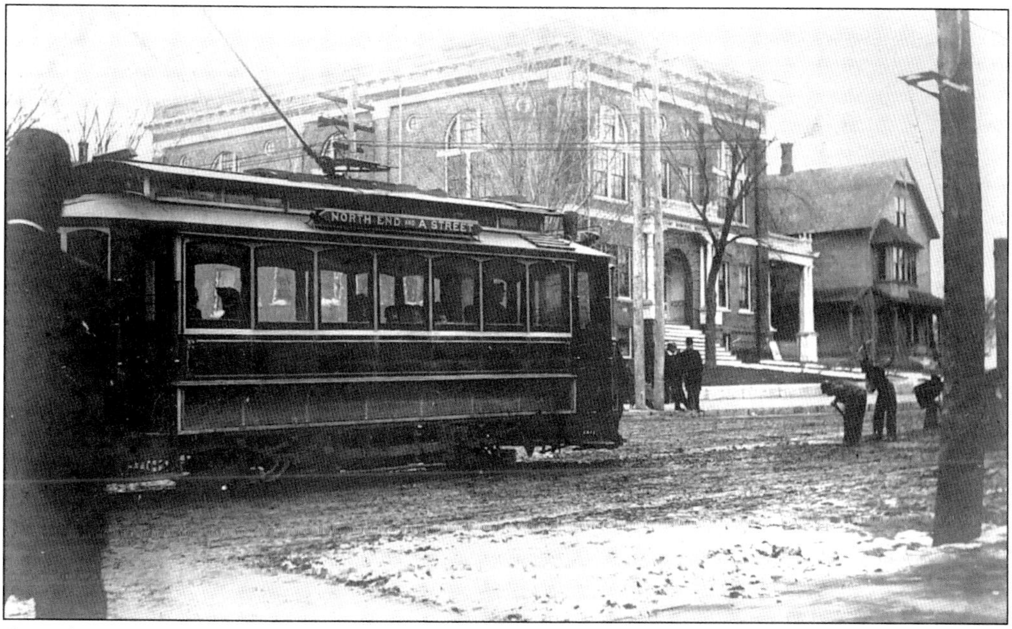

A track gang, carried to West Derry in one of the Laconia Car Company single-truck closed cars of 1895, clears the rails of ice in front of the Adams Memorial Building. A thaw must have been followed by a hard freeze, since there is little snow to be seen.

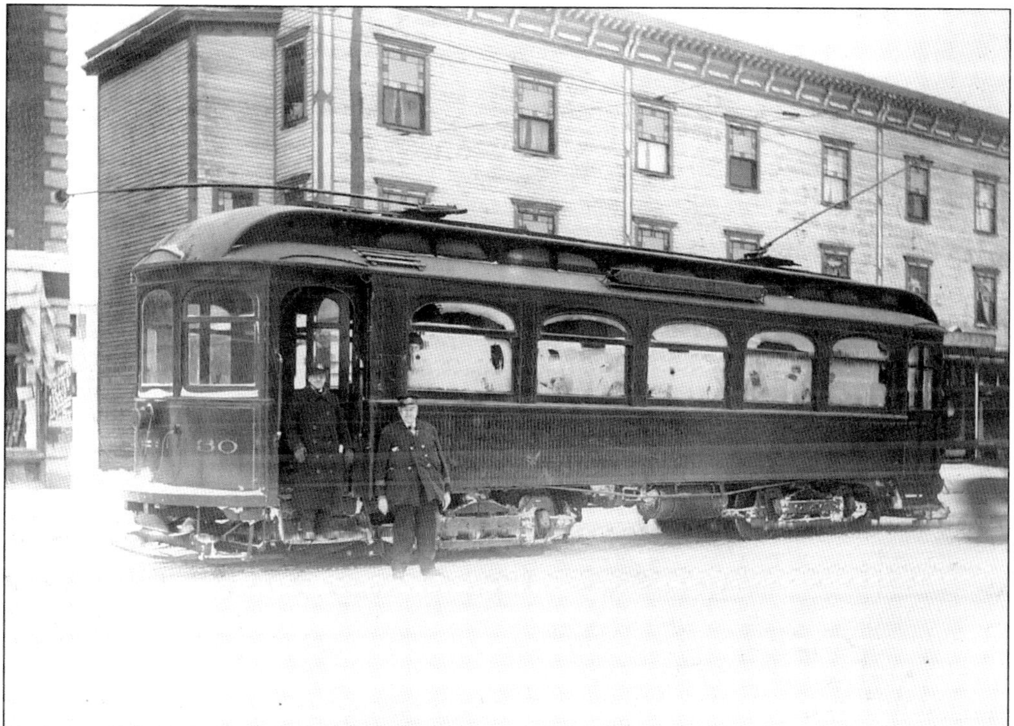

All the side windows are frosted as Rapid No. 30 is posed for a photographer on West Broadway, West Derry. The interior of the car was nicely warmed by electric heaters, and passengers rode in comfort.

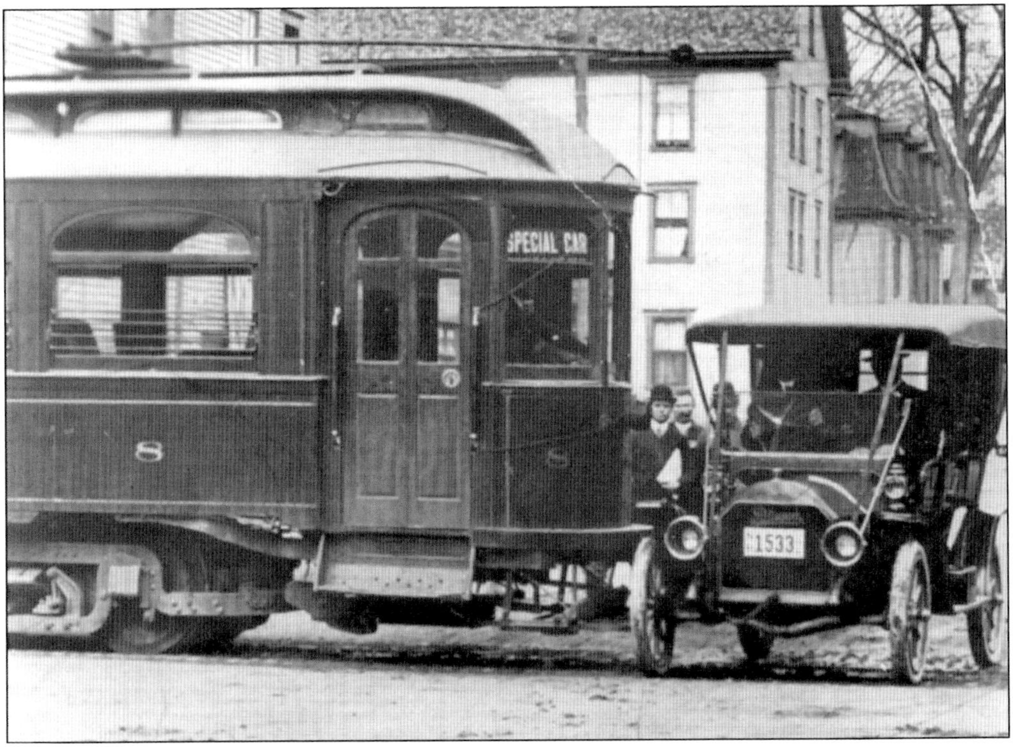

This obviously is a posed photograph of a supposed collision between Manchester & Derry No. 8 and an automobile. It appeared on the front cover of a Manchester trolley guide published on January 14, 1914.

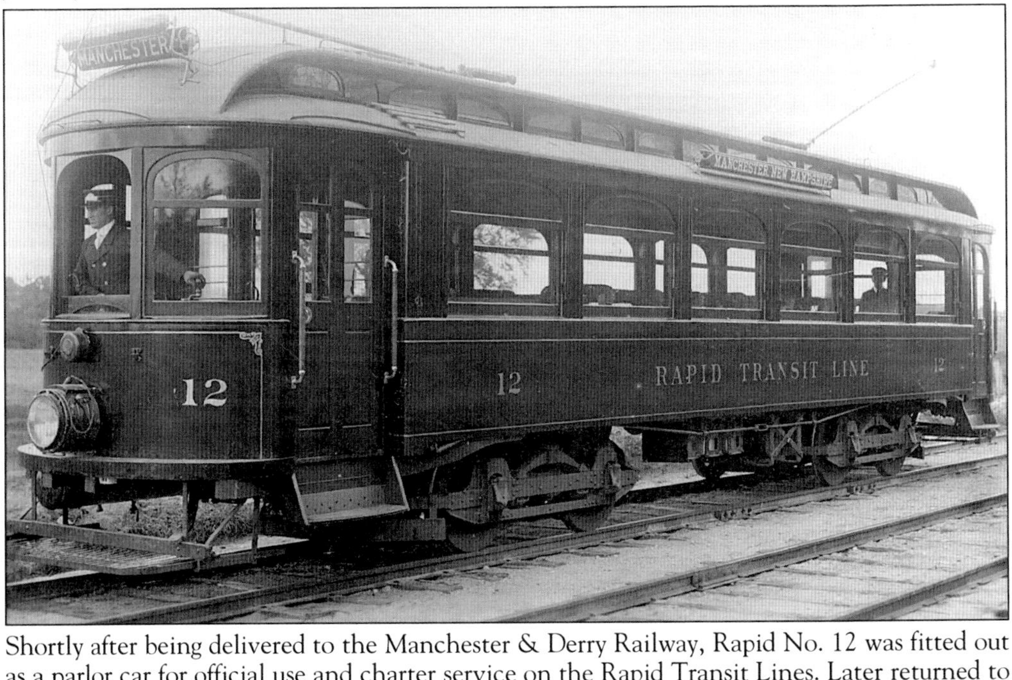

Shortly after being delivered to the Manchester & Derry Railway, Rapid No. 12 was fitted out as a parlor car for official use and charter service on the Rapid Transit Lines. Later returned to its original configuration, No. 12 remained in regular service until September 1931.

Nine

FAREWELL

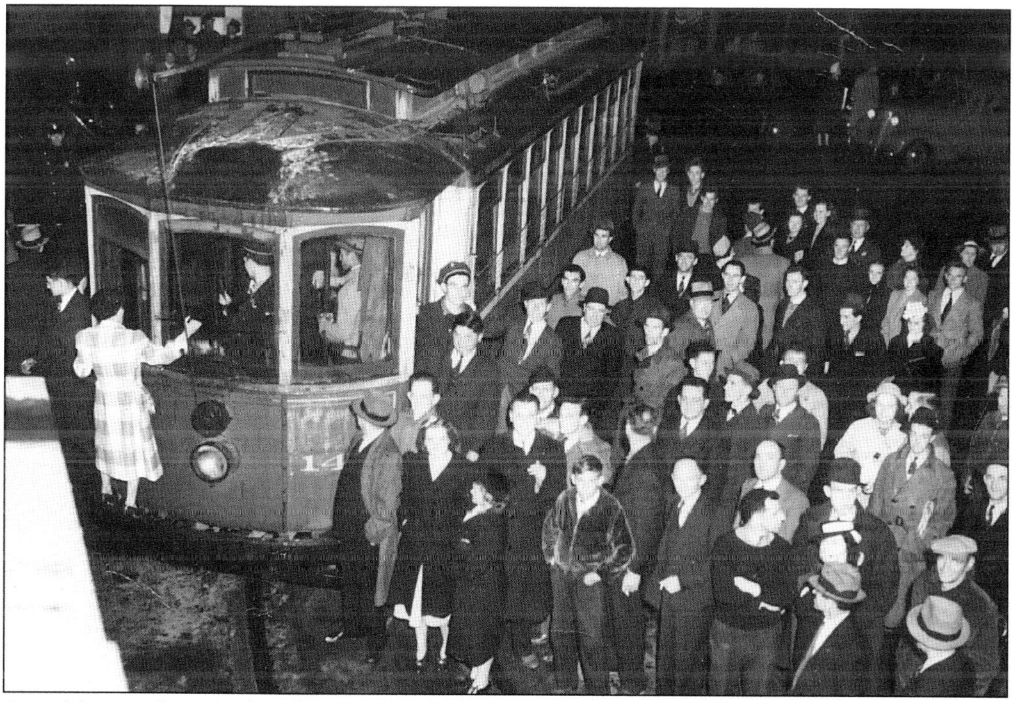

A sizable crowd was on hand to witness the arrival of the last cars at the Traction Street carbarns on the final day of trolley service, May 25, 1940. Somewhat the worse for wear (the hole in the vestibule hood cannot be explained), the car is one of the 138–144 class purchased secondhand in Connecticut in 1919. It was junked later in 1940.

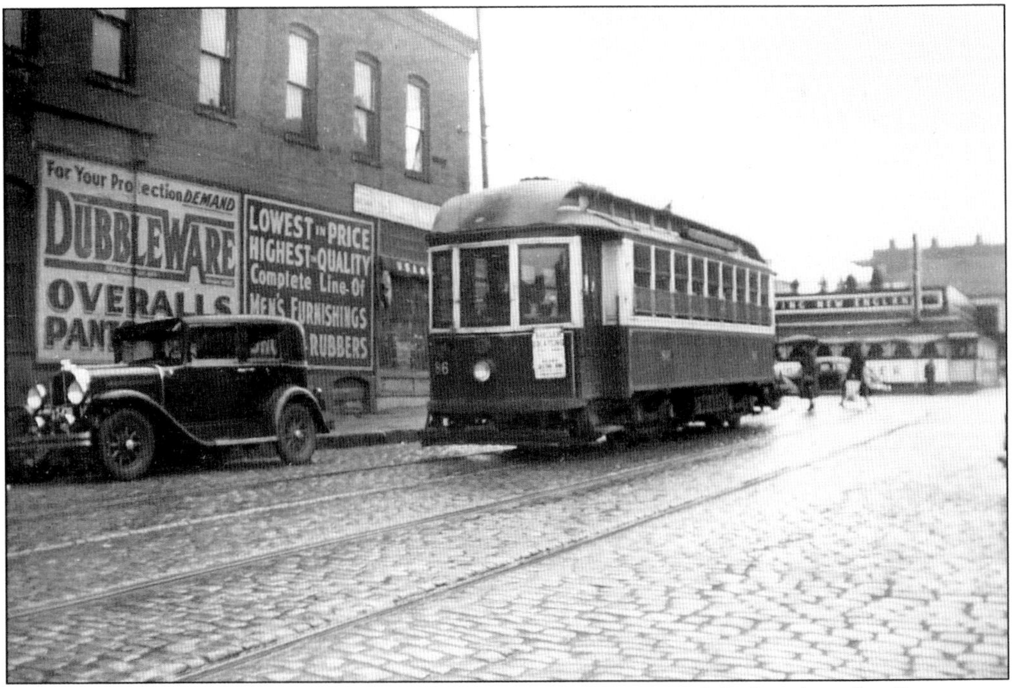

Bill Maier was on hand with his camera on May 25, 1940, to record the last day of trolley service in the Queen City. Car No. 86, heading for either St. Joseph Cemetery or Pinardville, is on Traction Street near Elm Street.

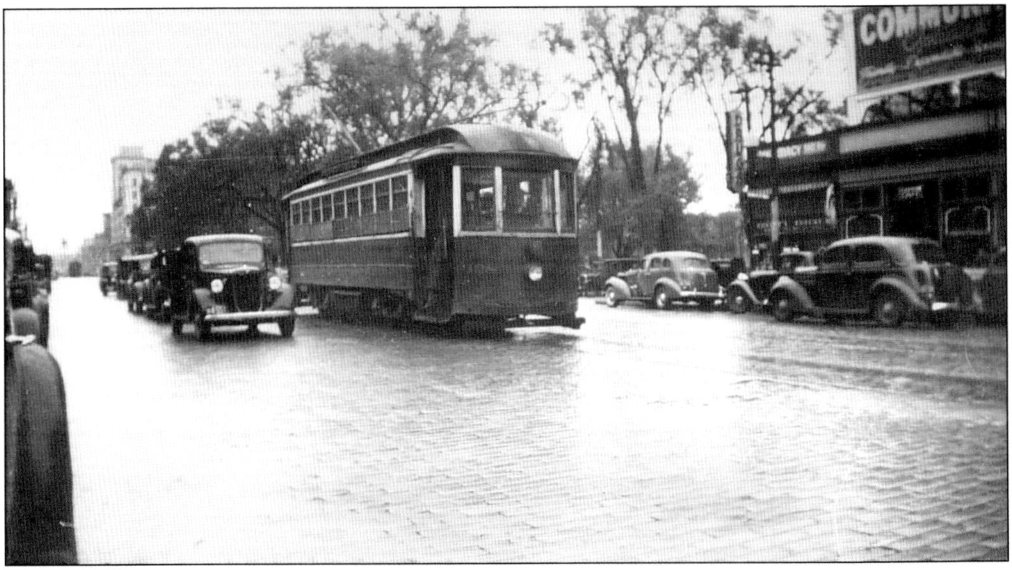

The cobblestone paving of Elm Street appears wet, as No. 128 pauses at the Transfer Station on May 25, 1940. Buses were in operation in the Queen City the following morning.